HIDING FROM THE
UNSPOKEN TRUTH

WHY LIVE YOUR LIFE WHOLE LIFE AS A LIE... WHEN THE REAL TRUTH COULD BE RIGHT IN YOUR FACE.

DAPPER DON

authorHOUSE

AuthorHouse™
1663 Liberty Drive
Bloomington, IN 47403
www.authorhouse.com
Phone: 1 (800) 839-8640

Published by AuthorHouse 07/01/2020

ISBN: 978-1-7283-6663-0 (sc)
ISBN: 978-1-7283-6664-7 (e)

Print information available on the last page.

This book is printed on acid-free paper.

PREFACE

I didn't write this book for clout, or negative attention ... This book was written for the healing purpose of self, and also for motivational purposes. This book was meant for the quiet middle schooler in the back that thinks the bad names he hears about himself in the hallways is all he'll ever be in life or for the college girl that is still working and fixing those inner parts of herself. Some names and details in this book have been changed for confidentiality. Others have been named due to their relationship with me. All of us as individuals are fighting with demons and issues so I hope it wouldn't kill you, as the reader, to be respectful and acknowledge that what happened IN THIS BOOK was in the past. My momma told me that y'all wouldn't need this disclaimer, but f*ck that because I wasted too much time putting my opinions in the ears of sheep. If you came here for the gossip and drama, I hope you are literate enough to find it. If the book is too much to bear, hopefully it can be of use to someone else.

- Thank you to my family members, friends & a special thank you to all the haters that made this book possible.

PROLOGUE

As I took a few sips from the cold-water fountain in my reading classroom, desperately waiting for the alarm to signal for the next class period, I peeked over to the bean bags in our reading corner, and behold there she was…

Her curly hair was glossed and even out with the wavy patterns from the crown down and lathered over with silky hair gel, her caramel Puerto-Rican skin was sun-kissed by God and all the angels, and her smooth black eyes batted in my direction when I looked in her presence as if to say, "Try me all you want." She was too spicy for my own taste, but I had to at least try because you don't know what could happen when you try. I looked toward one of my guys (gesturing with the coolest of head nods),indicating "I was about to work my magic" and made my move when I spotted an opening, walking with my palms sweaty as ever. Before I could finish what I had to say, she giggled and said sorry, because she had a crush on the guy who was twirling his Jesus piece on his neck on the beanbags. The class began to jeer and point in my direction and I dashed towards the bathroom, right next to the partition separating the adjoined classroom; trying to wipe away the falling tears from my face. She liked this guy over me; was I not handsome enough? I was so distraught and strangled by my insecure thoughts, that I barely heard the doorknob rattle and my friend whispered my name, asking if I was okay. "She didn't deserve the heart shaped box of chocolates for Valentine's Day that I had planned to get her from Walmart" I thought as I blew into what was left of the tissue in my hand.

My friend opened the door with a box of tissues that he held out for me to use and reassuringly told me, "It's okay, it happens to the best of us, bro" but is it really the best of us that sadness and pain come too? I squinted toward that cool kid's direction who seemed to be very indifferent about the newfound crush that was placed on him. He didn't care that this gorgeous hispanic angel cared about him. Would I ever find a girl that appreciated me for who I was, or would this be my first of many rejections to come?

CHAPTER 1

I was born at a hospital in Tampa, Florida and weighed in at a diminutive 2 pounds and 1 ounce. I was so shockingly small that I fit in my dad's palms. I was visited by relatives and my parent's church friends and soon my hospital room was decorated with flowers and cards. I wasn't allowed to be around other children because of my undeveloped lungs. I was given two shots to prevent illness and when my heart and lungs had stopped, I was put on a breathing machine.

I resided in the NICU clinging to life by a thread. When I reached three pounds and twenty ounces, my father snuck me out and took me to my first meeting, a business deal he was working to close on a nearby mall. When I was finally discharged from the hospital, I was whisked away our 4,000 square foot house in Kingshyre, a gated subdivision in the suburbs of Tampa. There was a room painted blue just for me, where I was surrounded by stuffed animals, including my favorite, Winnie the Pooh in his red t-shirt.

My mother was working as a medical doctor at an office in downtown Tampa and my father was working at the bank and closing business deals on the side. Seeing that their work schedules kept them increasingly away from home when I turned one, my mother went out of her way to inquire at the spanish church she had attended to make sure I was properly homeschooled and could become bilingual over time. The people in the church found a babysitter and called my mother to come and meet the babysitter they had found for her. When I started talking, I called her Titi.

My earliest childhood memories with Titi at home are of starting my morning by getting out of bed, eating breakfast and still wearing pajamas in front of the living room to begin whatever classwork that I had for the day. My mother would leave a bunch of DVD's for Titi, designed for visual homeschooling kids from a prerecorded lesson. Each disc, depending on the grade level, began with all the children in the classroom taking their seats, going over the national anthem and jumping right into the classwork of the day. When the teacher on screen would ask a question out loud, I would be prompted by Titi, to raise my hand and answer in a timely fashion.

My mother also left worksheets for me to trace cursive letters, practice math and sound out pronunciations. If I behaved well enough for the day, Titi and I would ride out together to the zoo where she let me run around freely feeding the goats, roar at the lions and staring in awe at the orangutans and monkeys swinging around on branches.

At home, throughout the week, Titi made sure I was well taken care of and in good spirits, bathing me and preparing me lunch: grilled cheese sandwiches, yellow arroz con andules, and homemade spaghetti with meatballs. She was patient with my Spanish, teaching me a new word everyday and having me write down the sentences so my enunciation and pronunciation would be clearer.

When I felt ill or my asthma would flare up, Titi checked my temperature, gave me the right medicine along with a bowl of soup and would sing a Spanish lullaby. As I laid my head to rest on my pillow, she gently scratched my back until I was lulled into a deep sleep. If I had cut myself or skinned my knee outside playing, she pulled me to the side singing the traditonal Spanish rhyme "Sana Sana Colito de rana, si no sanas hoy, Sanaras manana." (Heal, heal little frog's tail. If you don't heal today, you will heal tomorrow.)On the weekends with my mom and dad, I would go on walks around the neighborhood with both of my dogs Cocoa (a chocolate setter- retriever mix) and Bronx (a spoiled Pomeranian that was a present to my mom from my dad.) Cocoa would chase the squirrels and fetch sticks and tennis balls while Bronx pattered the sidewalk, probably thinking he was the best thing since sliced bread and wasn't made for all the running and chasing that Cocoa enjoyed.

I do feel like I'm forgetting something or someone…. oh yeah. My dream of being an only child was ruined when a bundle of trouble meaning my sister Lauren came into the world. She played with my toys before she had her own because " you have to share with your sister, she's your only sister…" When I was around five years old, I was blessed by my parents with a mini yellow Hummer and Harley Davidson which I raced throughout the whole neighborhood, zooming in and out of the neighbors driveways and exiting the neighborhood gates challenging anyone to race me as soon as they had reached the gates to leave and bust a U-turn back to my driveway to park my Hummer next to my parents cars.

It wasn't just Titi who would visit the house from time to time; I had close friends I would see in the area. My godbrother Bryce and his sister would come over to the house for playdates and my Spider- Man themed birthday parties. My friend Vez and his family lived down the road in another gated community and Dad would drive us over to check in for Super Bowl parties, BBQ's, Fourth of July or just to "let all the kids come over".

Sometimes we walked outside to the neighborhood pool which had waterslides and mushroom fountain towers. Back at their house, my sister would hang out with his sister Maria playing with dolls or whatever. Depending on whether we wanted to stay inside or go outside the house, Vez and I would play Lego Batman in his game room or one-on-one basketball on his garage hoop, or practice cannonballs off the side of their backyard pool… Sometimes we would meet up at the family YMCA off Compton Drive. We would play basketball with the older guys while on the other side of the partition the girls played volleyball.

If I were lucky enough to be on the right side of the town, our parents would take us to see Mr. and Mrs. Evans so my sister could hang out with both of their girls, Destiny and Triniti. At the park near their house, I would watch as Mr. Evans and my dad played five-on-five on the outdoor court or launch spiral passes back and forth to me but I can't throw a spiral correctly to this day. By the end of third grade, my mother saw it was time for me to just grow up and stop being homeschooled. Around the same time, she found a better workplace for her practice further downtown. It was less of a hassle for her to fight traffic every morning but if I'm being honest, I wasn't fond when I heard that we were getting ready to move to downtown Tampa. Even though my sister and I were getting older, it hurt that I had to leave childhood memories and friends behind- and even our dogs. Cocoa and Bronx had recently escaped from the garage because of my mom's worsening allergies. It hurt that I had to leave childhood friends and memories behind me. To this day, I don't know if maybe my dad who let the garage door open so Cocoa and Bronx would get out the neighborhood; never to be seen again. Maybe he did it because my mom's allergies were bad and he wanted to make her happy... but it made me sad.

There were so many memories and attachments in the area that I didn't want to let go. I had my first swimming classes down the road, and after picking me up to go home where my mom would let me get two M&M cookies. I used to have nightmares of not being able to swim or drowning because in my first few classes I struggled to keep up with my instructor and felt like I was always about to drown literally. I always felt some type of pressure, like I couldn't be good enough for anybody.

There was Mickey D's up the street from the house where my dad would order three Big Breakfasts with Hotcakes for my sister and myself. I would wolf down my pancakes so we'd have enough time to go to the Wildcat's gym where he played basketball with his guys from time to time. Last but not least, I can't forget the old SDA Mount Calvary Church right across the street that my parents had taken me to since I was a baby, surrounding me with people I would come to know as church family.But alas, my parents had their minds made up and as I looked out the backseat window past the shell gas station off the corner, the Publix in the plaza and slumped my head as I watched everything that I used to know fade away on the interstate.

CHAPTER 2

THE BIG MOVE DOWNTOWN

When we finally arrived at the house in Tampa Heights, I could see from a first glance of the outside of the property why my parents had ended up choosing this house. It looked like something out of a landscaping magazine and it resembled the white mini-mansion in the movie Belly that DMX and Nas lived in. The balcony outstretched over the front driveway and the driveway extended into the grass, could fit six cars if you made it stretch from side to side.

Opening that metal front door, you would first notice that the house has see-through glass and an outside concrete wall surrounding the property; to ensure secure privacy until the neighbors got that trampoline for their kids. If you continued down the concrete sidewalk towards the massive plot of dirt and grass that we called our backyard, and turned to the left, you would notice a gate. If pushed, the gate allowed a car to be placed in the back to act as a second driveway.

Coming through the front door, there is a white metal staircase, leading up to my shared bedroom and bathroom with my sister, and to the far left in the next room was our playroom with space for our books and clothes. The very far right is our parents master bedroom, leading outside of their room is the balcony.

Downstairs to the left was the living room, soon to be fitted in with the 50" black television and our family piano. Hiding from the cut to the right was the guest room with wood laminate flooring and a full bathroom. Then we had the space for a pool table and a plasma screen television on the wall, and the bathroom past the hallway leading into the kitchen with stone cut counters and stone floor. Now that I'm done making this "Welcome to my MTV crib" introduction, let's move on, shall we?

Ater traumatizing me with the story of Cocoa and Bronx taking off and becoming alligator food back at Kingshyre, Dad decided it was time he got the family a friendly border collie that we came to know as Tofy (Toe-Fee). His white coat was speckled over with cinnamon brown spots over his white body and tail. Tofy wasn't as well trained as Cocoa was but was sure good at attacking any four-legged creature that stepped foot in our backyard. Tofy's victims would range from the squirrels that mistimed their jump from our wall and landed in Tofy's personal space to one of our neighbor's twenty five cats that Tofy had his eyes on. I imagined that my dad was in for a surprise, when the cat lady came to our door asking if he had seen where "Blackie" had gone, and he calmly replied with his fingers crossed that the cat may have only ran away.

Actually those fingers were tightly crossed, as if hours before we hadn't noticed the small mound near our playground set that Tofy kicked some dirt over. For a cold-blooded murderer, Tofy wasn't keen on following commands that we gave him and resorted to just bouncing around on everyone who came outside and playing in the grass in the yard. On our family walks around the neighborhood, Tofy proved to be too strong for Lauren as he bolted down the corner with Lauren dragging on the sidewalk as Dad and I chased after them both yelling, "pull your hands back on the leash, Lauren!"

My mother's animal allergy seemed to intensify with the addition of Tofy to our family, and with no barrier to contain him from sneaking to the front where my mother was found tending to her long bamboo stalks. Sometimes I would come downstairs in the daytime and be in for a surprise as my eyes followed the white and brown blur outrunning my mother's bamboo staff until Tofy made it to the very back of the house. Unfortunately, Tofy didn't stay too long because my mother's allergies overturned our pleas to keep the dog "just a little while" and was given up to my dad's cousin, John before I finished up eighth grade.

My mom and dad made sure that I was stocked up with toys thanks to Uncle Glen, my dad's friend from college. Then I was later showered with video games for my personal Gameboy and the Nintendo Wii in the living room. My dad stayed home for a period of time and his love for his son and seeing his son interact with the toys he brought back to the house turned slowly into sheer disappointment as he heard Spider-Man, Woody, and all the toys I collected hit the floor from the balcony weekend after weekend.

My father would usually interrupt me while I was playing to say, "Why do you keep breaking up the toys?" "You can't be gentle with them?" I would respond with "Dad, Spider-Man was trying to save the good guys from the bank but got caught in the explosion on the way out." "That's why he broke his leg on the steps!" When I would have my friends over my house to play with some toys and they would notice that He-Man was missing his sword and shield or Batman missing his cape, the final conclusion was that it had gotten real and somebody probably didn't escape the danger in time.

My mother bought me a shiny black Nintendo Gameboy Advance as a gift for me when I was about eight years old, with the complete travel Nintendo case and a few game cartridges along with it. The first game I ever played was Super Mario Bros. 3 and I was hooked to that game like a moth on a porch light, traveling down green pipes and exploring the level until the music, that initiates the time is running out, starts to play. It was like I had a crack addiction the way I rushed to get to the finish line. I was so happy when I got the 1UP or the game prize at the end of each level. I would play on the game until I heard my mom's footsteps and would fake sleep until she went back to her room so I could pull the Gameboy from under my pillowcase.

The games I carried around on a weekly basis were TMNT 2 Battle Nexus, NickToons Freeze Frame Frenzy, Finding Nemo, Mario Kart Super Circuit and Donkey Kong. I became self absorbed in my own space and didn't let my sister have a turn on my Gameboy, so my mother would have to make that second trip soon after and get her a purple Gameboy Advance. I kept up with my Gameboy until my spanish math teacher would confiscate it in class and end up giving it up to her daughter. After school, I would watch through the door window that same day afterschool, dying inside as her daughter sat in her mother's chair playing MY GAME. The Nintendo Wii was intended for the whole family to play in the living room, but my mom messed up when she got some games for me which were Super Mario Galaxy, Mario Kart & Sonic and the Secret Rings. I ended up booting my sister off the Wii while she was playing Wii Sports & after that, she put up less of a fight for her turn on the TV.

The latest I ever stayed up playing on the Wii was on a Sunday morning. I was playing Mario Kart racing through the laps in 1st place, when I heard a noise in the background. I dismissed it for the smoke detector that needed batteries and kept playing until I heard my mother's voice about 12 feet from me. "Do you know what time it is?", she asks. "No, what is it?", I replied. "It's 2:30 AM in the morning, Go to bed." "Nobody wants to hear all that on the television." My bloody red eyes squint at the flashing green numbers on the analog clock on top of the television. "We need that clock to get fixed?" "Mom I'm almost done, can I do this last par- "No, Eddy turn it off and go to bed." And when my mom spoke in that tone, it was that on that.

My mother and dad played their own active roles in the home showing us love and conditioning habits to shape us to be the well mannered kids they wanted us to be. My father was a gentleman and a lover by nature, obvious traits he gained from his Christian mother and sisters in New York and tried his very best to instill those same qualities into me. He would tell me every week that I was a very handsome young man, even though I don't see it to this day, with gorgeous eyes that I got from himself and my mother's skin complexion.

He groomed me in the art of making sure the woman is well taken care of, how to properly opening doors (even if the woman doesn't acknowledge you or say thank you afterwards) moving out of my seat to let another woman sit down and lifting my mother or sister to make sure they got in the house safely. He made sure that he took advantage of the time I was with my mother to sweet talk her into getting what he wanted from her. A typical Sunday evening would play out where my dad would call me upstairs into the master bedroom, pause the R&B he was listening to and tell me "Son I need you to go and tell your mother, *Sweet lady* can I help you with the dishes?

"But dad I can't call her a sweet lady!", I replied. That's weird! Then he responded with, "Son, do what I asked." As I hurried down the steps thinking on the best way to keep my composure, I approached my mother washing breakfast dishes and stuttered my lines through like a shaky train on a stable railroad track. "Sweet, sweet lady can I wash the rest of the dishes for you?" All you could hear in the background was soft clapping and "Yes, Yes Good Job son." Afterwards my dad would have another mastermind plan for me as soon as I returned upstairs to be in my own room. "Son i need you to tell your mother hey sweet, sweet lady you look so beautiful today, is it possible that I can get a sweet sample of your Rocky Road ice cream?"

I ran back downstairs and halfway through stammering through my lines, my mother would exclaim halfway to tell my dad to get his own ice cream. I stifled a laugh, before stepping into the room awaiting his shocked face in the bedroom, once he saw I walked back up empty handed. "Where's my ice cream, son? "Dad, the sweet, sweet lady said you have to get it your-..."You had one job, son…"

My mother was very health conscious about the kind of food that we ate at home, being that was part of her professional career. Her Jamican father and mother practiced "Health is wealth" at a very young age for her. Soy-Milk was a substitute for cow milk and our school lunches were in the form of peanut butter jelly or tuna sandwiches, Wheat Thins or Ritz crackers along with some red apples or a bunch of grapes.

Our weekend breakfasts consisted of Aunt Jemima whole wheat pancakes, oatmeal, grits and eggs, or just regular cold cereal with the usual Morning Star chicken patties, sausages, or imitation bacon aka "striplets" on the side.

Dad had his selected playlist from artists like Michael Jackson, Outkast, Nelly, Tyrese, Kanye playing from his HP laptop and served us our plates. If my mom served us our food before he got his, he would tip-toe through the stone kitchen floor towards his unexpected victims, tap each of us on the shoulder and grab a spoon or fork full of food as we turned our heads for a brief second the other way.

If we had uttered our cry of " Mom, he's taking our food", his usual retort would be to the both of us, "God doesn't like selfish" or "Let me have my own small portion" and made us look like the bad guys every time. This became the catalyst for me developing trust issues to anyone that tried to get close to me at all. On the occasional Saturday evenings coming from church, my mom would host game nights in the open living room or our wooden kitchen table where we would bring out the board games such as Monopoly, Connect 4 and sometimes, Operation. I would grow tired of the board games and slink towards the tv or my room as my sister and mother would cheat, I mean alternate, from being the banker and property owners.

When we weren't yelling over who decided to escape jail so they could pass GO, my mom would put the two of us on the schedule for extra curricular activities. That would be taking us to the Tampa Bay Patel Conservatory and putting me on the youth choir that would sing for the holidays while my sister would take dance and ballet classes.

Mom purchased a " Piano for Young Beginner" book, which was the first of many, for the house so we could be gifted as she was on the piano after school. The three of us all participated in the taekwondo classes and my mother purchased the sparring gear and hand to hand sparring book for us to all practice when we got home. We never did but she put in more work than both of us and it showed by the questions she asked about her form & stance during every session that we had to attend together as a unit.

All that ended when she became pregnant with her third child and had to cease working at her office, even though she would fight back with the doctors at the hospital about how long she should be resting and how many days off work she would be taking. Upon hearing the news, my sister and I would pray before going to sleep and waking up in the morning, praying for a little sister or a little brother to spoil and take under the other's wing. The longer the months went by, the longer we prayed until our mother sat us down in our living room for the big reveal.

My sister and I both closed our eyes and crossed our fingers as my mother had prepared us with a drum roll. Then my mother exclaimed that I was going to have a little brother added to the family. Oh Boy I jumped for joy and did cartwheels around the living room as my sister cried into her lap, trying to figure out why she wasn't getting the sister she wanted. Oh well, guess we see someone didn't pray hard enough to get the sibling they wanted.

As I got adjusted into being in downtown Tampa, my father tried to enroll my sister and I into different places to keep us occupied and hanging around more kids. I was out at the Boys and Girls Club, the playgrounds at parks, played basketball and swam at the Y.M.C.A but my most ingrained memory was about eight years old attending a daycare center off 22nd street that was run by my dad's friend Starr. I told my dad goodbye as he dropped me off and promised to "See You Later, buddy" as I rushed through the doors to find the best corner to play with toys and nap in.

I was unbothered and carefree as could be until one day, this one mischievous kid came in and had "pantsed" me in front of everyone. Now this mischievous kid preyed on other victims at the camp that he knew other kids for his own enjoyment so I didn't hear any other kids making fun of, but I felt that he had it out for me anytime I was standing up doing our group activities. On the way home in my dad's SUV, I profusely cried out my frustrations and, being the protective, loving dad that he is, "He'll talk to Ms. Starr and make sure it's taken care of."

Unbeknownst to him, my patience had already run out and my beating heart was slowing down with the chilling rise of my negative emotions flowing through my body. I wanted all the smoke with this kid. He wasn't going to get away with pantsing me in everyone so that they all knew I was wearing Fruit of The Loom undies. I came into the camp the following day with a serene air about myself, I knew he couldn't catch me slipping this time. We went through the normal routine and when all the kids did their stand up activities, I peered out of the corner of my peripheral to see the kid creeping to each guileless down the row until he got to me and couldn't seem to get the job done as my pants were tightly held by my belt.

As I saw the desperation in his face as he ran back to his previous spot, I laughed knowing I had him right where I wanted him. When Ms. Starr let us out for recess, I sprinted up to him near the slide with a handful of mulch; and while he was rubbing the dirt out of his irritated eyes, I gave him a quick two piece without warning. My father was called as soon as possible and drove through traffic expeditiously to reach me and find out if I had gotten hurt during our little scuffle. As he walked with me towards his car ride home, he was trying to scold me on the ride home saying, "Didn't I tell you that I would take care of him for you?" for my own actions, pleased that I wouldn't have to deal with that kid anymore.

CHAPTER 3

YOU'RE A SEVENTH DAY ADVENTIST?

My mother and father were both raised as Seventh Day Adventists and upon graduating from college and getting married, they were both placed with the responsibility of putting Proverbs 22:6 in full effect. The verse states that you must "train up a child in the way he should go: and when he is old, he will not depart from it." Shortly after moving to Tampa Heights, there was a new church location so every Saturday morning, I would be awakened by gospel music blasting from downstairs and would calmly lay in the bed thinking to myself, "I can wait until my sister gets dressed or finally start to get ready while everyone is eating breakfast downstairs", because I enjoyed the peace of being alone while everyone was running around figuring out who was racing to get out the door first.

Sometimes, my dad felt like interrupting my breakfast before it was halfway done was the best time to give me a quick lineup or trim my mustache with his clippers. Our church was less than twenty minutes out away so once we reached the destination, my sister and I were escorted to the children's church room as my mother and father waved bye and went inside the sanctuary. The children's church was run by this lady named Brittany B. along with two older women who were very helpful. We sat down with all the kids and were given popcorn and snacks that we munched while Veggie Tales and other kids church programs played on the VHS.

When the younger kids dispersed and were moved to their other classrooms, we sat around in a circle and introduced ourselves. As I sat with my friends, trying to analyze who was going to be the wisecrack that ruined the introduction process for our teachers and made us roll out of our chairs with uncontrollable laughter. This kid named Quinton who couldn't contain himself by trying to be the funny guy everytime Ms. Bing came around the room. "What's Your Name?" "My Name's Eddie!" " My Name's Samantha." Before she could finish asking, "And what's your nam- Quint would stand up from his chair and exclaim "My name's Black!!"

While my friends and I died laughing to ease the tension, the teachers wouldn't find the situation funny and ended up moving "Black" away until we finished our arts and crafts and everyone came together to close out in prayer and return to their parents either in the fellowship hall, where we would go to eat after the benediction, or right outside the children's church door. Before I opened the church doors, I had to mentally decide which side of the church I would choose to sit at. Would I go to the right where my friends are or to the left where the adults would have an open space just for me? Then there was my dad tapping on my shoulder and walking me down with an usher hand in hand to the pew he had reserved for our family? I had options.

The service would be led out by a call for new visitors, amazing praise and worship, and then an introduction for the speaker of the hour, which was usually our senior pastor who was a well noted man that always gave an enriching sermon to those who listened, whether it was the people that had only come for Easter and stayed for about thirty minutes or those who followed him on the church's livestream.

The sermons may have filled those that needed the word that morning with the Holy ghost, but they always put me in a deep slumber that left me drooling on my friends shoulders. And then there were church lies that I used to believe as a youth like "I won't be too long up here OR I'll keep my eyes on the clock to make sure I'll wrap up by lunch."

By the benediction, the pastor would be waiting by the church doors with the elders to shake the hands of those that were blessed that sabbath morning. Those who stayed strolled down to the fellowship hall would receive the prepared lunch and occasional desserts from the hardworking women in the kitchen or the choir room to review the youth and adult choir parts in preparation for next week.

My friends in church were those that I would develop a special kinship through our mutual love for each other and God. Some would come and go, like Harold, whose mother made sure our youth choir and children plays left an unforgettable mark on our brains, or Kyle, who was a close friend on the pee-wee basketball squad and would ball out when my dad would take some of the guys outside of church to play with tougher competition. But my church squad was a group of people that I had been acquainted with since day one. There was PJ, the most grounded and firmest guy of the group who was often looked towards as a leader out of the whole crew. His dad was the one who led our SEC (Southern Eastern Conference) drum choir on our many Pathfinder camp meetings and meetups for parades with success.

Then you had Jonathan who was my JV basketball rival and the flamboyant one out of the whole group. He loved to show out with his crazy hairstyles, basketball shoes, skills with the drums and never backed down from anyone. Then you had Devion, who seemed to have a sneaky and mean persona on the outside, but showed a softer side when she would shove and push people out the way all her friends when they stood in front of a microwave too long because "Move, because you can get cancer from standing in front of it too long!"

Jada was one of the smartest light-skinned girls I knew and was well versed in her bible texts so we couldn't leave her out of the group. Aaron had the most nonchalant and humble attitude about him, which is why girls would flock to him as the "Chip Skylark" of the group. I remember our camp meetings when I would find this dude on a trail walking with M&M and Skittles on his shoulders (That's when those matching racing jackets looked cool. Must've been nice, Aaron!)

Last but certainly not least, I met Migale in my last few years of middle school and there was never a moment I couldn't die laughing at this goofy dude, even if we both were in the heat of trouble. In the earlier stages of our friendship, I used to wait for him during the church's summer vacation bible school. The girls would come by and say "You waiting for your friend on the bike again?" *"You know he's not going to show up."* And sometimes he didn't, but when I saw him biking through the parking lot towards me, I swear my mood changed from upside down to rightside up. Our bond would strengthen through months of Ms. Sherry's youth program and sitting on the sidelines of the church varsity basketball games. In addition to that, Migale also took the time to teach me phrases and curse words in Patois.

Remember John how I played rock, paper, scissors in the church sanctuary for that Puerto Rican girl to date me? Even though I beat you that day, you knew before I went to go talk to her that she liked me the whole time. All the girls used to gang up on me and make a scene for me to be with her. I'd always find one of my guys to duck me off in the bathroom stall or hide me when I went down the hallway at the wrong time but sometimes I would get ambushed shortly after hearing "WHERE ARE YOU GOING?" I didn't have an issue with being a couple with anyone, but in due time, I realized that I was more of a 1 v. 1 guy to talk and make the sparks fly. That's why everything,especially that kiss in front of the gym, was so awkward because the rumors that were spread by everyone except the adults, were going around like cold fries in a greasy fast food bag.

I had a love and hate relationship with the guys I grew up with at church, whether we were joking around during AYS in the sanctuary or cleaning up the fellowship hall after our lunch. A perfect example of this was when my dad's family came over for my brother's 1st birthday. All the girls grouped up near the front of the house for a group picture and as I showed my friends the pictures, expecting all the responses they gave me. "Damn, she's bad bro!" " Can I date her and be your cousin-in- law?" I smiled, knowing that all my cousins were already beautiful and my friends were showing genuine love towards them.

Then there was that one guy because it's always the one guy in the group that has some slick comment coming out of his mouth. "Damn, everybody looks great,but what happened to you?" At that moment, I'm stumped because I had no comeback and couldn't go to my friends who already covered their mouths in a "Damn bro" sort of shock. I replied back to the guy,"I mean my dad and mom happened. I don't know what else you want me to say lol." It can be your own guys that do your dirty sometimes, but I still hung out with the crew time and time again because they helped me get out of trouble and made sure I felt included in church activities.

If my parents had received an invitation to one of their friend's houses, Lauren and I were always eager to get some food and warm TLC from the church family that we'd meet there, When we would go to see Uncle Walter and Aunt Vivian, the overhead chimes would ring above the doormat and Uncle Walter would greet us with a heartwarming hug and let us run into the house, already fumigating with the mouth- watering smell of food. Aunt Vivian had her signature banana nut bread out of the oven ready to go, and their children, Wally and Kyky were upstairs cleaning their room or helping set up the table. Wally was the laid back one who dapped me up and went back and forth with me on small talk on sports, school and girls. Kyky… When I first met her at the house, I was lost for words and developed a crush that was *tout de suite* due to her similar resemblance to Rihanna with low cuts and overall beauty.

I hope some of you guys keep your laughs to yourself, because I know for a fact that some of y'all thought she was drop dead gorgeous as soon as you saw her walk through those church doors. Every time she came and hugged me, my mind drifted on the wedding bells in my head. I was able to sleep over a few nights when I didn't have school and the family was very supportive to my parents, to which I was always grateful for.

When I went over to the Powell's house for Sabbath lunch, there was a well spirited and heavenly presence that took over. It didn't matter if I got my butt whooped and I was crying on the way over there or complained about "my stomach is killing me" through the whole sermon. As soon as I stepped foot in that house, my whole mood perked up. The kitchen and dining room was the restaurant and the Powells (and their children, if they were already in the kitchen) were the chefs. They stopped cooking for a short time to give us hugs or kisses and then went right back to making magic over the stove.

Our family history with the Powell's travels back to a hospital visit after my mom had just given birth to the greatest gift of them all, which was yours truly. They brought enough food for my mom and dad to make it through being in the hospital for so long and became our adopted grandparents from that point on.. Now the dishes they would prepare for after church lunch were scrumptious. The mac and cheese was fixed up like heaven and stuck to the ridges in the dish bowl.The vegetables and greens always left a savory juicy taste on my tongue. But the veggie meat that went with that good gravy?! I'd trade all the fast food in the world for one dish of veggie meat to take home. There wasn't much for me to do after I had my plate clean so I would usually ask Grandma Powell if I could play on her piano or her computer in the back to go on Veggietales.com.

When we all came together and said grace over the food on the table, my eyes were already peering towards the meal I was about to devour. As soon as I heard that Amen, there was no stopping me from reaching the kitchen with a plate in hand. Getting seconds and thirds proved to be no challenge as Grandma Powell always told me "You can have as much as you like." The only catch was, I had to tell the worm in my stomach to calm down before the dessert, so I did not cry on the way home. As the dishes started making their way to the sink, and then people started to make their way to the couches, only if they were not in a rush to go home. I would be educating Grandpa and Grandma Powell's grandchildren on the background of action figures or sitting around reading Christian books on the living room carpet.

If our family were one of the last few guests to leave, my sister and I would join Grandpa Powell outside to his swinging bench or tire swing where he'd spin and push us until he couldn't anymore. He sat down with us outside and talked to us about God, and important life lessons on how to stay on the right path. He even promised me that one of these days when we had time over at his house, he was going to teach me how to fish on the lake right outside in the backyard. I waited on that day every time we came over until his untimely passing in 2009.

The funeral was a sad one for everyone to attend to and sitting in that pew towards the back, and as my emotions inflated like a hot air balloon, I couldn't stand it any longer. I left the church crying mid-way through the service because he was really gone from this earth and I couldn't believe that I carried so much emotion for a person who wasn't even blood-related. I wanted to whoop cancer's ass so bad and I wish it was an actual person rather than a plaguing illness, so I could stomp and kick its ribs and lungs out. Years later, I can't even bring a slight memory to my sister's recollection without her lashing out at me for speaking in memory of him. It took a very long time for the pain and aching in my heart to go away. I just hoped that God had some unknown reason for putting that pain in my heart and hopefully he'd watch over the family and continue to bless them after this was all said and done.

CHAPTER 4

GROWING PAINS

As my parents got prepared to enroll us in school, I would wonder aloud, while trying on school clothes at Walmart, how many friends I could make and if the cafeteria food would be edible for breakfast or school lunch. We made the extra trip to the grocery store when my mother grabbed a red lunchbox and my own matching canteen from the shelves. My dad always made sure I couldn't get that extra fifteen minutes of sleep with my school uniform on in the bed, so he made it a mission to wake me up an hour and thirty minutes earlier, to work on homework I hadn't finished, iron my clothes or make my lunch in the morning. To all the people wondering why I was always up at random times in the morning, you can thank my dad for that.

My parents would alternate their days with dropping us off in the morning with my father walking across from the parking lot to the black gates and giving my sister a wet kiss . I would yell "Stop trying to embarass me" before he grabbed me feet away from classmates and their parents and lay a wet one on my face before yelling "Have a good day son" while crossing the street back to his matte black Lexus Rx 300. My mother was less dramatic, waiting until she pulled up to the front gate to tell us to have a good day today in the car and then pull right off after we got out of the car.

My fourth and fifth grade year was an academic success, making honor roll with A's and B's on my report cards. I was noted by teachers and kids around as one of the smartest kids in my class and I carried that with pride, knowing I could be called on with usually the right answer, and if not, I'd try to have the problem solved before the person with the final right answer spoke up.

I read books like Maniac Magee, Drums, Girls and Dangerous Pie, Artemis Fowl, Percy Jackson series, The Extraordinary Adventures of Alfred Kropp and Diary of the Wimpy kid series. Reading books was my escape from the world when the video games weren't in my hands. After a good amount of reading,I guess, that's why in my writing class in school, I was so impassioned in writing my own stories and would have three pages front to back stapled for classwork. I wouldn't pay attention to the kids walking in for the next class because I was going to finish my story, whether I had a paragraph or two sentences in my head left. However, going into my fifth and sixth grade year, I always felt like an alien around my peers because my social skills were subpar with the nerds and the popular kids alike, being homeschooled for that long. I was invading everyone's "personal bubble" with my own breath smelling a mixture of Crest toothpaste, chocolate milk and Cinnamon Toast Crunch from the school breakfast line.

Although we had the same red and black uniforms, all the kids from the hood had the fresh white Air Force 1's, Air Max 90's and 95's and I felt inadequate with my AirWalks and Converse from Payless. I couldn't muster the courage to speak to the cutest girls in my class unless my pencil broke or we were paired in a group project. When I was engaged in conversation with people, my eyes would never align with theirs and my head would be parallel with the ground and my voice quivered and not be audible for the person who was listening to me. Desperate to fit in and seek validation so I could have some friends, I would confront my frustrations to my parents every other afternoon. I never told them that I would have precognitions on the way to school, because what 12 year old that claims he knows where his teacher would be standing at a projector in a certain area from the blackboard and see from a first person point of view where all of his classmates would be sitting in their desks and writing on their papers.

Their first few times, I thought I was just dreaming until weeks or a month later everything played out the way within that deja vu- like moment in class. I kept my X-Men power a secret to myself because my parents were already worried about how my esteem was affecting my schoolwork and then their son was seeing visions before he went to school? Nah, they didn't have to know about that."My father told me to practice my speech in the mirror, handed me a Dale Carnegie book titled "How to Win Friends and Influence People" and began to tell me encouraging words and to keep my head up high before I walked into school every morning. I trained myself mentally anytime I was walking in between classes or to the lunchroom to avoid the "What's up, Megamind?" or even "Honey, whereeeee's my Super SUIT?!" I hated hearing the every-other-day comparison between Eddie Murphy and myself until I saw the film " Boomerang" and the wake-up scene to "Coming To America". So the next time I walked by one of my instigators, I waited until our shoulders crossed paths and I'd tell him "Appreciate bro" & " Yeah I know", to the suddenly, confused kid who thought he was going to pull one over me that week.

By the end of the school day, I would be chilling in the CarRiders section near the after school gate or by the tables next to the office, I'd have to be very cautious of my father trying to sneak up on me. I had to learn the hard way of having my back turned talking to my friends until I got this chill on my neck and seconds later, a voice rupts from the front entrance "SON!" " My Handsome Son, how are you my baby boy?!" Then he proceeds to pull me in a tight embrace as I tried to run away asking me if I was behaving myself, if he didn't approach Mckenna or Imani, these two girls that he had kept tabs on me and embarrassed me in front of them, patiently listening to their full day report of what I was up to and if anybody tried to bully me that day. Titi would take the place of my mother picking me up around 2:30, before my mother started picking me up from the HOST program, and had the CarRider poster displayed on her windshield patiently for my sister and I to enter with her.

I remember trying to run as fast as I could to her car and hide in the backseat as I felt the onlooking eyes from behind the gates follow me towards Isabel's red Chevy Cobalt. She would look back before pulling off to ask me "How was your day mi amor/sweetheart?" I replied with," I don't want to talk about it, can we hurry up and go home now? As I tried to duck down and hide from the spectating kids, I began to become increasingly anxious about the kids that were probably thinking and pointing at me already, " That's his mom right?" "He has a white grandma?" Titi would drive back to the house and watch us until around 6pm. If my mom didn't work overtime or wasn't running late, she had to return back to her house and had to take us because we were obviously too young to stay in the house. There wasn't much to do at Titi's but sit on the couch and eat, dreaming about why my mom was taking so long after finishing my homework or getting lulled to sleep while watching "Gordo Y La Flaca" on Telemundo.

I had a decent amount of friends that I gained within the time I stayed in middle school, who helped me with my homework, picked up the ball when I stammered through the group project speeches, and ran alongside with me on Coach S's mile runs just outside of the school. There was Von, who also stood in as our band teacher, Mr. Hero's main percussionist, who was the first few black kids I became friends with instantaneously. We always rushed through Mr. K's science work and copied the Bill Nye video notes so we could compete against each other on Bloons Towers 2 and the other games on Coolmath.com until the class bell rang. When Mr. Hero wasn't looking and I could stop fake playing my trombone, I'd put it to the side to run to the drum set, where Von would *hide on the side* of the room and let me play until I heard Mr. Hero coming back from the back, running and knocking over a couple chairs in the process. There was Riley who started in the beginning band at the same time as I did. We were both pretty close in skill level, which is surprising because he worked on his Essentials of Music Theory book way more than I did. He was the Gerry to my Julius and never had an unpleasant word to say about me. He had never in my presence said anything racist behind my back and when he had the chance, helped me out in reading music sheets. He understood just how meticulous Mr. Hero was about playing the music correctly no matter how hard it was.

I formed a bond with three other classmates that went by Logan, Nayla, and Bianca when we were selected by the mayor Pam to be part of her Mayor's book talk show. We went to a studio not that far from the school where we were given about three or four books and were recommended to reach each book for the selected month, so when the Book Talk aired; we would be ready to go. The day we would meet up at the television studio, I would be reading through the second and third book in my dad's backseat because I would have already had the scheduled one for that session down pat. The only problem I had was the nervousness I felt as soon as those cameras in the room started rolling.

My anxiety kicked in as Mayor Pam asked us questions about each chapter and it's development… my hands start getting clammy, I tangle and untangle with the mic attached to my shirt after the first book session, but my friends told me they had their doubts and even forgot certain parts of the book and had to improv right on the spot. After that, I kept my head up and was able to provide great feedback with confidence. When it was all said and done, we were presented with a certificate and a photo with the Mayor. She used to call me "King Edward" after each airing of the show, and my dad ate it up every time. I was just glad to be able to show my love for reading to another audience other than my parents and family members that had watched me read chapter books at the age of five.

Around the 6th or 7th grade, a friend of mine pulled me to the side to show me a saved porn video he had pulled up on his cellphone. Being sheltered as a child by the protective wings of my parents, I had no idea that standing next to my friend watching the next few clips from his phone unknowingly changed my life for the better and for the worse. But before I tell you how I developed a compulsive addiction to pornography that nearly tore my emotional being and grip on reality, you'll have to follow my transition through my final moments of middle school to my freshman year of high school. My parents ended up divorcing but ended up living under the same roof, at least until my 8th grade year. My mother believes my dad was complacent at the time and couldn't be the go-to team member to balance her lifestyle. She tried to suggest marriage counseling but my father refused and she handed him the papers.

My father had helped a lot of people since I was little, jump started the business in real estate, and property flipping and his friends had gone to become millionaires; leaving my mother to wonder, how come that success didn't happen for us? My father tells that the economy was harsh on both of their pockets and the properties they both had right in Ybor. I remember sitting in that baking car in the backseat as my parents waited outside for their tenants to discuss issues with the rent and the bills that were coming through. My mother had accused him of cheating, although he felt nothing but her being cold and unemotional towards his feelings. I didn't care about who messed with who or what words needed to be said; because they would realize too late that they were too far in the marriage to even turn around and go back. Gone were the days of Gasparilla and MLK parades where our dad used to hold us high for the beads and pelted candy.

I couldn't get back the times where I used to get called into my dad's room to watch Jack Baier on 24 or dance with matching fedoras to Ne-Yo's "Champagne Life". Gone were the heart shaped chocolate boxes on Valentines Day or the breakfast-on-a-tray for my mother on Mother's Day. I no longer saw my friends come over by the house to play video games on the Nintendo Wii or basketball in the backyard. Realizing that the 16 years of marriage my parents had together was coming to a halt, I started to see the world not as black and white but with specks of grey in the sky. My parents were one of the many divorced couples in my family and it opened my eyes to the fact that there is no guarantee of marriages sealing any type of commitment. My mom would move out shortly after and my dad would soon fall suit out the door, moving in at a relative's apartment.

Throughout seventh grade, almost every day I sat down at my friend's lunch table, worked through my homework assignments and tried to create a process of elimination on any of the possible outcomes of why girls could not even bat an eyelash in my direction. I sure didn't have any faith in myself but if one girl comes out of her comfort zone to make me feel special, I'd feel like I was on the top of the world, even if it was just for an hour or two. My dad once told me after school, he had girl problems around my age when he was going to school.

Growing up in the projects of BX, NY, he was only focused on watching out for his siblings and maintaining his grades. " I might have got a kiss or a girlfriend here and there, but it was nothing serious." But when he got into his freshman year in college, he told himself that this would be his breakout year and he'd be himself, he continued. My mother always told me I was handsome, and I had to believe that and have the confidence to go with it, son. He went on to tell me that soon he would go on to date five of the most beautiful girls on campus and build his social circle of classmates and long time friends.

Nope I wasn't going for it; my mind wasn't set to think that everything he had told me would soon come to pass and I would have all the girls falling for me. But sooner rather than later, I met the one girl that may just be the one for me... Leah. She was a girl that has band classes that merged with the ones I was taking. Leah had very fair chocolate skin, a wide Colgate smile, and was friendly to nearly everyone she met. She was younger than me by two years and she was dating one of my classmates at the time, who was an elite student athlete, D1 basketball level at the time.

Her boyfriend was one of the guys I was cool with, although he had a stigmatism that had made him fidget and twitch randomly in public. I had grown to like this girl for some time now, so I wasn't just going to let her someone else pass up my chance of getting to her. It didn't matter that we didn't have any other classes together or that she was slightly taller than me because I hadn't reached my growth spurt yet, I had my goal set on tunnel vision to get her to like me.

After band class every day, I looked for Von and gave him some crumpled up papers that contained lines of poetry that I work on poetry that I work on days prior for her. "Aye bro I know you got to go up to the 3rd floor but she's got that math class that she walks straight across too." "I need you to stop at the second floor before she walks into class and give this to her." He stops me as he puts his drumsticks and music pack to examine each line, I guess to really see if I was serious about this. "Nah, you are going to *make me late* trying to make me *play messenger*." "Von you know I'm not that confident enough man, I need you to- Where are you going?"

Von replied with, "To class, bro." " I'll give her this letter, but you got to figure out what to do with the rest." "Good luck." It always was a Hit and Miss with this kid to get something I needed done… Like *bro you got a loose screw or something?* My answer came in the form of another young lady who went by the name, *Jessica*. (Jessica's *version of how we met* is vaguely different, where she claims I met her in the 5th grade, which was her 3rd grade year.)

Jessica was a very shy brown skinned girl (who was more on the darker side at the time) who seemed to be very close with Leah due to the fact they would go to Jessica's house every other day until Leah's parents would come to pick her up. I introduced myself to Jessica one day and explained my situation by trying to spit some game, which she quickly understood since she was around Leah all the time. She became my eyes while I was her ears for every conversation that involved myself or the girl I cared about. I trusted her over time and we became close acquaintances. If we *saw each other*, it would be a simple hello and *goodbye to each other*. She claims I used to bully her back in the day, which I don't have any memory of doing so.

Fast forward to my final day of 8th grade where I posted up downstairs with my friends that were sobbing and hugging each other. I didn't have as many class signatures on my grey school spirit shirt as some people did, filling up from the neck collar down. I thought about all the memories that I had with this school, the pot brownies that had been passed out in the cafeteria that would lead everyone falling asleep and hysterically laughing in class (I didn't take one because my gut told me not too and I saw this kid named Perry running around grabbing a third brownie), the time I performed for the Jazz 1 band for MPA at the Florida State Fair. The scholastic book fairs, where I would sit in the back hiding with books while everyone was able to walk out with one and my parents couldn't give me the money to pick one out and take home.

The steel drum band I played was led by Mr. Hero's friend, Mr. Jenkins or the numerous Student of the week awards our school principal Liz Uppercue handed me on stage for perfect attendance. I mean, it's nearly impossible to miss days or fake sickness when you have a mom for a doctor. I snapped back into reality as kids from 6th & 7th grade ran up unexpectedly to show love and give me hugs, crying that I wouldn't be here to see them leave 8th grade when their time came. As I glanced around to see all the familiar faces of Kyle, Tempestt, Darius, and Beau go over the fun times they all had together, I thought about the high-school that I would be attending next. I knew Von was going to Jefferson, which was near the theater our Jazz and Regular bands would perform. Maybe I could tag along wit*h him* if both of our parents could compromise on having me stay there.

As my mind drifts, I'm quickly brought back to reality by a Sudden big hug from Leah and then a side hug from Jessica, both exclaiming that they were going to miss seeing me at school. I couldn't help but smile that the *girl I was in love with* & *my best friend* reached out to me before I left the campus with my pride left in the dust. My dad breaks up the happy moment to take a couple pictures with my friends and hands me a Samsung Galaxy, as we were leaving, whispering that would be my phone for the next couple years. He stops walking on the right side of the sidewalk & tells me he was incredibly proud that I was moving on to the next chapter of my life and couldn't wait to see what life had in store for me. Back at my mother's house, the joy I was feeling to be reunited with one or two classmates in high school after that summer was killed off by the news that I would be flying up to Pennsylvania for boarding school. "What about the friends I have here?" I asked my mom. "What do you mean Grandmother Vilma and Uncle Sam helped me get into the school?" She calmly explained that she had gone to private Christian schools when she was our age, which had gotten her right and had planned to send us when the time was right for us to go.

I couldn't believe her audacity of trying *to* slip this under my nose after I had made promises with my friends to have future classes together. As we went to Target and the mall to buy trunks, clothes, toiletries, I prayed restlessly for a sign from God. I begged for a flat tire on the road, or a declined card in the checkout… Like God, please stop this crazy lady from making me leave Tampa because I don't want to leave all my friends and memories here. But when my mom had everything set for me, I was visited by my dad's church friend aunt Julia before I left my mother's house in Florida. Ms. Sherry reached out to Aunt Julia to give me some clothes and send some love my way. I didn't expect to get the same shirt, pants, and socks that were in the same style of fashion that her son Solomon wore to church at the time. I had to hold back the tears sitting on the couch because Ms. Sherry was a tough person on the outside that I forgot how caring and passionate she can be, but then again, she was the coach of the varsity basketball team at church so being a softy wasn't part of her personality.

I gave aunt Julia a tight squeeze of a hug that was meant for both her and Ms Sherry, to distract myself from how upset I was for going off to school and tried to focus on the love that everybody was sending my way. I told Aunt Julia goodnight and packed my set of clothes into my suitcase.

CHAPTER 5

SOMEWHERE IN PENNSYLVANIA...

The next weeks leading up until my flight to Pennsylvania was such a blur that I couldn't try to remember any of the details in between if I tried too. My mother was on a schedule to get me to the private school and make it back to Florida with time to spare. She went to *Enterprise* to get her rental car and as she focused on the road ahead, I watched the trees, confederate flags and houses by the street zip by my window as we followed the automated voice of the GPS towards the school campus. My mother helped me with my bags, and we walked through the sliding doors of the boy's dormitory to be greeted by the head dean of the dormitory, who was a short Jamaican man dressed in a very dapper manner. He gives us a short tour of the recreation room, bathrooms, the freshman wing leading to the sophomore wing on our left and the junior wing following into the senior wing down to our right.

My roommate had not arrived yet, so just like the other freshmen that had started unpacking their things in their rooms with their parents, I started taking out my bed sheets and hanging up my clothes in my closet.

I turned to a voice at the door to see a stout lightskin kid peeking through the doorway with his mother at his side. He introduces himself as Jonas and we both shake hands and I move out the way to let his mother and relatives get his stuff into the room. We exchanged small talk as he claimed the left side of the room, only to find out that he's from Washington D.C. and I'm older than him by about a year.

After we organized and put the room somewhat together, Jonas made his way around to meet the rest of our classmates and I followed my mom around the manicured grass outside towards the school building. She discusses the curriculum with my science, religion, and algebra teachers and how to get in contact with her in case my grades start to drop below average. Then after checking to see how many hours she has left; my mom exits the school building and continues her tour towards the girl dorm and continues her tour and circles around it towards the back to enter the school cafe.

As we snack on blueberry muffins, she informs me to keep in contact with her, if need be or anything goes wrong at school so she can be up there ASAP. I feel homesick each step leading up to her hugging me goodbye and getting to her car, but if she says it's only for one year then I should tough it out and I'll make it out in one piece, right?

Wrong! I should've known what was up as soon as my mom drove off. The first red flag was when I noticed that I was the only person from Florida at that school. Nobody that came to that school during the years 2013-2014 was from Orlando, Tallahassee, or Miami. The only girl that was close to Florida was a girl in my class that hailed from Texas. There were people from New Jersey, the DMV (who would rep the area code 301, Philly, Connecticut, New York, Michigan, pretty much every state except Florida. From freshman to seniors, the guys were able to form cliques with each other based on their area code and rep each other under Instagram posts (#201, #718, #213 and so forth).To add fuel to the fire, the upperclassmen had this tradition for claiming and looking out for freshman sophomores and juniors that were under the wing (campus families).

They called each other mom, dad, daughter, and son at each event and took "family" photos for school events and holidays. As if the kids that dressed up outside of school and church needed more of a reason to look fresh. I would walk to school, cafeteria, campus church on Saturdays, and back to the dorm with a mask on my face looking and smiling happy through the praise and worship while hiding the neuroticism behind it when I was in the privacy of my own room.

Jonas and I had a *love/hate relationship* inside our room that unknowingly created the building blocks for our friendship long after freshman year. He only referred to me as "Roommate" after our first physical fights to ensure there wouldn't be any attachment between the two of us. Had he not put me on to *Childish Gambino, 48 Laws of Power,* the *Dr. Who* series or let me use his PlayStation Vita when he wasn't in the room, I would've snuffed him with one of his three pillows on those evil nights that I was looking away from my computer and looking in his direction. We were both messy teenagers and Jonas was honestly, the only one between the two of us that would take responsibility for our mess. It would become an obstacle we had to constantly hurdle over as the dean and the R.A. would prevent us from going to any campus activities for the night due to how trashy our room managed to be; even if we cleaned the weekend before.

I couldn't help but come from school sometimes and *sing those first few lines* from Frank Ocean's song, *Thinkin' Bout You*, after opening my room door because a tornado looked as if it came through our door before it was time for breakfast. Jonas suggested that if we changed the physical arrangement of our room, because maybe our room wouldn't be getting so dirty if we put our bed here, desks this way and then sweep and mop after we were done cleaning. We changed that small room so many times that I think the Property Brothers should have given us a call to be on their show. And the room always ended up being messy every week, so changing the inside of it really did no justice for our cause. When it was time to go to bed, I'd poke Jonas in the stomach to make sure he was asleep then tip-toe over to the computer, trying to grab the wireless keyboard off the desk as quietly as possible and logged into my Mac desktop right away.

As I typed *P-O-R* into the search engine, I glanced over to see if my roommate had woken up from all that tossing and turning, he was doing in his bed. When I was confident that he was still oblivious to my current mischief, I continued my quest to make it through at least five videos and then would head off to bed. No sooner had I gotten to the two minute mark of the third video when I received a pillow to the back of my head and a "Aye man go to sleep, we got school tomorrow and it's way too early for you to be up!" Stunned, I shut down my computer and laid in bed trying to calculate where I went wrong in the moment, and then closed my eyes, trying to forget it all in the morning.

{Floating Demon}

Did you ever get bullied by anybody on the campus? Did you get into any big fights or was it just people seeing you with the "ones"?

There were different occasions that I had to hold my own between my first semester and the second semester so I *can't really pinpoint* when someone really got in my face and we had beef. There were fights in the rec room where it went from people watching tv and playing video games to an all out brawl in the middle of the room.

When leaving the cafeteria for the night after eating dinner, I headed out with a couple of friends back to the dorm . Sometimes if I needed a breath of fresh air, I would walk alone on that trail to shake off all the energy I felt around being with those people in the cafeteria. Imagine my surprise when I was walking on a breezy September evening and all I hear behind me is *"They're coming!"*. I turned back to see all the seniors chasing after the freshman and sophomores and they were all headed in the same direction. I got tackled and slammed on the ground without any realization on how I ended up on the grass quickly. As I curled up into a ball, I peeked after I watched everyone taking similar punishments on the ground and only the strongest member of our class duked it out with one or two seniors at the same time.

My roommate comes and pushes the junior steadily kicking my chest in, causing him to stumble back and I fought back with my roommate until I realized we were going to get outnumbered and took off to the dorm as if my asthma wasn't spiking through my lungs, sucking the air out like a Capri Sun. These battles would come at random and could only be recognized through whispers either in the dorm or out in the night from the cafeteria. Sometimes, somebody was talking sh*t and all the upperclassman had to put that guy in check in the usual battlefield just outside of the school. I took off as soon as I heard running footsteps by the trees because I wasn't staying to see anybody's heads get knocked down in the grass or the bodies get slammed down with emphasis. I know a couple people that begged me to stay and hold my own against the upperclassmen before they too met their fate. *But less than half of these guys didn't have my back when I got hassled in my own room, so what makes you think I'm going to stay and get beat up now? This ain't* 300 *and I can't be going out bad and get put in a sweaty chokehold because "I'm supposed to have y'all backs."*

My roommate and I heard that this guy from our class from a guy wanted to come meet him in his room. We walk down into this guy's room and instead of being greeted with snacks or getting dapped up, we glance over at the guy like we felt the same thing or something... He was already whaling on someone and *in the* split second that we came in, the guy splits between us to the open door like *a* wide receiver heading toward the end zone.

Jonas gets grabbed within a moment's notice and held down onto the bed, squirming to get away. I drowned out the pained squealing noises from my roommate and focused on making a quick escape plan. The window in front of me is suicide because it's right in front of the bed. Jonas is getting his ass whooped, and the other two freshmen in the room pulled me back in as soon as I managed to get past one of them to open the door. I wait for an opening and I rush to the door, but I barely had the leg and arm out the crack of the door when I got dragged back into the room.

The sophomore flexes his wrist back and cracks the belt on the bed and I dodge and weave, holding onto the comforter of the bed to soften the hits on my sides and legs. After he had his fill of torture, the guy proceeds to exit the room, leaving the two of us to recover from his never-ending blows. That wasn't my last encounter with that dude. Not long after, I find myself banging on one of Jonas's friends' doors desperate to get in. "Come on, A.J." "Hurry up and open the door!" As he lets me in, I catch my breath and tell him that *I need somewhere to hide* because this dude is coming for me and *he already knows where my room is.* A.J. opens the door and all I can see from my angle is two pairs of sneakers and a brown leather belt hanging to the floor.

He tells the sophomore that I haven't been over here lately & points in the opposite direction, suggesting he check over there. As the door closes, I whisper to A.J. if the guy left and he tells me that the coast is clear. I dap him up for the help and look both ways before I dash towards my room to the left, which was moved into the sophomore wing of the dorm.

Another instance was when I came to my room from the cafeteria to find my Mac desktop missing from the usual spot on my desk. I quickly suspected my roommate had something to do with its disappearance. Here's why: There was a girl by the name of "Diamond" who had a train run on her a couple summers back by a group of guys in a bathroom. (Choo-Choo!). She had a Skype account and the rumor was getting passed around quickly that she was giving out webcam shows. One of my classmates got a hold of her information, but couldn't install Skype on his computer.

However, I had Skype pre-installed so I could reach my mother if I needed to via her iPhone. Jonas, A.J. and another guy put their heads together to use my computer to video chat this girl. I didn't have a problem with them trying to reach her the first time, but when they kicked me out before the call started, I harbored some hatred towards these guys because my computer was getting eye raped for some chick that they would get tired of eventually.

Back in the present moment, I was walking into my room trying to figure out where these fools could have taken my computer when I peep A.J.'s head looking in from the hallway. I took off down the hallway and wedged my foot against their door from closing, but all three bodies pushing on the door were a lot of weight for me to push back against, so I moved my leg back when I gave out and the door slammed in my face. I banged on the door to be let in and to no avail, they ignored all the noise and yelling, I was making. The dean on the night shift asks me from the office, "What all the ruckus was about?" and I tell him that it was nothing and I'd be making my way back to my room. I didn't even make it to the halfway point between the freshman and sophomore wing when I stopped to put my back on the wall and slid down with my head in my hands crying. "God, why do you let these things happen to me?" "I hate it here and nothing ever goes the way I want it to."

"After that incident, I made sure I enabled some password protection on my computer and stayed back from going to dinner at the cafeteria a few times to ensure that these fools didn't take my computer again. I deleted all the messages and blocked Diamond from my account, after I tried calling out of curiosity and seeing she didn't answer.

{Floating Angel}

Did you ever fall in love with anyone? Were you ever rejected by any girls or did some find you cute or attractive?

Remember Jessica and Leah, the two girls that I ended up being friends with from school? I began talking to Leah after she broke up with her boyfriend, and I also got Jessica's Kik from Leah because I remembered that little girl that was kind to me and gave me a hug on my last day of school. Everything was going smoothly so far, all the days I used to be leaving school, singing Marvin's Room (I'm just saying you could do better... Tell me, have you heard that lately). *It* paid off now I got the girl *I* wanted. I could sense the way some distance between us so I switched over to talking with Jessica more now that she was my best friend. We discussed favorite colors (mine being black and red and Jess's being purple and black) and the videos she sent me of her *running track* with high hopes that I could *show up to her track meets* one day. All the *conversations and video calling* would catch up to me when *Leah confronts Jessica* privately on why she couldn't get a hold of me and why I was *"entertaining"* Jessica more on the phone than her.

Jessica, being the petty person that she is, sends her the screenshots of our messages back and forth while telling Leah that she didn't have any feelings towards me and if I remember correctly, why is Leah acting like she cares now when I was doing all the chasing and writing poetry and she didn't care back then? Meanwhile, I didn't even know this argument was even had until later, so I distanced myself from Jessica and put her on to one of the guys at my school so I could keep out of trouble with Leah. I went back to Leah to work on our communication issues, *even though there was an obvious rift in the relationship after that argument.*

The girls that would frequent the campus were *nubian goddesses* that would be seen with their *beautiful natural hair* out in full effect, skin color varying from *dark chocolate to light caramel* with a *fragrance of shea butter* and light perfume in the air. Being around these young women built an attraction for proud confident black women that I have to this day. Unfortunately I still carried the *" HEY, where's my hug at"* mentality that hadn't disappeared from middle school, so any attempt of showing any confidence to talk to one of these girls would be deemed cringeworthy. I'd make a U-turn back to where I was headed to deflect any embarrassment that I was causing towards myself. I felt like nobody was going to willing to give me a chance outside of being acquainted or being friends in school and I'd daydream occasionally about getting kidnapped by females to their dorm only to return back to my room with lipstick kisses on *my face and neck with a sly grin on my face*; awaiting any nosey guys to ask me what happened so I could easily respond with "Oh nothing happened, I just got a little lost coming back here, but you can mind your business though."

The girls in my class were decent but I had no eyes for anyone, despite what others may think, and seemed a bit snobbish by talking to guys that were the popular ones in my class.I did meet this one girl from Maryland who had changed my opinion on girls for the rest of my time there. We exchanged small talk from the one on one conversations at the cafeteria and some of the guys urged me to jump out of my comfort zone and try to date her, even though I didn't feel like I was worth having a relationship anyway.

We exchanged small talk from the one on one conversations at the cafeteria and some of the guys urged me to jump out of my comfort zone and try to date her. Fast forward to December when this grand winter banquet is being hosted at the pavilion on the school campus. *I reached out to my dad on the phone to tell him, It was about to go down.*

The day finally comes when we are gathered out in the lobby looking like the Ocean Eleven crew. I had to switch out of my shirt twice to find the right match for my outfit and a heavy jacket to pair well with the suit I had underneath. When the head dean leads us out the dorm across the snow and road towards the building, I think about *the* speech I rehearsed in my head for the girl on how cool she was to be around and talk to in class. We began marching through the ankle deep snow towards this pavilion to enjoy fellowship with both young men and women and the programs they had planned, like special guest singers and songs from everyone to dance to.

Upon arriving, I hang back from the crowd to find a good seat to avoid all the festivities and couples dancing around me. When the opportunity presents itself, I shoot my shot across the table and as it goes around the rim, I await the girl's response as she takes it all in. She sat up in her seat at the table, pushed her chair back and politely rejected me in front of the whole class. To add the cherry on the top of the melting ice cream sundae, she ridiculed me on the fact that I shouldn't have gone to my father for advice, not that it would make a difference on the rejection she just gave me. I got up from the table and sprinted to the bathroom, the Hoover dam tears already streaming down my face. A.J, Jonas and another guy come through minutes later to my side for a bro to bro moment on how these girls are for any and everybody, and that it was her loss that she missed out on me, not mine.

After heading back to my room after the event had ended, it dawned on me that someone had to go behind my back for her to reveal that information about my dad trying to help me out and try to talk to her. I realized that day was a wakeup call for why I was better off keeping to myself and losing the need to crush on any girls that are out of my league.I reached out to that same girl during the summer on Kik to redeem myself and she apologized due to the fact *she had really meant no hard feelings by turning me down*, but it was already too late because the damage had already been done, and *there was no going back from the savage I would soon turn into.*

Floating Angel : What were your happiest moments of your freshman year? Were there any people special to you that came to visit you?

Honestly, the first person I can think off the top had to be my dad. He showed up after numerous calls I made, which meant a lot to me even if he had to leave in a short amount of time. He made sure I had suits for church and long sleeve shirts to combat the cold weather. I couldn't be anything less than grateful to see him physically there when he said he would be.

My cousin Reyna and her parents, Uncle Rob & Aunt Carmen had to come second. I never expected Reyna to come on random visits to give me a heartfelt hug, or suprise me with birthday cupcakes and check up on me in the campus church. It kept me in good spirits and out of the depression that I wallowed in. On school breaks, my godparents opened their doors for me to stay over. There aren't any amount of words that can really express how much appreciation and gratitude I have towards them.I remember one Saturday morning being on the sophomore wing, I emerged out of my room and investigated my closet in hopes for a good outfit for church. I was taking personal photoshoots before and after church service and with the confidence the shoots gave me, I was looking for more variety and styles in the outfits I had. To no avail, none of the outfits I was looking for had the colors I needed to pop with the suit I was wearing.

I knocked on my neighbor's door across from my room and some guy named Josh opened the door while putting his suit together on his bed. I asked for a pocket square or tie and on cue, a door opened to my right with a pocket square hanging out. I said thank you to the outstretched hand and followed Josh in my room as he tried to make sense of the outfit, I was putting together. He laid out his own ties and handkerchiefs on my bed and details why this outfit colors compliment with the colors that are on the pocket squares and will pair well with black shoes rather than my suede brown shoes.Now by this point, I already took fashion tips and styling points from alumnists and the juniors and seniors, but for a sophomore that I socialize with to borrow his clothes because I was missing the extra pieces to make my suit pop? It was the small things, the small moments that meant the most to me.

If I needed something to laugh, I'd watch Dave Chapelle, Kevin Hart, Bernie Mac Kings Of Comedy, George Lopez, and Eddie Murphy's Delirious on Youtube over and over until my stomach started hurting from laughing. The journaling I did on my computer and on my own individual time gave me peace. I became my own therapist for my own thoughts, my own consultant when I got bullied or experienced heartbreak, when I was stressed beyond anyone else's or was in a good mood and wanted to write about it. I had to minimize my word documents and hide them in the face of company because anytime Jonas's friends busted through the room with him leading the pack, they used to stop over my shoulder and ask, "Damn why you got six pages of writing?" " Are you working on homework or something? Then sometimes they scoff or laugh and say "What are you trying to write a book or something?" (Well it was for my own mental stability to keep me sane. Now this is a book and I get the last laugh.) I timestamped each entry from the moment Microsoft Word popped up on my screen, and I used an online mp3 converter and collected all the songs I needed by the time I went to bed for the day.

My playlist included Kendrick Lamar's Good Kid MAAD City, Chance The Rapper's Acid Rap, Joey Bada$$ 1999 mixtape, Marvin Gaye's What's Goin' On and I Want You album. Sometimes I'd throw some Speaker Knockerz or the Weeknd in the mix if I had a writing block.

When I finally had the opportunity to go back to Florida on one of my breaks, my cousin Gabriel gave me his old PS2 from his then girlfriend's apartment in a dusty red and black Nike duffle bag. The games that came in the console were State Of Emergency, Grand Theft Auto 3, and God of War 2. I played it back in school every other time I didn't have any homework left and the deans could get the rec room open for me.

I was always gracious to let anyone in the dorm play GTA until one of the tiles from the rec room ceiling fell and hit my console while I was in my room switching something out. Smh and I left GTA running in the playstation, so when I turned around to clean it off the console, no one tried to stop and help. I didn't touch the PS2 until I came back to Florida for my sophomore year of high school. The hymns and prayers we had together as young men were spiritually soothing for the soul. Yes we did wrestle and argue, some of us never let go of grudges that we held against each other since August but when we stepped into that prayer room, you couldn't fight that calm peace that washes over you like a cool shower after a long day.

I tried to keep my mouth closed and not sing for as long as possible, but when the dean started giving me this glare of disapproval, while all the guys were singing "We are Soldiers"; I had no other choice but to join in too.

I can't forget all the times where we would go over the scriptures individually and talk about what parts of the verses meant the most to us and how it applied to each of us that week, whether it was God helping someone get that class grade from an F to an A or exclaiming with great news that someone back home had been healed from cancer. It felt peaceful seeing everyone happy and knowing that some higher power really looks out for us, even when we went about the day depressed or feeling evil.

The last few months of school for me was a dream come true and I spent them well deservingly. The majority of the two hundred dollars my dad had given to me in hand were spent on Papa John pizza boxes, medium cheese with no toppings. I'd walk down the hallway, sometimes passing out slices happily knowing I wouldn't see any of these clowns next year and other days running straight to my room to treat each stringy cheesy slice with the Tender Loving Care my stomach deserved.

On that final day, my mother pulled up on the side entrance and as we loaded everything into her rental car, I could taste the sweet freedom of home just waiting for me on the other side of that airport. Soon as I arrived that week, I reached out to my friends on messenger to let them know the kid was back in Florida and here to stay.

My church group chat was overflowing with enthusiasm knowing that I would be seeing them every Saturday at church like nothing changed. Jessica and Leah worked out their differences and was happy that I was in town, hoping to catch me out sometime so we could go hang out at United Skates or the mall. Someone reached out to me from the boarding academy and asked about whether I was going to be making a trip to the school for the following semester.

"Bro the girls coming up this year are looking better and the school is going to renovate the gym!" "You sure you don't want to come back?" While this guy is dropping reason after reason, Jamie Foxx playing the piano while dropping F-bombs was playing in my head. I replied with "Nah I'm good bro" and smiled because I was at peace, appreciating the fact I was back home and nowhere else.

CHAPTER 6

BACK HOME FOR GOOD?

My mother would receive GQ subscribed magazines as she placed the mail on the kitchen counter and as I would come across them, I asked permission to "borrow" the magazine the day of. I flipped through the pages, stopping occasionally to admire a chocolate lady in a bikini on the beach until I found the Style and Grooming articles.

I wrote down everything from outfits for weddings to cologne and socks for any social event and taped the papers along my bedroom wall because my mom would want her magazines back every couple of days and I needed a visual of what I planned to wear in the future.

The goals I had written on the papers taped around the walls included a number of things- By 27 years of age, I'd have all the imported fitted suits I need in my suit closet of my house along with the seven pairs of dress shoes to go with the outfit of the day. I'd have a muscle car before 25 and a certain number of custom sneakers around my house before I reached my early 30's. When I wasn't shuffling through my playlist on my computer or writing in my personal diary, I was getting busy on my phone responding to the girls and friends I had on my phone. Unbeknownst to family and friends, except for a few close ones, I had a selective number of girls I was talking to on the phone that I had found through Kik messenger and would be flirtatious with a few. Some girls were in Florida and others were long distance.

It was on that Samsung where I practiced speaking a love language to girls that were drawn to the figurative language I spoke. I had enough confidence in myself and in the words that I used that were alluring and appealing that in the affirmations I made to these young women and *some* would get aroused by the promises and loyalty I showed throughout the days and months that passed. Granted, making love with someone's mental and spiritual doesn't work on everyone (some girls want an athlete or a hood n*gga) because not everyone is going to get attracted to you, but the ones that I did get? Lawd have mercy! I had a physical type of girl that I was attracted to but if the girl in question was willing and trusting in me, I didn't shut her down regardless of her skin complexion or body.

I found out some girls that *acted shy and stuck up in public* would get comfortable enough around me to show that she was really a freak behind closed doors and had that well done "mac n' cheese". Others were skinny on their Instagram pictures but really had the yams when those pants came off. I didn't get attracted to any girls that came off too easy to me, because that would've turned me off too quick. I enjoyed a challenge, a girl that got looked over by guys that just wanted to get his nut off real quick. Pardon me, if that last sentence seemed too uncut and explicit, but it was the truth. Now the question you may be asking is why did I talk to girls over the phone, when I could just unmask that bravado in person and be my true self?

I enjoyed being a mystery, an enigma because when I tried to be myself around certain girls I was attracted to, it seemed like a guy would always "cock-block" my advances. In my head, I never got rejected or walked with my head low, like I did when I stepped out of my comfort zone but I guess that's what I get for trying to not be introverted. When I was on my phone, I didn't have my friends try to match me with a girl they saw because " you guys both look like nerds with glasses."

I was in a better state of content when I saw less of "Oh you're just a brother to me" and "Ew, we can only be friends because I don't like you like that" and more of "I've been holding back how much you turn me on" and "I love you because you genuinely care about me and I can put my trust behind that." Anything that I hated about myself, was something that I would mentally battle with when I stared into the bathroom mirror and soon ended up vanishing when I was able to pour my heart out to young women that returned the favor back.

When I went over to my dad's girlfriend's house for the summer, I was caked up over Leah on Oovoo. I used my dad's laptop to video call her and reply to each other's message throughout the evening when we would be online. Everything was going so good with the relationship up until she had broken my heart and it shattered to pieces. It all started late at nine in the afternoon when I saw the words "we need to talk" pop up on the screen. I knew what that was leading to and I tried to divert the situation by saying "I guess, or I don't know", hoping she would revisit the issue another day or another week.

As she detailed the issue of "space" that allowed us to grow apart from each other since I got into boarding school in 2013, she quickly got to the point and told me she had a newfound crush on another guy.

Before she sent me the picture and told me his name, my heart sank and I flashbacked to a point when I had told her about the yacht trips my dad "was working on taking me" and asking her to join so we could be chair to chair next to the railing and enjoy the view. That was way before I learned about my dad's financial situation and that parents don't always have it together like they tell you when you are naive as a kid. I deleted our conversations and cried like heartbroken Tobey Maguire in Spider-Man 3. I moped around the house for the next few days, watching Izzie massage my dad's bald head and lotion his legs on the couch thinking, "that's the type of comfort and love

I need in my life right now." "I won't ever settle again until I make sure I got that security in any kind of relationship."

It seemed effortless in my eyes the way my dad bonded with the pretty women in his life, looking out for each other's kids and being in mutual agreement when the other adult wasn't physically present in the area.It was a couple days later when I remembered how Jessica had said back when I was in Pennsylvania, that Leah wasn't into all the chasing that I was doing because she knew who she wanted but she entertained me for the time being. I reached out to my best friend to see if she could help me get over this pain I was feeling and if she wasn't seeing anybody, I'd probably holla at her too. Lately, Jess had been suicidal over some issues that she was facing by herself and been cutting herself for the past month, which I didn't know until she texted in context about everything that she was going through at that point.

I broke down to her about how I was feeling depressed about my issues after my breakup and had been eyeing the prescription pills in the bathroom with the thoughts of *"how many will it take for me to blackout and forget the unbearable pain?"*

I told her that I couldn't see how the world would be a better place if she just ended her life and sent her multiple paragraphs urging her to quit cutting. I wouldn't feel better about myself if she ended her life right then and there. After she showed signs of improvement and was in a better mindstate, I vented my feelings of infatuation that I confined towards her.

After giving me short answers and leaving my messages on read, she told me that she wouldn't be easily convinced because of the "I'd jump over a cliff for you and you're just as great as the mountains and rivers" poems I wrote to Leah. The thing that got me was that it had been at least two years since that had happened and the girl still couldn't get over it. But I thought about it and said, well she did try to help me talk to her friend before all this sh*t collapsed. So I decided to put 110% in this girl to show her how loyal I could be if we were in a relationship.

The first thing we did that summer was make a pact between ourselves to secure a bond just between the two of us. She told me to never call her out her name or we would be done. I told her if she failed to respect me when I wasn't around, then she would lose me forever. Because I'll mentally lose you before I physically tell you I'm done with you. She was such a hard cookie to crack and it didn't help that we were both shy people that only opened up to people that already gained our trust (childhood friends and family included). I told her my middle name was Eugene, and let her know that she was the only person on this earth, besides my mother, that could call me by my government name. In return she told me her middle name was Lorraine, which came from her grandmother so it was settled. She always made it a thing to be slick when she finally got comfortable on Oovoo.

If I felt like being an asshole, I'd call her boychest or a bum and she called me forehead and jiggaboo. It became enjoyable, knowing she wouldn't get sensitive or offended. Even so, we still drew a line on when to chill out and be respectful to each other.

I stayed up through all the kitchen cleaning and dishwashing that she did on the phone and would willingly play a third wheel on those late nights when her crush was playing hard to get to be with her. Jessica got to see first hand on the camera that I was a bad dancer and would only go inside the kitchen to make some cereal or a grilled cheese sandwich.

I occasionally saw her brother try to take her phone from her when he bust through her room and hid behind my hoodie or turned the camera off while he's trying to figure out who the guy was on his sister's line. "Oooh, you gotta be quicker than that!" While she'd walk around the house to the phone if I ever saw her mom around in the kitchen, I always spoke to her mother respectfully and always told Jess to tell her I said hello if she didn't come through. I knew she was starting to feel me when I'd start talking about her and she'd blush and cover up her face or bit the lip on the right side of her face. If I ever got her mad and she didn't look in my direction, her childhood friend Gabby would take her phone and text me "you need to fix this or go apologize to her and tell her how you messed up." I'd try to fight back my point and say, "But it wasn't my fau-."

But Gabby would come back with, "It doesn't matter, so you better go fix it and apologize." Guess you can't debate because a woman will end up having her way when she wants too.

Going into sophomore year of high school was a weird transition from being independently on my own and having people I was staying with watching over my shoulder to living with my brother and my sister. I couldn't get over the fact of my mother trading her beautiful locks for a shorter natural fade. I guess it was an emotional and mental phase of her leaving the divorce because of how symbolic hair is to women. I used to go through album books in the house, mesmerized by how great my mom's hair looked in her post college days.

My mother drove me down to Hillsborough High and as we stood in the long line, she went over SAT testing in hopes that I inch closer towards scholarships for college. I wasn't interested in college and wanted the school year to rush and get over with. The classes I received were Psychology, Drivers Ed, World History, English, Physical Science, Computer Skills and Digital Media Fundamentals, just off the top of my head. My mom made sure I would remember the bus schedule and where to walk from the back of the house on Plymouth Street to the nearby park and wait on the corner for the bus in the morning. The bus would circle from my stop on Ola Avenue after running through the last few backstreets to pick the other kids up and then go straight down on North Florida Avenue; to make a straight shot to the school until we pulled up into the back entrance.

The school's back parking lot was filled row to row with cars from lowriders to Toyota Camry's with official teen driver bumpers on the back windshield. Then the GTR's and low suspension Honda would roar into the lot, trying to impress anyone who watched the tire rubber leave marks on the street. In the morning, I sifted past the I.B. kids, the hispanics and the upperclassmen to get to the cafeteria and find a secluded spot for me to sit at. It was already enough hearing girls stuff down hot chips and yell "BEST FRIEND… I SAID BEST FRIEND COME HERE!!" I'm just looking at them as if to say in my head, "Like it's not even 7 AM, sit down somewhere over here yelling in my ear." I'd scan the walkways outside checking for who was going to start a fight so I could walk in the opposite direction and which upper class men dress tacky so I could walk by and give them some pointers.

Throughout the day, if I was talking to somebody while we were walking and if I notice something off about your outfit could be fixed like pulling your collar down or pin rolling your jeans instead having that big stupid cuff on your ankle; I'd ask about it and go straight to work on their outfit like Young Thug at the V Files show. I'd tell them to not buy that shirt from Pac- Sun again and recommend some shirt or jacket that would complement that same outfit. Sometimes I'd get stared at like, "You don't have a clean fit yourself, but you're giving me great advice on what to wear" and they would take my criticism and go with the flow.

Each week in the lunch area or in the school parking lot, There would be at least three fights. No one cared what administrator would break up the fight or how long the fight was going to last, soon as you saw the crowd from the cafeteria run outside or everyone already outside shift to one direction; you already knew what time it was. I was always told by my dad to never record or get in the middle of the fight if I get in trouble, but I either got the video from someone else that I knew or had a close call from someone as well.

Going down the hallway to my drivers ed course one day, a flying shoe came rocketing towards my head and I quickly side stepped out of the way to dodge it and the oncoming group of people that were fighting in front of me. The fights after school would put a hold on the after school bus drivers and I would watch from my window seat as the police officers went ahead to tackling or tasering the kids that wouldn't stop fighting. As the days and months passed, I became aware of the small changes around me. When I was in school, I saw people sneak off the back entrance to skip their classes or come from behind the stairwell I was walking towards after having sex. One guy tried to dap me up because I was holding the door saying "Appreciate it homie" and then tried to dap me up but all I could give him was a disgusted look. Don't touch me after you were all on that girl man.

Afterschool, I kept begging but my mother wouldn't compromise for me to get an allowance. I wish she did because I wasn't old enough to get a job & I didn't have the patience to keep waiting on my dad; he kept promising that he'd have it soon or it would be in my hands by the weekend. He kept telling me, I would need to "stop worrying about getting a job because he would provide anything I needed." *But you only can break a kid's promises so much before he starts to fill his head with doubt.*

Frustrated with not getting an agreement for some money, I talked to this one kid in my history class because he had some marijuana seeds he grew on his property. I figured that would be the temporary start for me to have some cash on the side. I hit him through messenger, and asked for proof because I don't want any duds that didn't grow in the ground. He shows what he had in his possession and we agree on a price. The last few minutes of class, I handed him the money and he put the baggie in my bookbag.

I went through the week on the bus wondering if K-9's could smell marijuana seeds and where would I plant the seeds at home because there was not a spot in the backyard that I could place it without the plant being discovered or dying without sunlight. I also did research on my computer and realized that *I wouldn't be able to have them last in my possession because of the lack of resources for it to grow.* So that weekend, I passed the seeds off to a close friend and flushed the bag down the toilet when I got back home.When the plants started showing progress and I smiled at the pictures on my phone, because what others saw as a drug or an herb, I saw future Christmas presents and sneakers that neither of my parents could afford.

That happiness was short lived when my friend texted me back a couple days later and I read the text that plants were male instead of female, so they were basically useless. I didn't see any use in trying to keep growing them, so I told him the best thing was to just get rid of them for the sake of us getting out of trouble. I was so hopeful of being profitable off the little hustle I just came up on, that I even went out of my way and found at least three people in school who were ready for some.

I just went to school with my head lower than ever because I just put my time into all that to get no return from it. I didn't see myself trying to get acquainted or find friends because every day I seemed like all the kids wanted to do was act out and fight whoever for any small reason, Naruto run between the tables and through the hallway, or be disruptive every day in every classroom. The only people I did end up being close friends with were two people that I saw on a day to day basis were Roberto, & Jean . I met Roberto in Mr. Bee's English class and our interaction with each other was slight with pairing for reading assignments and classwork done out of our blue Spring-board books. He sat in the far left corner of the classroom with his cousin Michelle and I sat towards the far- right middle table near Mr. Bee's desk with two Hispanic kids named Johnny and "Kalena". I was always the go to guy at our table, letting the two copy off my work when they came late because Johnny was either food in class, falling or cleaning off his Jordan's and "Kalena" had always been a polite person at our table, so when she got pregnant, I just wanted to get her up to speed with class to return the favor. From book reading out loud (Things Fall Apart) to taking quizzes, the class presented itself as an easy A had it not been for all the distractions around the room from time to time. You know the occasional Bluetooth speaker going off, yelling over the teacher, and getting kicked out of the classroom, only to be a fool right outside the door... the regular stuff.

Because Roberto and I weren't always partnered up in English class, I had to wait until we were in Physical Science in Ms. Pope's classroom to become better friends with him. In Ms. Pope's classroom, we had a lot of classwork taken from PowerPoints and videos, pop quizzes and online science labs that we worked on. I made sure I sat close to Roberto, because with all the kids that switched out of the class through both semesters; he was the only kid I was familiar with that had another class besides science with me. There was this Puerto Rican girl that he was cool with that I kept trying to press him to put me on with every day we were in class. She was quiet, only spoke Spanish to the other students that translated to Ms. Pope for her but understood English by ear very well in class. Now that I think about it, every black guy that was in that class tried to shoot their shot towards her. So I mustered up some courage in the hallway to shoot my shot and she looked back at me and called me a "crica."

I asked Roberto in class what it meant and when he told me, I was a little hurt, I ain't going to lie. It is kind of messed up when a cute Hispanic girl who acted like she was mute when she understands English made me go out of sad like that. But karma le hizo mal y el novio de ella la avergonzó so I didn't trip over her after I was done with that class. I just made up my mind to never go after Hispanic women, if they were all going to have that type of attitude. I met Jean in Ms. Carrey's Drivers ed class and unlike Roberto, that was the only class I had with Jean in school so I had to find time between driving silver Ford Fusions around the track or taking quizzes and classwork in the classroom to talk to him. He was one of the youngest guys in the class, so he couldn't get his permit right away that semester.

I forgot how Jean and Roberto ended up meeting but when all three of us got acquainted, we would meet up by the bike rack afterschool near Roberto's welding class, and I pleaded with both of them while they were unlocking their bikes to either let me ride one of their bikes and alternate each block to Roberto's house.

Have you ever seen a five foot five Salvadorian and a chubby dark skin Hatian alternating with their best friend on both of their handlebars on the way to the house? They would keep trying to kick me off because they said I was going to flatten their tires, but I wasn't going to just let them take off to the house and let me run behind them the whole time.

We biked through North Central Avenue, passed the McDonald's across the street, then headed down left on East Lake Street under the overpass, hit a right until we got on Nebraska's avenue, passed the church and ended up right on Roberto's street. Sometimes we'd stop for a couple minutes to mess with the Arab behind the counter of the corner store and grab as many hot Cheetos and Takis, honey buns that our growling stomachs could handle. I tried to reach in my back pocket anytime Roberto obliged to pay for my snacks that I picked out or offered too but he always turned me down and said I got you bro. I felt those "LA Capone vibes" for real.

As we approached the metal fence, Roberto shooed away his chickens to the back and Jean rubbed his hands like Birdman because he got fried chicken on his mind and I was standing in the back, just here to play Call of Duty and Modern Warfare with the bros. We squeezed past through the narrow hallway and kicked out Jeffrey, Roberto's little brother, because he couldn't be silent without revealing everybody's position in the video game we would all play together. We took our positions either on the side of Roberto's bed, or the floor. The rules were simple- Jean had to keep his shoes on because his feet smelled like rotten eggs, no cheating in the game (although Roberto tried to justify it because it was his Xbox), and to never overstay your visit unless it was rain, snow or some type of crime going on outside in the neighborhood. I would end up staying over longer than I should, because I felt alone at my mom's house. That was my only issue but it wasn't a huge concern to Roberto's mother because his family was that cool with me but at some point, I would get the hint that it was time for me to go.

Roberto, Jean and I made sure to stick out for each other. It didn't matter how hard it turned out for the three of us. If one was able to reach out to the other, we'd make sure we could talk out the stress or issue so we could make it through the days to come. Some mornings, we would all link up at Roberto's house or close to the apartments down a few blocks so we could all make it to school. If we set an appointed time to meet up, you better believe that we had to hustle to meet up or run like hell to school if I was late to the meet up spot.

I know I had to run a few times, running after their bikes like "slow down man I was only a few minutes late" but they weren't going to stop and make all of us late. Living with my mother in that yellow house off Highland Ave was anything short of enjoyable, in my eyes at least. Coming home, I would have to wait outside on the mat more than my few share times for Titi to come back with Ethan because I wasn't given a house key.

When I finally got inside, it was a straight shot to my room. No reason to stay in the living room because the only one who could watch Television for a long period of time was my brother. Why would I go to the kitchen if there was only Raisin Bran and Chocolate chip cookies in the pantry? My mother only went to Publix or Walmart occasionally but didn't hesitate to find someone to get the "high-end" dresses and high heels that she wore to work every day. I would rather not eat than eat dry cereal out of the bowl like potato chips, so I put my bag down and logged into my computer and went straight into my playlist so I could let the music play over the homework I had, the video games I was playing and the writing for my journals.When I was introduced to my mother's boyfriend, Life I didn't know what to take of him: a 6 foot tall bearded and dreadlocked African American male with tattoos all over his body.

Being the oldest out of the three of us and a momma's boy, I couldn't help but be judgemental towards this man. Where did she find him, was he a patient or some guy she met at a party? Did he get those tattoos in prison or did he get them out of jail? Is this supposed to be my mom's upgrade? I had a long conversation on the couch with my mom, months later when I could catch that sliver of time that she didn't dedicate her work into because my mom is a workaholic. I asked her, Do you plan to get married to him? And she quipped back with, "Maybe and if I do?" My face twisted with dissent and I couldn't help but be confused. Married to… him? I don't even know Life like that because he just came out of nowhere and I didn't have a chance to mentally heal from our parents divorce.

They bonded over time, with Life making trips to my mom's house or stopping at my mother's office before performing his Spoken Word poetry downtown. It would create a lot of awkward moments for my younger self, walking in the house to see my mom fixing his dreadlocks or practicing Wing Chun outside with LiFe as her partner. Then he would stop by while she was working to deliver flowers and lunch while she was at her office (Like I appreciate that you went out and got my mom some lunch but I'm over here starving too).

I felt like a distant third wheel because I was having no success with girls my age in person and constantly had to hear Life's poetry be played on the television, the car radio, listening to their open conversations… I didn't know whether to be depressed or angry so I mixed both emotions when I saw them together and kept it bottled up and didn't say anything to anyone. Where was my true love at?

My parents moved on and could find love for themselves but I couldn't even date or love someone who liked me for me. Life tried to form a respectable relationship with me, but I rejected any chances of him trying to build a bond with me, despite getting rides around his truck to see his family, the printing company he was working with to get his work published, and his open mic performances.

When my father found out that Life drove me to an inappropriate shop while I was well underaged at the time, he was infuriated and demanded that he would get him arrested for it as well. Life's intentions were not to leave me alone at the house but telling my father what had gone down only made the tension between my parents to escalate. I wish that I could've stayed by myself in that room. I had no recall of the whole incident, because I trained my subconscious to push down the bad memories, except that it was dark in that parking lot. Life only took me out to the house because no one was supposed to leave me home alone but my natural instincts told me to get out of the car and go find him.

I walked inside to look for him, and I was more surprised to see all the sex toys on all the shelves, and also the fact that I was surprised that no one asked for any I.D. as I entered the store. I thought to myself, "oh that's what they used in all those videos" and I quickly located Life who motioned for me to stay by the door while he went to the register.

The biggest wedge that was driven between my mother and I was when she had kicked me out of the house, due to the fact that I wasn't going with my father for the weekend. I was supposed to meet up with my father at Starbucks afterschool, where he would be sitting with his business casual attire and a cup of water next to his Macbook. I told myself that day, I wouldn't be going there for the simple fact that there was nothing for me at the apartment my dad was staying at.

Another boring Saturday and Sunday of feeling stuck and sleeping on the couch and being on my phone? I wasn't going for that bull crap again… I walked over to Roberto's house to meet up with him and Jean and we stayed over there for a decent amount of time playing Halo and Call Of Duty.

It was only when I checked my phone before heading out that I noticed the missed calls that were on my phone. I asked Roberto and Jean to tag along with me to the house to back up my whereabouts if my mom were to ask where I was at the time. I reached the house only to come to the empty driveway, which by now was not a surprise. I sat near the curb while my guys sat on the bikes, until Jean decided that he better take off before his dad comes from work cussing him out in Creole.

I looked at Roberto, and he had a look of concern on his face which quickly disappeared if to say "I wish I could stay but I can't" and he said he would text me when I got home. As he got on his bike and pedaled down the street home, I dragged my feet towards the front door and put my head in my knees because I was alone yet again. After my mother pulled in the driveway and finished bringing her work materials in, she began to berate me on why I wasn't with my father and why he couldn't come pick me up instead of leaving me running back to her house. My mother wanted a clear cut answer and I couldn't give it to her. I wished that day instead of getting frustrated with the issue at hand, she could have asked me why I didn't go with him in the first place? She told me to prepare my things, because I wasn't going to stay here in my house for the weekend. WHAT?! I tried to calm myself down and think quickly, where could I go if I couldn't stay with my mother?

I threw at least four days of clothes from my closet into an open suitcase and excused myself past my mother into the bathroom. I tried to force myself to use the bathroom, in hopes to stall and buy time enough where I needed to go. The shelter up the street? No, they have a lot of cats that roam in and out and I don't want anyone that would recognize me off the street to patronize me for not being with one of my parents. I couldn't go to Roberto's because his mother would have a fit if I stayed longer than I usually did during the school week so my only other option was Jean's. I emerged out of the bathroom, only to have my mother escort me towards the front door. "Can I get my suitcase first?" "Damn!" As the suitcase wheels rolled from the tiles in the hallway to the rug at the front door, I saw out of my peripheral vision to my left, the line of unlit candles on the counter.

In my mind, that only meant one thing, that she was waiting for Life to come on over and needed me out of the house so they could enjoy their quality time together. As the door shut and the locks clicked behind me, I stared past the front lawn thinking to myself, "Did it really have to get this far, Mom? I'm glad you're trying to get your rocks off and it's the weekend, but couldn't you find someone's house to drop me off at first?" I walked up to the bus stop and balanced myself on the curb as the oncoming traffic roared past me on my left.

Maybe I perceived the situation wrong and she just needed fifteen or twenty minutes to blow off steam? Then she'd let me back in right? I circled around the block and then checked my phone to run back towards the house, hoping I could make it back in time. I ran up past Life's Chevy truck in the driveway with my suitcase wheels hitting against my ankles and peered inside. The now lit candles were still lined up on the counter as I last saw them, with the flames dancing on the candle wicks before my eyes. Anger, anxiety, and fear all tugged at my heart at once and I didn't know if I should bang on the door or hurry to Jean's before it got dark.

I reached Jean's house and noticed his window was open but for some reason, the kid couldn't hear me calling his name. I picked up a couple of rocks near the fence and launched them around the bedroom window, because best believe if he wasn't going to hear that noise outside, someone else would. He stuck his head out and told me he would be downstairs as soon as he got his little brother to stop messing around with his TV setup. We sat down on his front porch on the chairs and he told me how he couldn't allow me to stay due to the preconception that his brother would snitch as soon as his parents came from work, and he was sorry but there was not enough room for me to *stay inside the house.* He wasn't willing to take that fight up with his parents either, so I told him okay... and ended up outside in his backyard that night. As the sky blacked out over the trees and houses, I knew I had to do one of two things: get comfortable with mother nature or make it work on one of these chairs if I was going to be putting my head somewhere for the night.

I raked the leaves back with my fingers until I created a "bed" to which I could lay up on and spread my shirts and pants out to the max, in order to ensure I would catch any dirt in between in case I started sleeping wild. My only issue was after I woke up during that night was finding somewhere to eat, and a place to clean my dirty behind off. I cleaned off the clothes I had laid out and folded them up into my suitcase. Before I took that left turn leaving the driveway, I looked up into Jean's bedroom window one last time. Was he aware that his friend had stayed the night in his backyard? Did he hear the noises beyond that back door or did he just dismiss it as a squirrel or cat running outside? It didn't matter because what was done already happened.

Walking down the street, my mind was moving like cogwheels jamming with the conflicting thoughts of where my mom would be this early on Saturday and how was I going to get back inside the house? I could've walked down to my family friends Uncle Walter and Aunt Vivian's house but I felt too dirty, too broken inside to even form the words that my heavy heart was holding back. How could I go to church today and feel God's presence when I can't see him working out my current situation? I went to the library to escape my thoughts and plan out my next moves until Sunday, when I could approach my mother again in hopes to get back inside. As I approached the library, I went straight to the bathroom and got straight to grooming myself and cleaning the dirt out of my hair and skin. As the soggy paper towels crumpled in my hands and made their way into the trash can, I placed my suitcase off in a corner; praying the officer in the library up front wouldn't confiscate it.

I went upstairs to find some graphic novels to bury my nose in, and push through each section of DC and Marvel characters, whether it be five comics about Spider-Man or a special edition of Batman and Superman. I felt a burning sensation at the back of my head and I turned to see a bunch of kids in the computer lab staring right back at me. I moved further down the aisle, picking up three more books to hide the embarrassment on my face.

I stayed for about two hours until I realized that again, this was supposed to be a detour because if the staff or security asked me how long I was going to be going back to the bathroom, and soon I would run out of excuses . I placed the books back on their respectful shelves and got my suitcase out the door rolling towards my mother's house. I almost immediately went straight to the backyard because I felt it would've been illogical to wait outside and feel like a huge disappointment all over again. That following Sunday, my mother let me back in and I washed up and got my clothes through the laundry as if the past two days hadn't happened and there was no bad blood between us.

CHAPTER 7

A NEW FRIEND?

Aside from Roberto and Jean, there was another person I brought into my small circle of friends, a guy named Daniel who came to school with his usual beat down Vans and cargo pants.

After we had a proper introduction, he made it a habit to ride past the school bus, and wink at me as if he was saying "You wish you were longboarding too, don't you?" I had one class with him, which was Psychology with Mr. D's class. Daniel would cause quite a disruption for anyone else trying to learn or actually ask questions because he would question every theory or conclusion on the case studies that we would go over as a class. I'd spend some days looking at him, like "bro, have you lost your f*cking mind?"

But it made class go by and it was our last period so I figured it helps to have that one person disrupt everything…. It ticked me off to have him as a friend, because he was so smart… but the way he carried on about things, made him seem full of it. Outside of class, he tried to get me to engage with the people around me; perhaps he thought it would help overcome my social awkwardness.

In one instance, he interrupted a girl eating her lunch to ask her what she would rate me on a scale of 1-10. I kept telling him not too because I wasn't the popular kid in school and didn't even know the girl. She made a face and asked me to take off my glasses, then crooked her neck to the left, only to say, "I guess he's a 7?! A 7?… oh hell nah, she didn't put any respeck on my name… out of all the girls in the section, he had to ask her?!

When we headed out after school, we always headed out from the back stairwell with the rest of our class. Daniel would drop his longboard and roll past the drug dealers, past the cops cars posted up next to the trees and headed down the road with me trailing not too far behind.

His house turned out to be twelve minutes from mine in walking distance, which made it convenient for us to go our separate ways. The first time I came over was his invitation to let me smoke marijuana for the first time ever. He gave me a quick tour of his home, which had a calm & Zen like vibe from the first floor to his room upstairs. There were bamboo stalks in the backyard, a glass vessel sink in the guest bathroom. I waited on the couch with his dogs at my feet until he came downstairs with the essentials- a smoking bowl, weed and a lighter on top of his rolling tray. He motioned for me to follow him outside which I reluctantly did so.

I watched from afar as he took his post by his fence and sparked up with his bowl in hand. I chanted in my head, "Light, Inhale, Exhale and repeat", just in case he decided I could do it myself from all the watching I was doing. He motioned me over and instructed me to nub my lips, so the smoke would flow through and not escape while I inhaled. I took a deep breath in, let the smoke flow through my lungs so I could let it exhale out my nose after about five seconds. Daniel wasn't satisfied so I took four more hits before we got back inside the house. He whooped me in Call Of Duty on his PS3, starting off with Team Deathmatch and ending with two rounds of Search and Destroy. He had the nerve to turn to me and ask, "Did your brain feel like eggs on a frying pan... like on those D.A.R.E. ads they showed in school?

To be honest, my eyes weren't scorching red but I could feel myself sinking into that couch while playing the game. He got up to start cooking some food and asked me if I wanted to help out. He tried to make some fried chicken and starts pulling out the seasoning and ingredients out of the fridge. He had Ab-Soul's albums Control System and These Days blasting, which I had never heard of before but I thought it wouldn't hurt to remember a couple lyrics to add later to my playlist. He presented me with some drumsticks on paper towels and offered some condiments to add with the fried chicken.

I told him goodbye and headed toward the door, but he stopped me to see my reaction to his cooking. Damnit! I looked at him, then the aluminum foil in my hands then back at him. He reassured me that if I didn't enjoy it, it wouldn't hurt his feelings so I took a bite.

Ladies and Gentleman, the flavor was um.. "sensational" as Future would've called it, in the sense that he used organic Whole Food ingredients to throw down on the whole meal. That was the first time on the way home that I felt no remorse in wasting fried chicken on the side; I hoped a squirrel or a stray dog would enjoy it better than I did. I know, there's starving kids in Africa but my palate needs more sodium than that.

I thought I wouldn't go back to his house after that, but his mom brought Popeyes on the way home and I was eternally grateful to see that box of chicken on the dining table. Some time later, my mom became very skeptical about my movements after school when our house got broken into for the first time. I claimed my innocence after I walked past all the cops in the driveway and let her know where my whereabouts were. But when her Ipad, Nikon camera, my sister's tablet went missing and then the second break-in would lead to my sister's bathroom window getting broken into... serious questions started getting asked.

Nothing got touched in my room the first time, but the second time around led to my suitcase being left open at the foot of my bed. I deduced from the angle they left the suitcase in, that they tried to toss my iMac desktop because it was on the other side of the bed.

It was too big to fit in there, though as I tried to put it in myself. So why leave my suitcase open in front of my bed and not take anything else? The following Saturday morning, my mother followed up on my claims and drove up to Daniel's house, with time to spare for the morning service. I begged and pleaded with the passenger to have her drive past and "Let's just go to church Mom! He was nowhere near the house!" But when my mom's mind is fixated on something, she ain't going to cross it off until she knows she has her answer. She knocked on the glass door and I watched sheepishly as Daniel's dogs ran to the front barking and instantly became calm when they recognized me through the glass.

I looked up to the bedroom window, although my gut was telling me that he was watching from afar in his room. Sure enough, I got a text later saying he had been watching from the cameras and if my mom had started trespassing around the house, he would have pelted her with BB gun pellets. I told him, don't trip, because my mom was just traumatized by the break-in we had and was making sure I was where I said I was.

I kept my distance from Daniel afterwards to keep my mom from asking any more questions. We kept our conversations strictly on Facebook or on the phone with talks about society, and our future aspirations. He harassed me about this girl I met on Kik who planned to come from Virginia and spoil me. In the words of Bernie Mac, "She wasn't attractive but she was good people though." Her mom was getting those military disability checks and even let this girl get a Mustang... I thought I was going to be a sugar baby until I found out she had a kid on the way. Gotta Blast!

In retaliation, I harassed him about the girl he lost his virginity (because she was a mutual friend) but he kept it romantic and civil, as any mature young man should. One quote Daniel left with me to remember before we would part ways, was one from Emiliano Zapata. "It is easier to die on your feet than live on your knees." Do you choose to be your own person or to conform to what others around you are already doing?

CHAPTER 8

"FOR BETTER OR FOR WORSE?"

The straw that broke the camel's back and then the second camel's back was the day Roberto, Jean and I decided to leave school the week prior to school testing and grab some Xbox controllers and batteries from the store. It started off when I overheard in class that a group of teachers were handing out papers excusing the smart kids that didn't have to take any tests and I was trying to get my hands on one. Unfortunately, none of the teachers in my classes were passing any out except for Geometry, but I just knew that I'd be home free if I got just one. Roberto and Jean didn't get any of the papers either but we put our knuckleheads togethers and said, we could just leave and if anyone asks, we had a project to work on.

Back at Roberto's crib, we get in the middle of playing Rust on MW2, & Roberto comes up with the brilliant idea to leave the house and grab some more batteries. The controller that we gave Jean was dying out and I had this feeling in my gut that I should stay back until they got back. But what would I say to Roberto's mom if she came from work before he and Jean did? These guys were my ticket to being out of school and it was either all of us or none of us at this point.

We took turns on the two bikes Roberto and Jean were using because Roberto's third bike needed a new chain. We were fine for the first ten minutes of taking different backroads until Roberto made a left and another a quick right. We were unaware that the neighborhood we were going through had a bunch of home invasions in the area, which explains all the police cruisers and Ford Interceptors parked up on the curbs around us. But we were getting closer to the store, as long as we got there and bought the batteries we could just head home and I heard the tires rumbling on the street behind me before I heard the engine rev towards us. I turned to see a Ford Interceptor hit a left a couple streets behind us and started speeding toward us.

My friends were already biking ahead and I didn't have one, so my legs didn't stand a chance against the SUV, with the front tires already passing by me and heading towards my friends bikes. The officer told us to stop and pulled over right on the curb, asking us for our ID's. I pulled out my driver's permit and Roberto pulled out his ID and Jean didn't have anything to his name. The officer told us that even though we were truant, he'd let us call our parents to get us off the hook. Roberto had a short conversation with his mom, my mom was super pissed and told me to meet her at the library parking lot near the school (That's when I knew I f*cked up). Jean's dad was working and would have to get him later.

Roberto and I watched as Jean hopped in that cruiser, and I let him ride his bike in front of me as we took the long way back home to his house. We didn't cop any AA batteries, and now we both have to get yelled at by both of our mom's; but at least now I had a bike to ride instead of walking all the way back to Roberto's .

It wasn't a total loss. I grabbed my bag and told Roberto to wish me luck as I headed out to meet with my mother. Upon arrival, I noticed that my mother's sister, Aunt Kay and her husband, Uncle Kevin were also in the backseat intently waiting. They had helped my mom send me to boarding school so what would be the consequence this time? All I could do was send a prayer up quickly as I got in the passenger side of my mom's Kia. Luckily, the talk didn't last as long as I hoped, and she was more worried for my safety than she was for my truancy that day. However, actions have their consequences and weeks later, she would go over to Roberto's house to speak to his mother so things would be cleared out. I stayed in the car, but I could tell by the tone of the conversation that coming over afterschool was going to come to a halt.

But I still came over, just because that was my brother didn't mean we wouldn't stop hanging out over some wack stuff. That May, I made it a mission to see Jessica on her last day of school. I ran past the big entrance doors to the stairs, and skipped three steps with each bound upwards. As soon I noticed no one was coming out the hallways, I hurried downstairs to the main office and asked if they knew which classroom she was coming out of. I turned around and there she was, staring right back at me. She hesitated to meet me inside because a guy she used to talk with dapped me up, so she stood sheepishly next to the pillar just outside the door. I looked at her in the eyes with butterflies in my chest and told her, *"Are you going to give me a hug* or *are you just going to stand there?"*

We share a tight embrace and on cue, Leah tries to bump her to the side to give me a hug. I watched as Jessica slowly blended in with the crowd, and I noticed her eyes looked melancholic. It was only for a brief moment, as the dismissal bell faded and a sea of red and black shirts began to crowd up in our space, but seeing that look on her face was all it took for me.

I feigned a look of concern as Leah rambles on about how she called my little brother her boyfriend and how school is going for her. And that's cool to hear and all but beloved, I didn't come here for you. I shifted off to the round stone tables and pulled Jessica close to me, because I was not going to let her get up and head home without letting her embrace me one last time. I kissed her forehead and headed toward her lips, but my pointy chin tipped her on the way down.

She chuckled at that awkward attempt and started to peck on my neck. I looked up to the heavens as she pressed her head on my chest, and I told God if he was watching, that he could take me straight to heaven by the end of the day. Because if I had that one person to love me unconditionally, make my endorphins dougie like John Wall, that would be enough. Jessica lets go because she sees her ride is there and I tell her to text me when she gets home.

Leah approaches me and tells me that she was watching and trying to make sure my hands didn't go further than where they were on her waist. "Mannn, bye Felicia!" "If you don't go somewhere…" When I got home in my room, the first text I sent out to Jess had said, "You know I ain't feel nun of those kisses you gave me?" "I'm pretty sure a mosquito had hit my neck or something." She replied back, "It felt like that because your neck dry as hell like those lips, Lol."

Ever since that day, I made sure cocoa butter vaseline was an essential from Wal-Mart because Jess would always tease me for how chapped my lips were. Our bond got closer, going into that summer and I made sure I was observant to all the small details about her when she was home or came back from her dance rehearsals.

The way she would clean the whole kitchen and if I was caught napping, she would reprimand me by whispering "You are going to stay up until I finish washing these dishes!" I would never forget the Oovoo calls at 9-10 AM with Jessica wrapped up in her blankets, telling me to keep my voice down because she was trying to keep her family relatives that were up early from having an excuse to come into her room. By the time one of her little cousins had busted through her door and invaded her privacy, I had already peaced out because I didn't want to hear all that noise.

Jessica made it a habit to show off her school outfits the evening before. First the pictures from Instagram closet pages so I could tell her, "No you're not wearing that, it's showing too much skin." I would get caught talking out my jaw, like I was her daddy or something lol, but she would call after school to show me that she had that same skin-tight outfit on.

This type of behavior would seem audacious to others, but I knew that she knew better; that deep down she wasn't a "puta" or harlot. She just enjoyed being that comfortable around me, because I never came off disrespectful. Yes, *I was direct* and sometimes forthright, but there were boundaries I didn't cross with her, because I wasn't raised to treat women like that. Other days, I kept my thoughts to myself when we both had a bad day or she would get excited mid-conversation and talk over me. She would criss- cross herself on the bed, probably thinking about how exasperated she would be if her dad asked from the kitchen to serve him another plate or how she was going to be stuck in the kitchen, cleaning all the dishes. I was over here thinking about how many girls blew up Drake's phone, to make sure they weren't going to get name dropped or as the chorus for a Billboard charting song (Hotline Bling or Child's Play).

Unfortunately, that summer ended on a bittersweet note when my mother made it crystal clear that I was on the waiting list for admission at another school. What she wasn't aware of is the fact that Jessica had begged her mother to let her go to the same highschool I attended, instead of the one that her mother had attended. My mother may have been trying to stray me out of trouble but what she didn't realize is that I held my own personal feelings to a higher regard than anyone else's agenda . God would be banging on the door of my heart for a while to tell me to let that pain go, and that it wasn't meant to be, but I never listened. Going to that school for that 2015-2016 term had me wearing that grudge out everyday, along with the tacky school uniform I would pick out the night before.

CHAPTER 9

SOLITARY CONFINED EMOTIONS

"I hate it here. I wanna go home."- Dre Parker (Karate Kid, 2010)

I didn't have a desire to make friends or show any real effort to keep up with my classes. I remember during that second month of school when I was walking down the hallway, this girl tells me to take off my grey turtleneck hoodie in order for the whole uniform to be shown. I waited 'til she turned the corner, mean- mugged her behind her back because, who was she really to tell me to take off my jacket?

It was only until I sat around a group of black guys by the names of Dre, Tyler, Casey, and a few others I don't recall and won't try to pretend like I do. I don't remember me at the table at lunch but when I sat down in my chair over to the far end of the table, I was in for a rude awakening of insults and comebacks getting hurled back and forth over lunch boxes and lunch trays on the table.

I began to laugh so I could feel included and instantaneously, "I know you ain't laughing" fires from the far left and I turn to see Tyler having his hand cooked towards my direction in a "I'm-bout-to-chew-you-boi" motion.

Before I continue, I'll go ahead and give everyone a proper introduction. Tyler was an overweight senior who always had a decent pair of shoes in rotation, whether it be Saucony's or crisp Jordan 4's. His roasting level was well over 9000 and to back up this claim, those who would try to dethrone him would be met by his phrase "You know how ugly you got to be." If you tried to sit in his chair, when he showed up late, or stuttered while trying to get a comeback and god help you if you made a crease on his sneakers; you would be his first victim on the chopping board.

Casey was a well rounded individual, who's seventy and counting sneaker collection made any competition that devoted themselves to surpass him look pitiful.However, he had to get back surgery a while back, making him unable to play basketball and never had a cellphone out to use in school (until he hopped in his mom's car); all of these "weaknesses" making him an easier target to prey on.

And Dre, (because I had to save the least for last) would come dressed to the table, like he was unprepared for any and everything. We roasted his Jordan's if the Jumpman looked off to the left, and the way his hair looked like if a group of Mexicans cut a whole yard of grass, but left a little on the side untouched.

However, Dre's deadliest weapon was putting people's business out on the table or afterschool in ways that shocked even Tyler because there were unwritten rules that Dre would say, F*ck it and keep going. This wasn't the table meant for bro hugs or reassurance so you would be off the hook until next week. Even bystanders from other tables that got fired down as well. You got exposed by a cheerleader that told everyone you had a vienna sausage in the DM's? Someone tried to fix your hairline with a permanent marker while you were asleep in class? Everything would be free game for us. I would try to write down anything I came up on paper when I got home and use it the day of, but they would rip it up in my face saying, "nah you better freestyle something over here." I would ponder each day as the laughter around me got rambunctious with time. Then it dawned on me that I would use a bible verse on Tyler.

I came to the table with an air of confidence, my chest poked out with both book bag straps over my shoulders. All eyes were on me and the silence got so tense that you could cut a sword through it. Tyler shrugs his shoulders and says out loud that I can go first, not that would it mean anything. Casey and 'Dre stifle their laughs but I drowned them out as my fingers raced through the Old and New Testament until I landed back on Genesis.

Everyone listened intently as I read the first couple days of creation, and I paused for some intense effect to look right in his face and tell him "That's why God made you look like..." and threw just about everything else I had at him. A smirk crept up on my face as the Oohs and "He used the bible on youuu, Tyler" swirled around the group. I had him right where I wanted and I'd finally get the respect I deserved. But why isn't he stumped? Tyler gave me a slow round of applause and said, "That was nice but now it's my turn" and proceeded to sink whatever pride I carried that day into my stomach.

He was like the anime villain the protagonist throws everything at only for the dust to clear, to see this guy dusting his shoulders off with only a scratch to the face. I didn't talk much to Jessica because she had to focus on being a freshman, even though I wasn't there to be there for her, and I had another girl named "Shaniqua" on my line that I met over the summer. It all started with a group chat Jessica decided to put me in and because no one was really talking about nothing, I started to put my poetry that I had in. Shaniqua was the only one digging it and I kept it cordial, even though she was a hoodrat complaining about how her ex was doing her wrong. Her closest friend had hit me up on Messenger and tried to set me up but I said no. They said please to which I said fine, although she wasn't cute to me at all.

Only person I had my eyes on was Jessica but she was dating this older dude named Kam. I could tell that he was head over heels because he wouldn't stop gushing his love for her in the group chat. Just sapping, like we get it bro, you got the girl already. Fast forward to when Shaniqua and I started to get to know each other and build a relationship. We would go back and forth about her drawings and my poetry, likes and dislikes because I ain't have nothing else to talk about if she wasn't sexting me. I was required to make her my profile picture on Messenger back, when making your girl your profile pic or putting some emojis for them was cool on Messenger. I would be getting roasted left and right by my friends and the church kids and not to mention Jessica who was on a social media break, came back for a shocker; but we'll get into that later.

We met in person a couple times, but only out of those two times, she would be comfortable enough to make a move on me. The first is when I walked down over to her house and she got me to meet her parents for the first time, who suggested afterwards she could just walk me back to the corner I came on. We ended up sneaking back around the block to this lake, where she led me around counterclockwise until we got to this huge tree and she had me lean back on it with my eyes closed. I'm thinking to myself, "I'm hype, I'm lit, this girl finna suck my..." and ended up getting assaulted with her little octopus tongue in my mouth.

Afterwards, I was flicking the roof of my mouth to get that hot dog water taste out while she was standing in front of me telling me that I was pretty decent at kissing. It started drizzling so she walked back home to get her umbrella and started to walk me back to the corner, with both our heads under the umbrella. We got to this section in the middle of the trees, with that post office being on my left and I guess she wanted to be "romantic" since the rain was coming down around us . Her breath didn't taste as bad this time around, I thought to myself, "maybe she had slipped some Crest in her mouth." Then it takes a hard left when she reaches into my pants & whispers in my ear that we should go back to a house or somewhere to get out of the rain.

Floating Angel: "*So you just going to let her rape you out here in the rain and you got no protection with ?*" "*You think you Michael Jackson bad huh, but all jokes aside, do what Jesus would do and tell her to go home.*"

Me: "*Well, Speedy Gonzalez needs to slow down with those hands, because she really hurting me bro like this ain't all I got.*" "*It's like that Spongebob episode where Sandy woke up from hibernating and ripped Patrick's head clean off.*"

Floating Devil: "*You turn around and walk home now…*" "*You're gonna be the saddest black kid in Florida, talking all that talk and getting no play going home.*" "*You better stop all that crying and Man up!*"

We moved out of the rain and waited for it to clear up, so I could get home but soon after, three guys on bikes rolled around in semi-circles just taunting the two of us. She kept looking at me to do something but I ain't Captain America, so she stood up to try to fight all three of them and they all biked off, with me not too far behind because I wasted my time today. The second occasion was during the night time, towards this ballpark where she waited at the dugout area. We start doing our thing, with her grinding on my pelvis and I'm kissing up on her chest until she says, "Nah my period coming on so I can't…"

Floating Devil: Excuse me? I didn't sneak out of my house to run over here, just to hear NOW that your period was coming on. You must have caught something or been smelling down there for you to be dry humping me and then stop now all of a sudden."

All of a sudden, the baseball field LED lights flashed down from the other end and circled around until they stopped on our end. I tried to squint and see if someone had been out there just watching us, while she clipped her bra back on so we could get the hell on. We ran a couple blocks down, then we made a right on a backroad where I would leave her, once she got a good distance ahead of me. To be fair, this wasn't a date and I won't be escorting anybody back to their house in the dark because I'm not Prince Charming.

She wouldn't talk to me for a good minute, because some older guy had ended up coming around the corner and stalked her for a good distance. But it's above me because if my mom would've found out I was out, I would have been out with the mosquitoes on that front porch. When I came back through my window I reeked outside and was out of breath, but I felt better knowing I got back in the house in one piece with everyone sleeping. Back in the present at school, things weren't looking too hot for me. I wasn't passing Algebra 2 Advanced, which I didn't care for anyway if I was being honest. I might as well have skipped all the afterschool tutor sessions, because the work I had on my papers would look nothing like the chapter tests we had to take.

I would walk the hallways with either Dre or Tyler after school and anytime some girl would walk by and smile in our direction, Tyler would make the same slick remark of saying "Wow you get all the girls, I'm trying to get like you bro." He knew damn well I wasn't spitting any game to anybody in that school. They didn't approach me so I didn't make a move to try to get them. The only girl I got out of my comfort zone to speak to was this light skin girl named D.W. in my painting class.

Unfortunately for me, she already had this crush on one of the guys at the school. When she found one day in class that I had some Jamiacan in my bloodline, she would call me *her cousin* and there was no turning back after that. It hurt deep down getting that curveball thrown at me, and I felt like I was sinking deep into the friendzone, like Chris from Get Out, trying to do everything I can to swim to the surface only to get pushed back down. And they wonder why I don't like speaking up now.

Afterschool I would walk to the bus stop with Dre to catch that Hart bus off Florida Avenue. My mom had gotten these passes in advance, so I stopped having the luxury of waiting for her to pick me up afterschool for the rest of the school year. 'Dre would have to work at Publix but we would get off at the same stop in Seminole Heights, so we just sat near each other to let the time pass while the bus made its runs. There would be fights, and the occasional drama but nothing would prepare me for the day Shaniqua and her sister would try to call me out from the back of the bus.

I took my spot near the front on the right side when I got on the bus and for a moment, everything was running smoothly;but less than half an hour goes by, I hear someone calling my name. I shake my head thinking I'm hearing voices until I hear a familiar "Eddy I know you hear me" coming from the far back.

At this point, 'Dre would make one of those "the noise barely comes out of my mouth" laughs and points on my shoulder for me to turn around. I look back to see Shaniqua's pregnant sister wave at me with Shaniqua's long neck behind making it pretty clear that she wanted me to talk. I did my best Kevin Hart ``Help Me'' impersonation, but Dre wanted me to take the L for that day. I got up slowly and made my walk towards the back of the bus, because if she made all my business known with loud mouth 'Dre on the bus; then a school transfer would have to be put into order.

I glared at her as she told me all she wanted to do was say hi, and asked what school I went to; as if I didn't have the school patch on my shirt. When she got off, I walked back to my seat and lied to 'Dre about who she was (like I need some stupid rumor to go around) and then made sure I texted her a paragraph when I got home to never pull that again in her life. I've never cussed someone out so politely before, so it was safe to say she didn't catch me outside slipping again.

CHAPTER 10

JOB HUNTING

There wasn't a day that I didn't get ridiculed by Tyler or Dre afterschool, once they found out I was trying to go out looking for jobs. "What happened to Sonic's, Ed?" "Ain't that the fifth time they said that they would have the manager call you back, Ed?" My dad would blow up my phone on the weekends for leaving my sister on that bus stop, but I told myself I was going to find a way to make everybody regret making fun of me for wearing the same worn down shoes.

I had to deal with people taking my red Air Force high tops and hiding them in the cabinet, so I couldn't find them when I stepped back into class. Captain D's, Mcdonald's, FinishLine, Shoepremacy, anything down Central or Fowler Ave got an application if they were hiring. I kept calling but I never got any call backs, or I would receive an email that I got passed up for someone else.

In the meantime, I reached out to this guy on Twitter by the name of "Rybvnks" when he was just custom painting shoes for sale. He gave me a couple tips and what tools I needed to startup but that's all he could do because he wasn't living anywhere close to where I currently was. I thought doing shoe customs could be a good side hustle and even got this senior named Jon paint an old pair of Air Forces black and gold to spark some inspiration in my heart. But my dad kept trying to force me against getting a job, "The only thing you need to do is work on your grades, so stop trying to chase for a 9-5 that can only get you $10 an hour son."

There was a hiring event for a theater within University Mall, so I took the bus and would keep asking the receptionist up front about any open positions until she saw how eager I was to get any open spot available. I switched out the hard toed church shoes for some Nike Janoskis for better comfort, but soon realized that they only made it harder for me to walk through the kitchen during the orientation. I was shown where the film reels were, how much time the cleaning crew would be allowed to clean the theater for the next film, and the discounts on the food for the people who just started like myself.

The position I was given was a runner for the people who ordered their food in the theater, but

I started off wiping seats and handing out mints by the door for those that were just leaving. My hours were 4pm to 10pm so my only focus upon arriving for my shift was to make sure I got done quick enough, so I could make it on the latest bus heading back to my house. A couple nights I'd get rained walking back to the house and would make inside with my socks and shoes soaked. I fell asleep once I made it on the bus, only to wake up with everyone off and the bus driver headed downtown.

It was going on 12 in the morning but I hopped off and walked those couple blocks back home, because my mom would be home working on her medical charts and never picked me up from the job.Regardless of how many times my mom yelled at me for coming home late, I was happy to have a job of my own. It was dangerous to walk that late at night on the streets, but nothing could take that sense of pride that I carried everyday to go to work and back home.On the bright side, I made a friend named C.J. (who didn't talk much, but would play a role in molding me my senior year of highschool) and got to grab some free quesadillas with fries at the end of my shift. My sister, Lauren had other plans well into the summer. She had reached out to my dad's side of the family one weekend, with her only wish to live up in Georgia because of all the Thanksgivings and Christmases she missed out on with her cousins, aunts, uncles and grandmother. I had no issue with this and even revised this letter of distress she had written on my mother's computer because of the multiple grammar issues.

She was emptying out her closet and had a suitcase packed well in advance, which was good for her. However, I wasn't informed by my sister that I would have to be leaving with her. I had nothing against seeing my family in Georgia, yet all of this had happened under my nose against my mother's wishes.I didn't pack anything at all, even when I heard that my cousin Anna and her mother, Aunt Evelyn were a couple hours away from picking us up from our mother's house. I had some loose ends to tie before I could even go anywhere. That morning I woke up and searched my kitchen cabinet for breakfast to eat, but to find only a box of Cinnamon Toast Crunch with no milk in the fridge was very common for my mom. I headed out from the back door to get an Egg Mcmuffin and texted 'Dre to meet me by the bus stop with his box of Retro Air Jordan 12's.

Leandre knew a bus driver that wanted an all black pair of Huaraches, which I had and Leandre would trade me his Retro Jordan 5's in exchange for them.

Seeing that I was leaving on such short notice, he decided that he would send his shoes to me while he was in college while I detailed his Retro 12's for him. He had paid me in the past for cleaning his Jordans, since I had a makeshift shoe cleaner kit with Shoe Crep and some cleaning supplies, so I figured why not? We met up and I rushed home with the shoebox tucked under my left arm, just as my As Auntie's Chrysler 300 pulled up to the curb, I bursted through the back door. I made sure I took my sweet time putting everything in my suitcase, as my sister called out my name from the living room begging for me to hurry up.

I met my sister and my mother at the front door and begged for my mother to hear my side of the story, that there was no way I would be leaving Florida over a scapegoat my sister was making her situation to be. Yes, she had to walk by herself home from church on numerous occasions, hasn't been able to see her dad's side family in years, and wanted a new experience for herself to be "grown."

But was anyone going to factor in how I felt about this sudden move to Georgia or did I have diva stamped on my forehead for all to see? I let out all my anger on my sister, letting her know how selfless she was and going to another state wasn't going to escape any of the issues that she had at home. As for my mother, I gave her the whole alphabet of curse words, as she tried to speak over me stating that her house wasn't a revolving door. My sister was already crying her alligator tears, so I shouldered myself past my mother through the open door because I didn't have time for the whole pity party that she was causing.

I got my suitcase in the trunk and prepared myself to sit in solitude for the whole ride, even when Anna stopped by the park up the street to switch her seats with her mom. I guess Aunt Evelyn figured it was better for her to wait at the park, so she wouldn't go off on my mom with whatever story my sister had come up with at this point. As the street signs and breeze past me in the car windows, I closed my eyes to reflect on the past and how far I had gotten to reach the point I was at now. During my sophomore year and junior year, people would reach out to me as some totem to vent to when the time got rough back at the house, when their depression would hit their lowest point or for relationship advice. Yet I had my own issues that I couldn't find the right people to trust with my own thoughts in my head.

In December 2015, I reached out to both of my parents with a screenshot of a penis enlargement pill that I had come across on the Internet. My dad quickly obliged to whoop my tail, but my mother took a higher road of informing me that life was too short to try to control something that could only be enhanced with surgery. I don't know about you, but to hear that I was too young to worry about something like that, I ended up feeling comfortable coming to my mother about anything if I felt like I'd get mocked by my dad for it first. Still I couldn't help but overhear girls in the classroom or be on Instagram exposing some guy's text messages about how his dad, grandpa, great-grandpa, and the whole family tree cursed him for not being well endowed. I don't play with the Internet or try to gossip with people's business like that, because personally I'd hate to see such an issue take a toll on someone like size did for me.

Then there was the murder of this kid named Lyfe. At the time I was still inwardly focused on self to burden with the issues at home, and wasn't really into meeting Lyfe when his father brought him around in the neighborhood. Don't get me wrong, because I heard he was a great kid and all, but the resentment of not having a father figure present at home, coupled with my "social skill issues" didn't make me budge towards meeting Lyfe. I used to watch him play basketball with my sister and his dad on the court from my bedroom, never thinking that he would one day see his life flash before his eyes from a robbery gone wrong.

I remember my mother telling me one morning before I headed out to school on a chilly school morning, " I had to go to Lyfe's burial service so please be careful on where you walk in the streets." I'd hate to see you get caught up or murdered out here." I waited until she walked back to her room and scoffed as I shut the front door behind myself. Thanks for the care, but I would be lying to myself if I would reciprocate it back, because I felt she only did that to cope with the grief of Lyfe's death. It's L'z Up Lyfe this way, but I still put my hood over my head everyday like there was no way I could be a Trayvon Martin story in the headlines. I was by no means active in the street, but I had no place for school either. I didn't want to belong anywhere except the solitude of my own world. I had this old quote from a Tyler the Creator interview on Instagram where he stated, "I want to be better than everyone because I hate everyone and I want them to know that.." And I tried to live by that mantra, steering clear out of the situations I had no business and just being vigilant of my surroundings.

My father and mother never eased away from confronting their marital issues in public settings, whether it was my mother running over my father's foot backing out of that public library or denying my father visitation to his children at her office. Thank God I never saw the cops involved. Every other weekend I wondered to myself riding with my mother or dad was "Is this what you get signed up for with marriage?

"So we just trade in the breakfast in beds and family memories for fighting over custodial rights in court and wishing jail for the other if they were to violate those rights?" As we rolled in a gas station in the present time, Aunt Evelyn began to stress to me the importance of chopping down the reddish brown nappy mess that was my hair. Hearing that put me in a better state of mind, that I didn't have to be a walking snowglobe of dandruff. As we started the car up to drive through the hour and a half that remained, I couldn't help thinking that maybe all this happening was for the better and I could have a chance to start my life over again.

CHAPTER 11

AIN'T NOTHING CHANGED..

"Home is the place where, when you have to go there, they have to take you in."-Robert Frost

Living with my aunt was an upgrade in comfort, but life was just as mundane to me as it was back in that yellow house in Seminole Heights. Her house was over in Locust Grove where a golf club was to the left of our street and the tennis court was adjoined with the pool with a waterslide. We were already familiar with the area, being that our cousins would race from our aunt's house with floaties and pool toys and were prepared to stay for hours and bask in the summer sun; once we were shriveled up like raisins in those pool chairs.

There weren't any complicated rules living with Aunt Evelyn, only to make sure that we were to clean up behind ourselves and not touch her snacks. I'm not saying I wasn't the reason she started hiding her snacks in her room, but we aren't going to speak on that. I sent off those Retro 12's to Dre once I had a ride to get to the post office and even sent him a text with the tracking number and address to his college. To this day, he swears that he didn't know what happened to the Retro 5's he promised and even sent a video via Snapchat of his own collection, proving they were no longer in his possession. I could've sold those shoes for a profit but I wasn't trying to hold onto Jordans that were bigger than my own shoe size if I wasn't going to wear them, if I'm being honest. But I had somewhere to sleep, a roof over my head and had to eat so I ended up counting up my blessings before I would be exiled to the school down the road.

My aunts and my grandma chipped in to make sure we would have all the essentials for school whether they had to go out to Wal-Mart or dug up some stuff from the garage. Everything was moving smoothly and my sister would occasionally fight over who's turn it was to wash the dishes that week, even when my aunt made a schedule over it. That sense of peace would be disrupted by the coming and going of my father, who made sure that his presence was felt through his aggressive texts and demands even in his physical absence. I can't pinpoint when the dynamic in that house shifted, whether it was the expiring food in the boxes he brought from the food bank or showing up unexpectedly to school counselor meetings when our grades did get rough.

It was one thing to leave a state to better our situation, but to have my dad put everyone in an emotional limbo when our focus should be on school. Sh*t, I felt like I was being suffocated by everything I thought I had escaped from the first go around.

He even made a notion to tell me that part of the reason I left Florida was the disrespectful attitude I gave my mother, although she told me it was to keep me from jail or death by the gun. But what do I know? My sister and I would walk out to the school bus stop, never walking in stride because depending on the type of day, one of us would be ahead of the other. A couple weeks in, my sister became quick friends with this girl, Nykiah who lived a couple houses down. I wasn't interested in making friends until about a month or so in, a guy named Lashawn moved into the neighborhood. He was just interested about being in school as I was, but that didn't automatically make him my friend. He just enjoyed being a goofball where he could fit in at any time. You still owe me 40 dollars for that essay, you bum.

CHAPTER 12

THROWN IN WITH THE LIONS....

The school I attended in Georgia had a middle school right around the corner, so it wasn't uncommon for anyone to have siblings or relatives that they grew up with, to end up reuniting in freshman year. The classes that I got were AP Statistics, Weight Training, Environmental Science, Human Anatomy, AP Literature, and Personal Fitness.

I didn't get a say-so in the options for classes in the counselor's office, but one thing I was grateful for was the fact I didn't have uniforms to wear anymore; not that any of the choices in my closet had gotten any versatile in the past year.

I would get chewed out for having bell bottom jeans, walking past the Special Ed doors only to hear "Don't forget you're supposed to be taking the short bus afterschool" or "I can tell you forgot your helmet with you today." If it wasn't about trying to get the answers for the classwork or the tests we took, I wasn't trying to pay it any mind. AP Statistics wasn't a hard class to pass unless you don't like math like I did, or just didn't put in the work from day one. The class's routine was simple: Copy the classwork displayed by the Powerpoint or the notes from the Elmo projector, do the homework assigned by the textbook pages, and study enough so you can maintain a high enough grade in the class. My math teacher would go over the answers for the homework, but my head was never in the right headspace to comprehend why I was erasing the wrong answer or rushing to fill in the empty line paper for.

I partnered up with this overweight mixed kid named Corey who was patient enough to help me review over each scatter plot graph, sample proportions and distributed variables; whether it was a test or review of classwork. After we got our papers back, he would take notice of the grade to the right corner of his paper and try to go over any questions he got wrong with me. "Aye bro, I got number 13 wrong because I didn't plot that fourth scatterplot in the right spot, what did you-" as I'm trying to erase any graph that resembled something similar to a strawberry PopTart. Over the course of both semesters, our seats would shift from the back to either end of the class, as "certain" people would withdraw or get a schedule change. Corey would roast me for my appearance, calling me "Scuba Goggles" for the majority of the first semester and I in turn, would slide a bank card between his belly rolls, only to tell him that the card was now overdrawn.

Outside of academics, Corey was a really chill dude that enjoyed listening to Big Sean. He was the goalie for the school soccer team and talked to me about his weight issues,female issues or problems at his job. He was the first guy that I confided my issues of being distant with having a girl (that being Jessica) and not being able to share that love in person.

Corey: *Alright bro let me see what you both are talking about.*

Floating Demon: *Iight before you give him the phone, just go through Snapchat to find a part, where you guys are just lovey-dovey over each other. Keep scrolling… HEY That's explicit, keep scrolling jackass. Alright, now give him the phone.*

Corey: *(scrolls his thumb down and nods his head with slight approval) I don't see a problem bro, you guys are talking like a couple.*

Me: *Well she's the type of girl that likes to be liked in person and right now, she has a boyfriend . I mean if I was there instead of Luella, she wouldn't have "that problem". But she knows my rule is simple: either we got something or we just kickin' it.*

After that Statistics class ended, I would head over to AP Literature across the hallway to the right. Now my Ap literature teacher was a very sweet lady and had a huge passion for books, plays and anything dealing with literature. My only issue was those socratic seminars for the books we read. Keiston aka "Mr. Luella" at the time, and I were copying off SparkNotes in the back, just going ham off the worksheet so by the time our group would get called, we were somewhat prepared. SparkNotes to my teacher was like what your average high school teacher thought about using Wikipedia for your homework; she was totally against it.

My literature teacher had a good heart and she wasn't a racist white teacher either… I think a lot of people took advantage of that but she was making her check either way, and didn't play when it came to working in the classroom. She pushed me far ahead then most of my teachers did when it came to doing work in her class, making sure my essays got done even if it was a little late and actually reading the material all the way. Keiston made sure he gave me the hardest time ever, because he always downplayed his athletic and academic skills out in person, but everyone made a big show especially when he did his official college signing in our media center. The asshole would always bully me in some way shape or form...He even lifted my chair up with one hand just to show off how strong he was. But he had the funniest Booty warrior from the Boondocks impression, and wasn't afraid to show it off in class when the opportunity presented itself .

Floating Demon: *Go ahead, show it off Keiston..*

Keiston: *I know who you are Chris Hansen. But see, I calls you Chris Handsome. I watch yo tv show all the time, so you can go ahead and bring them cameras and them polices waiting outside. It don't make me no different. Now I tell you what. I like ya and I want you. Now we can do this the easy way or do this the hard way. The choice is yours.*

Floating Angel : That video cracks me up everytime.

Keiston may have set me up for failure a couple times, when he tried to put me on with that hood midget across from our homeroom or stopping ahead of me when we did our little Naruto run from the cafeteria. But he was a good dude, despite the antics and I wish him nothing but success on his college endeavors. Weight Training was the only class that I really decided to take seriously with the weights, once Coach had got us done stretching in the cold. There were school wrestlers and football players that were already flexing weights so they could go hurry and play a quick pickup game on the court. I tried to dedicate myself to the weights, just to see if I could lift something and with some spotting from this kid Fernando, I was able to lift over my body weight and squatted somewhere in the 200's. Weight Lifting was cool and all but I really came to play ball, but leave it to all the hood negroes and guys that played soccer, (*cough Harry), to mess it up for everyone else that was waiting. The worst part is they would let Domani on the court, for the games that I would call next for. I claimed to them that they were dickriding him because he was T.I. 's son and they would tell me to stop complaining and crying because I wasn't playing in the pickup game.

Floating Demon: But they weren't the ones with their gym shorts and basketball sneakers waiting in the bleachers, while this light skin kid with jeans and timbs airball 3's and called foul every time he missed a shot. But I'm the crybaby? I'm glad he finally stuck to what was working: the music industry.

Floating Angel: Don't forget he did call you out on the bus afterschool, and say you were like the Michael Jordan commercial where he was balling out in the rain, snow, and still not be good enough to play forreal? And he had your sister and the people on the bus cracking up.

My Anatomy class was one of the only classes that I maintained a passing grade for both semesters. The teacher, Ms. Williams was an easy going black lady who anyone would be very grateful to have as a teacher, whether they were graduating or just passing through for a class credit. Just make sure you are studying for the suffix quizzes and tests that were based on the textbook readings we would have in any class period. Unfortunately for me, this was the same class that people would give me a hard time walking by that Special Ed classroom or hounding over my shoulder when I was scrolling through Flight Club on the school laptop. So my best friends were outside of this class, and I made sure I got my projects done. Ms. Williams told the best stories though, about carrying yourself outside of school, protecting yourself if you were sexually active because of anonymous students that would privately tell her about the diseases they carried...

You always got the sense that our anatomy teacher cared about the well-being of people by the way she talked and lectured individuals on being disciplined inside or outside the classroom. Back home, Aunt Evelyn was stepping up her game to make sure all five of us were well taken care of. Ebony, her oldest daughter had gotten home from Japan and went straight to work, but when she got a second job at the animal hospital, she would get the car as soon as Aunt Evelyn got off. Lauren started to regularly participate in the female basketball practice, which seemed to be such a grand excuse for her to be taking two showers daily.

Anna moved out with her boyfriend Corey, when she had enough money to move out on her own. Dad made his space wherever he could lay his head at, whether it be on the futon in my room or the grey chair posted in my sisters room. His more permanent resting place would be residing on the couch in the garage, due to his inability to secure his cousin's house further down the road. He ended up letting the Pough's, my sister's church friends that also moved to Georgia in the summer, rent out the house but would later cast the blame on my sister for having to endure the harsh conditions in that garage.

Floating Demon: If only he could foreshadow how that would cripple his relationships later down the road, he would've taken a different course of action. But hey f*ck it, let's piss everyone off if we are not happy!

Floating Angel:Between you and I, I would have made sure that garage was the last place to be in, in order to not place a scapegoat on someone who had nothing to do with the living conditions of my own. But to each his own, right?

Aunt Evelyn even began to cook homemade meals in the kitchen, which to the Garcia's was a surprise because "mommy hasn't been cooking since we were little, so you guys must be really special." There was meatloaf with mashed potatoes and vegetables, spaghetti, lasagna and the occasional baked chicken straight from the oven. Every week, we were feasting to the point I got tired of seeing the leftovers in the fridge and would stay in my room until aunty would call me out, begging me to come out or my food would get cold. The worst part of some of those exchanges is that my father would take advantage of that dinner time to express his discontent of not feeling respected in the house.

You couldn't blow your food on your fork or chew it hot and fast if he demanded to know why he couldn't get his good morning at 6:45 AM. If he started grilling my sister on the spot and saw that he couldn't get either one of us to respond, he'd bring Aunt Evelyn to his side; and try to list out everything from past to present on *WHY we were the problem*. I didn't have to watch an episode of Scared Straight or feed my eyes on Atlanta's Love & Hip Hop for some drama and entertainment. They should have come over and paid me for the mess I had to put up with. I couldn't escape and go eat in my room, "you gonna get roaches in your room, and you need to eat out here!" If I didn't speak when all I wanted to do was eat, I was the problem… So I got through with my food and went straight to my phone in my room, as soon as I cleared off my plate.

CHAPTER 13

ON MY PHONE LIKE IT AIN'T NOTHING...

My social circle was tight as it was, being that I wasn't rushing to make any friends. These people in real life weren't pressing me about how I was really feeling here and I could care less because I was already conditioned to keep my own opinions and thoughts in my head. If the effort wasn't reciprocated my way or in a positive light, you could bet your weekly paycheck I was not budging to help with anything. My dad kept telling me I was making myself socially awkward on my own, but he hadn't made it better with taking my shoes, computer and phone repeatedly to prove that I would get on top of my school work and Credit Recovery if it was the last thing I did.

Floating Demon: *Did I forget to mention I didn't pass that math class back in Florida? That 55 in that second semester would haunt a negro until my dad made a routine to canceling anything that would emotionally benefit me for the moment, in order to ensure I got that online work done.*

So I made small talk with everyone, leaving me little time to get my homework done but I enjoyed the small moments I had with my peers back home. With D.W., I would delight myself in conjuring up stories each call on Skype that she would answer from her laptop on her bed. It could've been a fictional story about a boy and a girl that fell in love and met up in a cafeteria or library next to a dark alleyway.

She sat intently and begged for more details as the story would carry on with my imagination sweating it out on my treadmill of a brain. "Did they have sex?" "Did she get into a fight with him?" I would have to tell her to chill out because I was making up the story as I went, but that's how most of my best stories came out anyway.If I wasn't telling any of my fictional stories, she would let me pour out my childhood experiences that had to deal with my Caribbean bloodline. I told D.W. about trips to Orlando, Florida that I would go visit my grandmother Vilma and her second husband, Sam (preferably, Uncle Sam as I called him from time to time).

All I did in Orlando was wake up around seven in the morning, read my devotional with my grandparents and try to entertain myself as they would head into the kitchen to make breakfast for the next hour or so. We couldn't run straight to the kitchen because everything had a systematic routine of how things were to be run: everyone ate at the same time when all the food was prepared, and we would coup up in the house until we would drive out to a book center, or play in the pool as soon as it warmed up during the day outside. The house was run, (no disrespect to my elders), for older folks that were just as refined as they were.

I made sure I cut my dinner with my fork and my knife in the right hand, and I made sure that the right utensils were used for salads, or soups. It was bad enough that I was picky about anything I didn't have a custom for eating at home. The first time I ate bun 'n cheese, I could've sworn it was the end piece of Sun-Maid Raisin Bread. I couldn't swallow down the first two bites without my grandmother coming behind me clicking her tongue and scolding me in with her heavy accent. " Eat Up man!" "Why do you play with your food like so?" "Grandma I thought it was raisin bread, what is thisss.." "It's bun n cheese, so eat UP!"

There were no pets for me to feed any of the food I didn't enjoy, and I sure couldn't dump the food out due to my grandma being out in the kitchen or watching the news from the open living room. Sometimes I had to put on my big boy pants and make sure that plate was cleaned from end to end if she was sitting in front of me. My breakout moment was when we got to go to Jamaica for the first time. When we touched down in Montego Bay, we stayed in a hostel and the breakfast was the bomb. Best pancakes and sawfish that I could ever put in my mouth. We would go down to the beach where the waves looked mesmerizing and were untraceable of pollution so I could get my hands on some festival bread.

Who knew Caribbean dumplings that were handcrafted by God's hands only to be passed down to elderly rasta men under tents persuading us to come try some, because everyone loves it! I visited my cousin Zach who walked with me through the red dirt clouds and detailed every bit of how he had sex with some girl from his church when he invited her to his house. I asked him if he had any intentions of getting caught and he said they were only fooling around, playing Mom and Dad until his mom caught him in the bed. My eyes rolled as I could only imagine the asswhooping that was waiting for him, but I paused in the street as the thought occurred to me… "Can you really get down like that in Jamaica or you really got to know someone like he did to get freaky like that?"

Back in Orlando, getting up for church was really a grind in itself to be present.

My sister and I had to have our clothes pressed and ironed, already in the garage before my grandparents made it into their cars. It was something different about falling asleep on the plush BMW seats to the monotonous narration of the radio, and then waking up only to be ushered towards the Sabbath school room inside.

My facial expressions could never hide that I didn't want to be in the room nor did I try to mask it.

If my grandparents had to pick up my great-grandmother from her retirement home on the way home, it would be almost certain that I had to sit next to her in the sanctuary. I always fell asleep, but to feel that tap on my shoulder with a chilling whisper in my ear say "did yah pee ya pants?" by benediction traumatized me everytime I woke up out of my slumber.

Floating Angel: *I know, I know. I peed in my pants while sleeping, laugh it up. I couldn't help but forget about the "don't use the bathroom in your sleep" rule, but the service was sooo long and dragged out each altar call and praise of worship.*

My great grandmother never let this go, until I finally had the balls to move away from her in service to sit next to my grandmother. Funny how my bathroom problems went away shortly after that, but I still had to sit with her when we had our sabbath family dinner at the house.

My chest felt tight and compressed, knowing that my "secret" could be brought up at any moment, as I passed the dishes and trays for the gravy, rice, yams, and salad on the table. If I ever had to stay over at her house due to some emergency, I had to come mentally prepared with reading some tabloids in her small apartment or scan over all the copies of Madea movies she had in her TV chest. I did have step cousins, if that was a thing because of Uncle Sam's family that lived in New Jersey. Mikey, Sammy, and Prissy were his grandchildren that he had much pride in being his only ones. When they came over, we were actively doing things for us to avoid being in the house all week. Six Flags, Sea World, and Busch Gardens if they came down to see us... we were always making sure we had fun.

Like I said though, it was very uneventful and colorless living in Locust Grove. I'm in one of the safest neighborhoods in Georgia, but I have nothing to look forward to but the recorded fights in the school bathrooms, failed assignments and tests that I had to correct so my grade would look just a little better for that month, and the fights in the cafeteria and just outside the school buses.

That all changed in December 2016 when I got a snap on Snapchat from a girl that I went to school with that I'll call Stephanie... only it wasn't Stephanie that was on the other end of her phone, but her girlfriend at the time named Jasmine. We introduced ourselves and she said that since her girlfriend had her phone cracked, she would be filling in to make sure her snapchat streak wasn't broken. I offered her my Snapchat so we could have a streak of our own and I kept it moving after that.

The first literal conversation Jasmine and I had was a complaint about a random guy that wouldn't respect her privacy in class at all. "He sent me an inappropriate picture and it's small and I don't like it at all." It was odd now that I think back to how I felt an urge to be protective, but I responded back to her naturally that had I gone to her school, I would have beat the guy up so it wouldn't happen again. She thanked me kindly for that reassuring thought and we soon became best friends. The snaps we would send each other on a daily basis were platonic but I took a liking to her because she had a very cheerful and optimistic outlook on life.

You couldn't tell by how she carried herself that nothing was wrong in her personal life, because her heart was too big and keen on loving anyone and everything. She asked if we could be BFF's while hugging a teddy bear with a heart attached and I said sure, why not?

After a while I said, *Yo where have you been shorty my whole life? I was waiting for a friend like you to pop up in my life.* She replied, "I was waiting for you n*gga…" "Where were you hiding out at?"

It wasn't too long before we started posting each other on our story, thankful that we were creating a beautiful friendship. I learned through Jasmine emotions on topics she spoke on, that she was still trying to figure out life herself, and wasn't in a rush to do so. She had her family and her dog, so the little life she enjoyed was appreciated.

Once Stephanie became aware of the bond that we shared, which I don't know who she heard from because it obviously wasn't me; she confronted me about the situation through Snapchat when she had gotten her phone fixed. I wasn't sweating the small things that girls got emotionally pressed over but once I saw that forehead with that headband over that school desk, I knew it was going to be an issue from her.

She demanded to know why I insisted on knowing why I had called her girlfriend "baby girl" or "princess" behind her back.

Floating Angel: Now I should make it known to the readers that when I met this Stephanie back in Florida, she had a relationship that was well known through that small school with a different girl at the time.

Another sweet person by the way, who I didn't dare have a chance to meet because Stephanie was just as non-approachable as I was to the people around her. She had her little friends and didn't really talk to anyone.

Did I purposely flirt with her girlfriend? I mean I am a petty person and she is a very attractive looking person but I should have respected the relationship, regardless of the direction of how my feelings were being portrayed at the time.

Floating Demon: Nah F-ck that. Stephanie was the same rude girl every time I came into Ms. Young's English class late with some McDonald's and an iced coffee in my hand. Always had something negative to say, talking about "I bet you stole that before you walked over here." They got cameras and do I look like I would "Boonk gang" an Egg McMuffin?

I even offered her some and she's going to make a face like I didn't think about her in the first place. So yes I did flirt with her girlfriend AND I LIKED IT.

I also got in hot water with Jessica for posting Jasmine on my Snapchat, because that girl simply wasn't her.

I tried to resolve that situation by putting the two of them in a group chat, explaining that A) Jessica couldn't get mad because she had a boyfriend so get over it if you are not going to breakup with him and B) so she would get to know her in the future as a *good friend of mine*. Jasmine would try to warn me against doing it, that she felt that she would be intruding on the relationship between Jessica and I. But I insisted either we're gonna be like Timon, Pumba and Simba in this b*tch because somebody had to set some boundaries. We were getting too old to be going on with these petty arguments on who hates who in a group chat.

On January 19th (or was it the 20th), I was on Oovoo with Jessica until I heard my aunt yelling at me in a berated manner, telling me to help my father with the boxes that he had in his friend Brian's car trunk. I reluctantly got up out of my chair and went to her first demanding why I had to help him bring in the expired food from the Food Bank once again.

It was always the same routine, helping my father bring the boxes into the kitchen and stock everything up as if the fridge and pantry were not packed.

My father was the only one making these trips and I was growing tired of no one else speaking on the extra food in the house. I knew I wasn't the only one tired of seeing the expired food in the house but no one said anything to him except me.

As I dropped off the first box, I shoulder bumped my father, unaware that he would trail me on me walking back to the car as he pressed in my ear. I wasn't ready for the shove against the passenger side of the car, but I was going out like a coward, and I didn't care if he had over 60 pounds on me. I had heart and to get knocked down, because he felt that I was being disrespectful to him, I wasn't going to go out like that. We hit the dirt and I never laid a punch on him, but kept shoving him off me as I hit the tree bark hard on my back. My aunt yelled for us to stop as she noticed the commotion we were causing in the dark and screamed as she noticed the huge dent on her car.

I walked past both of them yelling over each other, letting them settle it out like the twin siblings they were. I reached my room and immediately let my rage loose, throwing everything around and letting my fists hit anything that couldn't hit me back. Jessica was begging me to stop yelling and getting angry but I couldn't hear her as I kicked down my blackboard.. That was until she ended the call and the sound made me look at the blank screen of the desktop.

Floating Angel: You know she hates anyone yelling at her, even if it was indirectly you idiot…

Floating Demon: Now look at her, gone all because you are getting mad and can't control your anger. Stop trying to call her back, you idiot, you loser… You don't know when to stop hurting people's feelings. And stop calling because she's not going to pick up.

I put my hands over my head and breathed out slowly. I tried the breathing technique that my grandma told me. "Just count to ten and it will all be over soon." Jess always tried to help me out, always got me to talk to my dad, even when she knew I carried a lot of resentment in my heart. "Please go do what he wants and don't be rude." It wasn't even the fact that I had feelings for the girl, but just to hear her calm me down and let me know everything would be all right for the moment; even if it was just for the moment.

My conversations with Jasmine came to a halt as Stephanie pressed on her harder and harder with the idea of respecting the relationship that she was still in. We used to argue about her dog Zeus trying to butt in our conversation while she was in the bathroom or talk some meaningful stuff about the environment, entertainment industry and any of our favorite celebs or musical artists. Now I just get emails about how she has to block me and how she enjoyed the friendship when it was uninterrupted with all these distractions that life just ends up throwing your way. I was just stuck again, feeling like I was alone with no one to talk to.

Floating Demon: *Here we go with the "woe is me story." How about you just get some girls on your belt so you can stop crying? You're not even eighteen yet and you are over here waiting for a soulmate for crying out loud. You just got to enjoy life and hope that if she ever comes for your miserable lame behind, she'll be there through the thick and the thin. The real ones will be there for you in spirit, even when you are no longer alive to see them anymore.*

CHAPTER 14

DON'T FORGET THE FAMILY....

I'll have to make this detour in the book and introduce you to my father's side of the family because I don't mean to fill this book with meaningless words or space. I got to shout at least a couple people out if I'm going to bash some others in this book. My dad's side of the family enjoyed Thanksgiving the same as any traditional black family did. You know how it is with black families. Cooking weeks ahead making sure the collard greens were cleaned thoroughly and the candy yams and mac n cheese were filled up in the pans. We dressed up in our matching family colors and pulled up to my aunt Lynette's house in the most sensible fashion. Everyone is saying grace, praying over the food, and dancing along to the music in the living room.

No one was worried about any outside interference because we just wanted to enjoy the fellowship of our family around us. I sat down on the couch with my plate of food, just observing everything around me. How the rest of my family reacted to each of my cousins previous or current girlfriends, and who came in looking like they planned their outfit and who just threw something together that the last time. I was ready for all the celebration and things to go down so we could all have a good time and go home.

Then we'd dive right into cutting the cake, sing the Happy birthday song for my dad and Aunt Evelyn, watch the people that left early for work or things they had to take care of outside of the family... Same old stuff, nothing really changed. So I'll take the liberty of introducing the family members that did play a key role in this story.

Everyone really did, but there were some things that people did more than others have stuck with me throughout my journey here. In my younger years, I shared experiences with my cousins that were in their late teens or early twenties that had a lasting impression on how I viewed them. For example, my cousin Ryan was a young man who didn't have much to say about anything unless it was pertinent at the moment. It wasn't much you could tell about Ryan only that he minded his business and stayed to himself, much like I did. I remember a few Thanksgivings ago when he had left his laptop sitting on the glass table in the living room. I scrolled through, being the nosey little kid I was, only to find that he had been talking to some girl about me interrupting his space and interrupting his gaming experience.

I felt hurt and instinctively ran over to my father in the kitchen, so he could handle my big bad cousin that wouldn't share and be nice to me. Ryan reluctantly gave in at times but I still wasn't allowed to play any video games if he didn't give me any permission. I know he was pissed to come home from work to see that his PS2 was warm from usage and I would never give myself enough time to turn the PlayStation off as he pulled into the driveway.

When I went over to his house that he shared with his sister Ashley, I asked if he was watching Naruto when clearly a Naruto episode was currently on screen in front of us. He mean mugs me as if to say, "Did you really just say what I think you just said?" I whispered to my cousin Shon next to me, that Ryan was just passive aggressive and Shon bursted out in laughter. At least someone had a sense of humor. Shon was the family man, the poet and worked as a truck driver in New York for the most part. He was more a lover than a fighter than anything and made people around him feel like their potential or purpose of living in the world was to shoot for the stars. He even wrote a poem called "Chocolate You, You Chocolate You" which was just centered around how beautiful and gracious black women are.

Our dad's side of the family was the type to showcase how talented we were and showed our talents a lot during the holidays, because if you weren't gifted with some kind of skill in the family, what were you really doing? My cousins, Alex and Tory started a group called F4 troop (or was it just F4) along with my sister and I, where we performed gospel songs at my grandmother's church. We disbanded because we honestly got tired of hearing "One More Song F4 troop" because we were only teenagers that only had three songs rehearsed.

It wasn't some mass tabernacle choir, just us four kids. The adults ate it up though and it made my grandma happy, so as long as I saw her smiling in the end, it made all the difference. My older cousins had their own agendas and if they were headed out to the club or to the mall, I could never tag along because I had to watch the younger kids. And by watching the kids, I mean let them play on my phone because you can only ask "Do you have games on your phone?" so many times before I gave in. I never really found a perfect space to be at, seeing that I couldn't hang around the older guys. Being around the girls because one minute I would be sitting in their room to get away from the little kids, only to feel all eyes beaming on me because of the gossip they were sharing or because they had to change their clothes and wouldn't let me back in after that.

I guess being a loner just fit in my description of how I was viewing life, because I just carried around the wave of where people wanted me to go. Downstairs, Upstairs, "Please take the trash out and help us clean the kitchen…" As the hours passed by, my mind was only concentrated on getting back home into my bed, where I'd be able to revive myself from all the energy I was around that day.

CHAPTER 15

SPRING BREAK 2017

It was March and it meant one thing: another holiday that I could cut up and finally be out of the house and forget about that Credit Recovery that was nowhere close to getting done. Aunt Evelyn had told us that she was planning to take us out to St. Petersburg to visit Gabriel and his wife, Dessy. I know she was excited to see her grandson, Gabriel Jr. so we had to be on our best behavior if Lauren and I were going to visit them in Tampa. On the way there, I made the mistake of choosing the passenger side knowing Aunt Evelyn would be counting on me to keep the landmarks and the cop cars that would be hiding out in the cut. As soon as we left Burger King, I caught the fooditis and fell asleep.

She wouldn't let me hear the end of it as soon as she heard me pick my head up from the window, but that was Aunt Evelyn for you. It wasn't the break of dawn when we arrived so I took our suitcases inside and took my spot on the couch with my blanket. Soon the wait for us to get into Tampa became too slow and long, so I decided to do some contract work with Gabriel on a house by the water. We had finished with the roof, and once the work was over, I hopped on a boat along with another contractor Gabriel had history with to go fishing by this overpass.

I was hugging onto the side of my boat so tightly, because my fear of drowning is so tough that I could get an anxiety attack from getting too close to the water. As the guys threw in their reels, I made sure I kept my balance in the middle of the boat because I couldn't dare fall over now. As my foot touched the boating dock as I stepped off, the joy of being on dry land again beat the exhausting work we had put in earlier to fix up the nice house for the white couple coming over.

Fast forward to when Gabriel drops us off at some mall parking lot and gives us a certain time frame of when we should be back in order to have a ride back to his house. "If we weren't there on time, then it is what it is after that," he said. Our first stop was to be at school because Lauren had some teachers she had wanted to meet and old friends she wanted to see.

We made our way to the school and she said hi to Mr. K and her younger friends that she had kept in touch with before she left middle school. With each classroom with a teacher that I hadn't met before, I waited until she finished saying her hello's to everyone before leaving. I made sure I got to meet Mr. Bigelow while he was testing some students and personally thank him for all the hard work he put me through in those writing classes. We headed downstairs to the office in search of Ms. Ambrose, the assistant principal of the school and a former teacher to some of my classmates because she had enough authority to call down our brother from his classroom. We waited in the chairs as he came through the door and jumped up and down, excited to see our brother in what had seemed an eternity.

Floating Demon: It's only been like 10 months bro. Just take your pictures and go do what you have to do. There were other places we had to be today, right?]

Floating Angel: Aye man, let them enjoy the moment. You see Lauren got him doing the dab for Snapchat?! Look at him go, he's growing up so fast!

We said our goodbyes to my brother and made our way to the next stop which was the second highschool we attended. We came through the visitation door, but unfortunately the people at the front desk were not as visitor friendly as the school we attended.

Apparently we did not make a visiting appointment ahead of time so my sisters options were limited to seeing anyone unless they physically came out to her. And I didn't have time to wait like that. So I took another glance at the receptionist, who had stopped lurking her eyes in our direction.We got off the bus stop to make our way towards the convenience store, Lauren had to buy a phone charger and we were about an hour so ahead of schedule. I threw some food in her direction while we were leaving because I caught her lacking and laughed as the seagulls around us started diving in her direction.

I might be her big brother and all but I had to get her back for taking her phone back when I was trying to let Jess know I was coming through to Hillsborough that morning. We took our seats on the next bus and had a quick conversation as we finally headed down Florida Avenue.

Lauren: We couldn't stay long enough for me to see my friends, and now we are going to see Jessica?...

Floating Demon: She does know those kids were having lunch when they came out? That we'd have to wait almost an hour later, for one of her little friends to come out, even if they did. But whatever...

Me: We ain't gonna stay that long, you can stay in the library or stay by me.

Lauren: AND she got a boyfriend?! I'm not staying around for this...

Me: You're gonna chill out or I'm going to leave you on this bus.

We walked over to the public library and waited for the time to pass by. A couple minutes passed but all the clock hands were more patient than my sister in the library chair next to me.

As soon as the clock hit 3PM, I nudged my sister to get up so we could get moving. I walked across the street and passed by all the kids rushing out from the sides and the front entrance, looking for Jessica. A familiar "What are you doing over here, Cabrón" came from the right side and I turned to see Roberto braking on his bike in time to dap me up. I gave him a look and said, "you know why I'm here bro." He grinned and said, yeah I do. "You know you looked better with her than the guy she is with now." I appreciated the compliment but if I didn't believe that, I wouldn't have showed up in the first place. I dapped him up one last time before telling him to bike back home safely.

Quick Flashback: I walked over to Roberto's house with a blue pencil box in hand. I'm in the eleventh grade and I've only been home for a couple hours but I had a couple letters that I wanted to give Jessica. I knocked on Roberto's door three times and he beckoned me to come over to the room. I stepped over all his siblings toys and put my pencil box next to his Xbox games. "Go ahead and read this over bro." He put his game on pause and skimmed through at least three pages that were front and back. "Bro she ain't worth all this work. She is dating some guy that claims he's going to shoot anybody over her."

I gave him a blank face to show that I truly didn't care about what "he thought about me" because if he wanted to see me about that, then we could handle that when it came to that point or it would be water under the bridge. Roberto sighed and told me to get rid of the other pages because it still wasn't worth it in his eyes and he would make sure she would get them as soon as he saw her in person.

I ripped the pages out of that pencil box, littering them across the curb in a brash frenzy. "Why was I such a simp?" "Why couldn't I get over her if she was just dating somebody else?" I had no idea that she would Facetime less than a year later to show that she still kept those pages on her drawer, right under her baby picture. I hoped she threw them away because they had to be somewhat old by now.

In the present time, I stood in the pavement chuckling on that memory, as it seems like sometimes you have to take the L in the moment for you to get a W later on. When it seemed like ten minutes had gone by, Jessica started to walk up towards the front entrance and then halted as if she had seen a ghost.

I couldn't hold back the smile that was coming across my face until it stopped in the middle once I saw who was with her. Her loud mouth friend Kelcie who was big enough to be her bodyguard, and could have by the way she was walking alongside her. I waited until Kelcie got out of Jessica's shadow and stayed my ground while Kelcie began chanting behind her "Ooooh you've got a man coming to see you!" "Wait until you know who finds out." I waited until Jessica approached me and I looked at her as if to say, "Bookie, don't you have any mature friends that you hang out with?" We embraced for a moment and she searched my eyes waiting to see if I was going to make the first move.

I began thinking back to the days when she told me about her boyfriend repeatedly accusing her of being a hoe, pushing her down the stairwell, and being very controlling. Did she feel better because she was with me and I respected her or because her boyfriend was too insecure to come meet me and tell me how he felt about me being friends with his girl? Even if she did have feelings for me, this wasn't the place nor the time to mess around, even if her boyfriend was a piece of sh*t.

She tried to take the black hood from over my face and I quickly removed it, showing that my hood was only there to keep my nappy hair from being exposed.

We moved to keep some separate distance away from Kelcie and made some small talk because for a girl who was ready to fight anybody that interfered with her personal space, she seemed pretty calm around me. She blamed the reason why she wasn't squaring up on me because of the period cycle that she was allegedly on, but her eyes lit up when she saw me, like a parent getting surprised by their child on their return from military deployment. Her mother pulled up in her Benz and I walked across to give her a hug one last time. My body felt stiff and awkward as I still felt shaken up from how her big mouth friend was staring me up and down. Like she was going to either expose me or try to eat me too.

Floating Demon: Oops, Sorry! Don't take it personal because it was a fat joke.

They drove off and if I remember correctly, her mother was looking over at Jess, saying that she was going to start an argument with her father and see why he didn't pull up on her when they were younger. Jessica shrugged her shoulders and said she didn't know I was going to do all that. Tell the truth and shame the devil because if there's one promise I'm willing to keep, it's that if I am able to show up, I will come through for anyone. I turned around only to see that my sister had disappeared from view. Damnit, I told her to stay in that area where I could see her. Now she's gone. I ran around the whole school, went up two blocks east and west.

Then I waited in the office to review security footage with the assistant principal from the outside, only to find no evidence that she was in that same location before I crossed the street. And I'm the one that wasn't able to hold on to the phone. After running around and asking some kids that were playing outside if they had seen her, I ran towards the nearby Dollar store only to find her casually walking further from the school. As I shook her down for not sticking by me, she calmly replied that she didn't see when I walked across the street and just moved out of the way.

As if I was going to trace back to where she went, like I'm Sherlock Holmes or something . My father reached out shortly to make sure we were okay and in one piece, and decided that we should reach out to our mother for a reunion over a reserved dinner. "Was he unaware that we are already on a timed schedule to make it back to St. Pete?" But we called anyway. And called, and called again to only receive a voicemail. So we headed over back to the parking lot, exhausted from all the walking around we were doing.

One afternoon, as everyone was going to sleep in the house and got settled down from work, I decided to make a phone call out to Aunt Lois, my grandfather's wife and my mentor. It was going towards nine in the afternoon, so the conversation had flipped the switch once she brought up the question of how I was getting by academically, being that the school year was almost over.

I started to break down emotionally saying, "I can't be the highschool graduate my family expects me to be." They are telling me that 150 seniors will not be able to graduate, and I'm included in that category. I don't know how to move right and I don't even see college being in my future. "Am I selfish for not wanting to pursue college right after highschool?" She told me to calm down, that I had to graduate because the finish line would make the difference for my family, because not finishing would be just as selfish as giving up. "But I didn't ask to be here!"

I continued with my rant to let her know that no one's ever taken time to consider what I wanted. It was always about getting an A here, passing this test here. She told me to calm down and we prayed. We prayed that I would close out 2017 strong, and with a level head so that everything coming my way would be a blessing that would only fuel my hunger for success because everyone wanted the best for me, but it's up to me to determine what the best would look like for me.

I dried my teary eyes and blew my nose out in some tissue I had placed on the glass counter. I could always count on Aunt Lois to let me know I was steering myself in the right direction, because if I wasn't able to carve the future I wanted, then someone else would try to have me work on theirs. And I couldn't stand to sit back while someone else had me working at a desk or looking at the time I wasted being unhappy doing things to make someone else happy. When was my time going to come? Was my mind rushing for the right answers or was I not asking the right questions? The day before we headed back to Georgia, we took a drive out to the beach with Dessy, Lauren, and myself. The weather was very windy and it took us a minute to find a good spot to put all the towels and food down. Lauren went in to go further out in the water and I kept my distance to the shore.

I would go back and forth in the sand, occasionally stepping back out when the water got too cold until I made the mistake of sinking too low into the ground when the tide started to come back in. I underestimated the speed of the tide and let one of the waves hit me smack in the face, ripping the Rec-Specs clear off my nose. As I wiped the sea salt from my eyes, I dived in yelling "my goggles, where did they go?" You see, in order to avoid getting teased at school, I would take the strap on the goggles and place them in my pocket so no one would be able to cause attention to me with the strap on. Only problem was I lost the back strap of those goggles and wasn't able to secure the goggles from falling off my face. The one time I needed the strap to the goggles, ended up costing me my eyesight.

I ran back to the chairs where Dessy and Aunt Evelyn were to let them know what had happened. Aunt Evelyn was upset for my carelessness because she knows how blind I could be without them and Dessy felt a bit of sympathy for me. But no one was going to let some inconvenience ruin the fun that they planned to have at the beach, all because I had lost my Rec-specs. So I waited in our beach chair while everyone was having fun so we could get the hell on home. I was able to get some new glasses and Thank God because that was the best "F- you to anyone that called me Scuba Goggles" present that I could ever ask from my dad.

Prom was around the corner and with school deadlines and assignments getting turned in, going out to dance and have fun was the last thing on my mind. I just wanted to get my diploma and cross that finish line.

I got my Credit Recovery out the way, thanks to Google, so my father could stop taking my belongings and watching me like a hawk over my every move on the computer to make sure I got my work done. I told my dad's girlfriend Lori that I had no interest in taking someone's daughter to prom but I guess they both went tone deaf around the thirtieth time I had said it. Lori asked me back at the house if I had anyone I knew at all that I could take to prom. I pondered as I thought about all the options that were available.None of the girls I was physically attracted to would consider me as a date to prom; they either wanted the guy that graduated ages after them ago or to go hang with their girlfriends. But you can't explain that common logic to adults if they want to see you go to prom that badly.So I called up Jessica on my phone and explained the whole situation to her. I told her not to be scared about the way that my dad's girlfriend was going to grill her because she will interrogate you like Detective Olivia Benson from Law & Order. But then she told me that she had it under control.

I asked if she was sure as they began to call me from the kitchen and she nodded her head yes. I sighed, because my intuition told me that this situation was going to take a hard left very soon. I handed Lori the phone, and it was like watching some poor animal get torn up on Animal Planet the way she had Jessica froze up on that phone camera. "Do you like him alot?" "How did you meet him?" "How old are you sweetie?" I facepalmed myself for even thinking that this was going to be a good idea and I turned to see my dad making a quizzical look on his face, when Lori asked for Jessica's age.

I knew this would be brought up in conversation very soon. And very soon would happen to be my birthday right around the corner.

CHAPTER 16

YOU'RE 18 NOW... AIN'T YOU?

I woke up to birthday texts, wishes and came back home from school to a Publix birthday cake from my Aunt Evelyn and Aunt Lynette. I hugged them both only to hear Aunt Evelyn telling me that I would have to go out with my dad later; he was planning a surprise that I would be attending with him at Applebees. I rolled my eyes, thinking what does this joker have for me now? I got a ride with Brian to pick up my father along the way and then head out to Applebees, like we couldn't have the celebratory talk at the table we would be seated at. My father gave me the whole coming of age talk, how proud he was for me to see 18 and then told me that one of these days, he couldn't wait for me to have one of these "grown men dinners" where I could talk about the women I would date and take out, as I got older and experienced more of life. I just nodded my head and ate the appetizers in front of me as he gave me game on being a bachelor with women, using coupons when they were necessary because nothing's wrong with balling on a budget if you play it right.

He told me about staying lowkey with the women that you are with, letting them know up front that it was just something slight and if a relationship were to come from it, then pursue it in the best fashion. He breaks into a quick story about taking a female friend of his back to his college room in college and breaking her down, only for his colleagues and friends to come to the room and ask what he was doing. My dad ended up telling them that they were just watching a good action movie on television,when they pressed him about the noises that she was making inside. They knew it was a lie but it's all about how you handle yourself under that pressure and if you will fold when they ask about your business.

My birthday dessert rolls in and the narrative quickly changes as he sits up in his seat, staring me down while my spoon clinks against the bowl and the ice cream melts with the fudge brownie. He brings up that I should have no business interfering with young women outside of my age gap, because I could face charges down the line and that was something I didn't want to look into in my adult life.

Floating Demon: He does know that younger girls will gravitate towards my appearance, regardless if I tell them no or not right? It's as if the guy has no hope in me handling my business with Jessica or something. Like I'll let her get me caught up or something.

I told my dad that younger women wouldn't be an issue, that he must be watching too much "How to Catch a Predator" to think I'd get involved in some mess like that. I started to feel a sickening sensation in my stomach and excused myself so I could go to the restroom and handle my business. I walked over to the sink and held my arms down for a quick breather.

Floating Angel: You got this bro. Just tell Jessica what your dad said, that you got to let her go because she's younger than you. You can't be getting caught up because it's going to ruin the future.

Floating Demon: You gotta be a special kind of b*tch to let your father tell what kind of girls you are going to talk to. This is your life, ain't it? You only live once, you better keep y'all business lowkey and tell the old man mind his business.

I texted her on Snapchat and waited. I waited, and waited until I saw her little Bitmoji pop up on the screen and I got a "Wow that's crazy." "It's up to you baby." I texted her back, "okay cool I'll talk to you later" and put my phone back in my phone and told my dad that it was handled, and that the most I would probably do with her is go out skating or bowling. As I tried to put that little cool guy bravado, I soon lost my appetite for any of my dessert at that point. It was time to go home and not worry about the events that just put my heart on an emotional rollercoaster in the bathroom. Just breathe and get back home, and it'll be over soon. Jess and I still ended up kicking it on Snapchat three days later, like the whole thing had never happened.

CHAPTER 17

GRADUATION DAY

Just when I thought it wouldn't happen, it happened. I was behind on my essays, failing AP Statistics after I bombed that E.O.Y. exam. I couldn't help but thank God for keeping me out of serious trouble, because if it wasn't bad grades I was worried about, it was staying out of everyone's way at home. I knew that my father would come through with his rants and my aunt would be on my ass to pass, and my family pitched in with ideas on how to tackle my projects when I just ran out of all the other options on my table. But I was graduating, and very soon I could put on that gown and that cap and walk the stage like it was nothing to me. Aunt Evelyn took some pictures with me in the driveway and then we got to school with time to spare. I rushed down the hallways, after finding my friends ready for the walk, looking for my homeroom teacher to get my bowtie right for the occasion.

It took us more than twenty minutes to get the right bow, but if Mr. Hightower wouldn't do it then who could? I sat on the bleachers in the gym with the rest of my graduating class, and started recording everyone around me; only to have my neighbor complain about having her face get recorded in the process. We walked outside to the fields like we had rehearsed over and over again and I couldn't help but smile as I noticed some of my family members to the left of me in the bleachers.

Floating Angel: We can pose and look good later in the photos. Just remember who you are doing this for. Remember who got you here and how happy you are to be here, finally graduating on time.

I sat down and waited for all the name calls to go by. Everyone was getting crunk and dancing on stage but as I rose up to shake my teachers hands, the whole noise I heard was my family going crazy for me. It was a little weak, compared to everyone else's cheers but it was my family rooting for me and that's all that mattered at the end of the day. I took my seat and waited for all the speeches and band music to go by. Suddenly I looked up to see someone had hit a ball in the back and we kept volleying it back and forth until the teachers had told us to cut it out.

Then there was the aroma of marijuana that was strong and pungent, yet no one complained about the smell as it wafted through everyone's noses like the aroma trail in the cartoons. When the confetti and caps had all flown up in the air, I rose up to go find my family and take pictures because I don't know like no anybody here like that and it's time for me to head out.

My mom showed up with my brother fashionably late, which I will blame for her favor the parking. We said our hi's and goodbyes as we walked our separate ways to the car. I could not wait to get home, that bed was calling my name. I went on Snapchat as I got in my room to review all the videos and pictures everyone had taken. I posted my pictures then slid to my messages, where I scrolled for Jasmine's name so I could show off my drip and collar cuffs.

Once she had been off her "probation", I made sure to screen record her snaps and post it on my story. We both had spent countless hours motivating the other to get our homework done but she did it and I was so proud of her. As she started to type her message from her phone, I was more than ecstatic to know she was proud of me for graduating and letting me know that I looked really good with my whole graduate attire. I thanked her and proceeded to end the night right with some well deserved rest.

CHAPTER 18

SUMMER OF 2017

I thought I would be able to kick back and relax as I thought I should. The hard part was out of the way and I got my old friend back, but life can be so full of curveballs. My dad had planned to take us out to D.C. so we could go out and walk around the streets, view museums and see the Pentagon.

I knew his only intentions were to see Lori because she lived there at the time, but go ahead Dad. I was tasked with finding my sister so we wouldn't miss the bus to get there, and the only reason I remember this is because I was getting snaps from Jas, stating that she received a note from her girlfriend about something I quoted a while back on Snapchat. I was walking my aunt's pitbull Black as I called her saying "Yo we got to put an end to this because this sh*t is getting out of hand." She agreed and I went through my whole story blocking and unadding anyone that had any ties to Stephanie or myself from Brooks, because at this point anyone could have snitched on me. The only two that I left alone were D.W. and Tyler because they were the only two people that really didn't mind how I carried my business. I walked down to Nykiah's house in search of my sister and turned to leave Black back at the house once I confirmed that was the house she was at.

I tried to get her to see that we had to leave with our bags, because if dad was trailing too far behind, then he would be making a mountain of a molehill. We finally got the hell on after she said her sorrow goodbyes and started walking in front of me, like I was the one who told her to pack her bags and leave. I had just as much of a choice to leave as she did, being that Aunt Evelyn wasn't at home to tell us we couldn't leave our belongings where they were. But go ahead and kill the messenger, I guess. Our dad approached us with Black's leash in one hand and started to go off on Lauren about how she left the house not letting anyone know where she would be headed off too. In hindsight, I think we both knew she was going to run away from the house to buy herself some time and he just wanted to yell at her for something. We rode on the Megabus for what seemed like hours until we got off and walked through a parking lot to reach a hotel. Only the hotel was just for directions and we started walking some more miles until we finally got a taxi cab to take us downtown.

After a walk, we made it to a pretty decent hotel that had a balcony view and the interior of the room wasn't too shabby. It was small but we would make do because we always did as Felders. The plan was to tour around and visit some museums, take pictures of landmarks and then go visit Lori at the end. I was trying to piece where she would come into play and as the days went past, we did a lot of walking and talking and more complaining. Then we took the liberty of choosing a restaurant/casino in D.C. to meet Lori and celebrate Lauren's birthday at the same time. After my dad and Lori walked across the boardwalks in the beach to make lovely cozy memories together on their camera phones, I couldn't help but once again question my purpose of being here in that exact moment.

Floating Demon: Ain't this some place you would take Jasmine out too? Look at the lights and the ferris wheel out to the left with the moon shining over the water and sand. She'd love this.

Floating Angel: Yeah, but she's taken, remember? I don't try to get down like that, or at least try to anyway. We are going to take all these pent up emotions to the chin and thug it out until we get back to Georgia.

Unfortunately for me, my dad had more surprises up his sleeve. We would go from hanging around his boo thang to staying with my Aunt Denair and cousin Colin and Debra for the rest of our time there. We had some help getting our things transported by our family and took a detour at my Uncle Tommy's house, whose hospitality is ever so graceful.

Once we left Maryland and headed off to New York, my father brought me over to my aunt's apartment and set living arrangements for us to stay there. Although she had a space for herself and gave her daughter 'Nika and her granddaughter Lovie, she made sure she had given us a spot to sleep as well. I got to watch Starz Power in the living room with my Aunt Denair as we snacked on popcorn.

On the days that I had the entire apartment to myself, I would go into my aunts room when 'Nika was too busy working on doing her clients hair after dropping her daughter off to school. If I wasn't catching up on Power or had a random movie playing, I would make sure I started up on this show called Dexter.

I never watched Dexter on certain days because I felt like there was too much commotion going on in the house or if my aunt would be coming in and out of her room. That show was my ultimate vice... the way he narrated stalking his victims to each house and how he would leave no loose ends behind, and the justification he would ultimately feel after mutilating his victims... It was dark but captivating, even if it was just a show. Dexter never let anything distract him from his work but my favorite episode was when he managed to get James Doakes killed because James was hot on his trail and made an investigation out of pure envy.

Floating Demon: He killed Doakes, the black cop? That's racist!

Floating Angel: It had nothing to do with race. Doakes got too close to Dexter's trail. If he had left him alone and let Dexter do his "work" in peace, maybe he would have managed to stay alive for the rest of the show.

My dad had looked around to get my sister and myself working and reached out to a woman named Melanie that co-owned a restaurant by the name of Forty North. It was a Jamaican cuisine restaurant that was rated five stars on their website. We had to wear all black uniforms with aprons and were given two blue towels as part of the orientation. My sister and I learned from a server named Jules, who gave us the proper techniques on walking our trays to a table, how to deal with the quick orders that came through as fast as they could through the kitchen and how the tables should be arranged before we closed up for the night.

Once I got the hang of working there and got to take some Jamaican food home back to whomever I was staying with, it was the bomb. The jerk chicken, oxtails, corn fritters and the occasional pasta in my to-go plate was a treat to take home. When we had birthday parties or celebrations to host, we went into gear like clockwork.

I got used to hustling and bustin' down tables with my peers, but the only person that really irked my nerves the most was Max, Melanie's eldest son.

Floating Demon: Max managed to get in the way of my tables, was overly polite and never knew how to leave people alone. He was too pushy and too confident about the little things that people didn't necessarily worry about. Like we get it, you love helping your mom but can I work here too?!

Floating Angel: I thought he was gay for the longest time. Especially after he made that remark about being ecstatic for the LGBTQ parade in New York. My man's emotions were all over the place.

Floating Angel: We did help him lose his virginity though, after we met..

Floating Demon: Why you jumping ahead in the book...Ugh You can't help but say too much anyway. I don't know why we let you speak up in this book.

Max was a nice kid, I will admit. But he did have his tendencies to be very childish. Many times I would ask him to relax and let me do my work, but he kept butting in my personal bubble. I'd get off the bus on the way with Jasmine talking to me via Snapchat or on the phone, making sure I was okay and getting to work safe. Sometimes the bus would let me off too soon or my phone would die and I'd have to trust my intuition on how to get where I wanted to go. After that, it was only a matter of time before I remembered the bus route and the sidewalks by pure memory. If walking on the road or the grass wasn't such a pain in New York, I would've driven there if I had a car. As soon as I walked up the stairs with my backpack on, I'd see Max about 15 feet in front of me just staring like there weren't tables he could have been cleaning. "Hey Jasmine... I'm going to call you back." "I got this kid who won't stop staring at me." Yeah I'll hit you up after I get off work.

I would ask his mom for permission to beat him up towards closing time and as long as there weren't any customers around, I would go ham on him. But this kid had to have Kung Fu Panda powers, because he absorbed all the hits with his stomach and neck every time I managed to run up on him. We only started to get along and stop bickering once my cousin Colin left because at that point, who else was going to keep me company? I ended up befriending his little brothers Logan and Luis because they were way more laid back than Max.

He'd have to wait until after I left the restaurant for good to develop a better friendship with me. At cousin Debra's house, I would either take my living quarters in the basement downstairs or the couch if I was able to sleep comfortably without any of my little cousin's toys laying around on the floor. Getting up to go pee and slipping on a lego block on the way to the door is not a fun experience. Sometimes the wifi would act up and I had to change the way I slept to make sure I got all five bars or four if I wasn't as lucky. Colin would spend his free time making music or producing his beats for any artists that he met at the studio. He was going to college for music production and I couldn't blame him. We talked about girls, what was good and bad weed, his favorite artists coming out NY all while he was cooking up heat in his room.

If we weren't going to work or staying in the house, we would go to the basketball court for some hoops. On one occasion, he ran a game of two versus two against some taller hispanic guys who were clearly way more athletic and skilled in basketball than us. I could tell that one of these guys were at least pro, if not college because his brother would always pass him the ball going into the paint. I wasn't going to guard him and I definitely was not going to play hard defense and break my glasses either. Then after they spanked us, we played a quick game of three versus three with some kids that were just around the block. Colin made up for all the shots I airballed and I got his rebounds if he made sure he would get open out in the perimeter for an easy pass. Then the game ended when one of the guys injured his hand after slipping on the hardcourt.

Floating Demon: And his idiot friend says to him, Damn bro how you gonna be able to jack off now? You're going to let the kid shake around in pain and not help him up?

Colin and I laughed on the way home, as the rain drizzled down on us and it was safe to say we had a good time playing basketball that day. I was trying my luck with this girl on Snapchat back in the basement, who was doing a lot of talk but not trying to back it up. I met her when I was on Kik messenger in Florida and we kept the conversation short and sweet as the time went by. She was staying in Gainesville at the time, so I figured once some time would go by, I could get some play if I went up there. She was being so petty and it got so annoying that I couldn't stand to f*ck with her. She did a lot of teasing with towel photos and didn't take any full body pictures, but was up front that she just wanted to see what I was working with.

She wasn't ashamed to say she watched Xvideos or did things from time to time, but it became clear within a month that she was going to either friendzone me or keep rejecting me. At least she kept it a buck tho.

Floating Demon: *I hated that girl, like a n*gga was trying to get in them guts and you over here saying no. I hated to play that nice guy role so long like "yes I really am so sorry about the fact that your boyfriend broke your heart." "I really feel bad that your best friend tried to rape you after school like why didn't you leave?"*

Floating Angel: *man you holding everybody up, I wanna know the juicy details.*

Floating Demon: *After the mixed messages, I had the opportunity of letting loose and teasing her with the fact that I got a stash on Snapchat. You know the My Eyes Only thing?*

Floating Angel: *Oh yeah so what did she say?*

Floating Demon: *She's gonna come back and tell me "Well I thought you were going to be small because you act like an emotional b*tch from time to time." And I was like, that's a new one. Had she stopped playing hard to get, this whole situation wouldn't have dragged out this long.*

Floating Angel: *Did you send her anything else?*

Floating Demon: *Yeah I did it, but only with the intentions of making her feel just as pissed off as I was. Either you're gonna show me them goods, let me beat or let me block you because you're a rude person for me to even be friends with.*

Floating Angel: *HAHAHA. You're a bold bold man, at least you are keeping it real.*

Towards August, Aunt Denair had already laid down the ground rules of staying with my Aunt Evelyn by the time I got back. I would have to start paying the rent at Aunt Evelyn's, now that I made enough at Melainie's restaurant, secured a bank card at Wells Fargo and made a plan to work until I got into college. Seemed pretty concrete, although I could have stayed in Georgia if I was going to be making a decent amount of money. I took both checks that were written out to me to a Check Cash store and I got heckled for it. "Why didn't you wait until you got home to put that money in the bank, if you earned enough cash in tips?"

I shrugged my shoulders, just walking in that $1,800 in my pants was a good feeling, and being able to spread it and count it in my hand in that apartment felt even better. If someone thought about robbing me, they'd have to fight me for it or mind their business.

I bid my farewell to Melainie and she was so eager for me to come back and continue to work at the restaurant that she suggested I make that move to New York and start to work here. I promised I would be back the next time I would be here, because the price of living in New York was higher but getting those checks and tips at this restaurant made it all worthwhile. I liked my coworkers, and I got to work behind the bar on a few occasions. Maybe if I had learned to mix drinks while serving guests that came in, my checks would have made a big difference.

Anyway, Dad had me running behind him that night as we took subways and walked through Chinatown, as if we were on the run or something. He told me to be on my best behavior and that he would be home soon after he got done with business in New York. I closed my eyes on the bus, as we headed for Georgia thinking about the money I left for Aunt Denair and the card I left for her hospitality. I hoped she enjoyed it.

CHAPTER 19

WORKING MAN, WORKING MAN... YEAH THAT'S ME!

The first thing Aunt Evelyn told me as we pulled out from the parking lot, was to specifically not roll the windows up because the AC would be going out for right now. I only stayed an extra month in New York after Lauren came back, so how much really changed while I was out of town? I couldn't get through the door without having to empty out all my clothes in the suitcase. We ran into a little bed bug epidemic before we left so I made sure I washed my clothes any chance I could and did it before I got on the bus. Aunt Evelyn wasn't hearing me though and I made sure I threw the clothes I had on in the washing machine.

Floating Angel: I even tried to warn her about dad staying over in NY, so that argument could be avoided. They still started all that yelling as soon as he came back, talking about "I promise you I did wash my clothes before I got here.." You hate to see it and you hate even more to say I told you so….

We went to Wells Fargo bank to make sure the cash I left at aunties apartment was there and as I waited for the numbers to appear on the keypad, the first thing I noticed was that there was some money missing from the account. I hesitated to do the math in my head, but then thought nothing of it because I would get it right back. We didn't make any big moves but I had to walk Black as part of the family routine. No one thought to put effort into making sure he got home trained as big as he was now, so you could imagine how pissed I was to smell dog pee and poop from that cage every morning I had to take him out.

Now I loved this dog to death, like he was my own, so don't get me wrong. He used to lay on me as I studied for my exams and gave me the comfort I needed. But when Ebony gave the family all the tips and tricks on how to train the dog, everyone was too focused on themselves to help him become fully trained. As for me, I had to wait until September to get a job so helping around the house, cutting the grass, and raking the leaves was the most I could do to help until someone decided to hire me . Apparently my grandmother knew a guy who was a McDonald's manager over in Locust Grove so he put my name in while I waited for my name to be in the system.

CHAPTER 20

MICKEY DEEZ NUTS: THE LOVE HIP & HOP SEASON THAT NEVER MADE IT TO TV...

My first couple weeks in Mickey D's was pretty hectic. I learned very quickly that not everything there was as simple as wrap the sandwiches, push them down and make the next sandwich. There was a prep station for condiments, pies, cookies and biscuits, the grill station with four grills in place, cooler, freezer, crew room for employees and stockroom for other boxes, cups and sauces. The manager over me put me right on the table and started to make a grilled chicken wrap, three big Macs, two Quarter Pounders and then walked away because he did it within six quick minutes and expected me to pick it up where he left off. But I was a bit too slow on the table and the other managers had to quickly push me over to the grill area, because I wasn't making the customers food fast enough.

The guy on the grill name was DJ who had also doubled as a crew trainer on the table. He went over how to wipe down everything per usage on the grills, cook everything up from frozen nuggets to McChicken up to speed with the Crew members on the tables, and where all the frozen meat products were in case I had to be working by myself. He trained me well enough to the point that he changed his schedule with the GM of the store, Mr. James, as soon as DJ saw that he could leave me by myself. It took me a while to get used to because I hated the constant pressure of making things fast for everyone, and when I slowed down, they would tell me to work faster to keep up with everyone. DJ and another crew member by the name of "Ant" would make a bet on me that I would stop doing all the extra cleaning and mopping I was doing for the whole restaurant. They both agreed on two weeks, but I already overheard them talking about me so I did a little over two weeks just so I could prove them wrong for doubting my work skills.

After that, I paid more attention to the pace I worked at more often because when I went to clean something, I wasn't doing it for them; I did it when I felt like it was necessary.One of the managers, "Z" would repeat this phrase over and over to me all the time when she got frustrated on how I was acting : "*I don't know what happened to him.*" "*He used to be all nice and polite and now he's mean and nasty to everybody.*" "*He wasn't like that when I worked here.*" And she wasn't wrong though, but when people keep pushing your buttons, sometimes you gotta let them know that you aren't just some pushover.

When I began the morning shift (5am-2pm), I made an effort to make sure that I was ready before Aunt Evelyn got outside to her car. On the days that it was too cold for her to go out or she wasn't able to, I took a Lyft or I walked all the way from the house to work. Sometimes I got lucky and Mr. Rok would pick me up on the walk there on his way to work. It beat freezing my butt off, but I knew that the hard work would one day pay off. I made friends within the workplace and I knew just based on the energy that they would reciprocate to me in certain scenarios, I would know whether I would stay away from them after a period of time or not.

One girl had asked for my jacket because she was cold next to the drive thru window. I asked what happened to the one she had and she responded, "I couldn't wear it because it was my little brother's jacket." I didn't care if she was lying or not because I worked on the hot grill, but I'd post her occasionally on Snapchat from October to see whether she'd let me keep my jacket or not. It reached the point where she told me at work that her boyfriend had smelled the scent on the jacket and asked "who's cologne was this on her jacket?" She had lied to him so he wouldn't be harassing her over a jacket that she had lent from me. Funny thing is when I left that job, I ended up bumping into him shortly after at my next job.

Floating Demon: I ended up shaking hands with this dude, smiling because little did he know that cologne he was smelling around her neck was from my jacket. Not that I liked her like that but it was funny how the situation did cause some pettiness.

I met this white boy named Carter who worked in maintenance and who was also struggling to find himself together as a young guy. He introduced me to Marcus who seemed to be about his business at the job. Marcus was older than me by at least 3 years, but once we established a love for video games and similar rap music, we became the best of friends.

Marcus put me onto songs with rappers, such as Pee-Wee Longway, MoneyMan and Polo G. We talked about collabing on video games, how to get the most out of Gamestop memberships and whether college was an option for the both of us. You can ask him in person about all the links I sent him on game designing or testing because of how desperate video game companies are in need for the next big development. I could see him making his own course of action and getting his bread from Ubisoft or Activision. He wanted to wait and create his own thing with one of his friends, but I figured I'd rather take advantage of making money with a big company than just grind. Marcus and his girl always made sure I got home in one piece, regardless of what they had handled outside of McDonalds.

91

My dad complained about some "funky aroma" coming from the car as soon as they pulled off but they never pressured me into doing anything I didn't want to. If I wasn't able to catch a ride with them or got a ride from my aunt, I made sure I could navigate my way back home. Speaking of funky aromas, while I was at work, I had been tempted by a few coworkers that shall not be named to smoke some weed all because we were all less than twenty minutes from the job & because it's Friday. "We are all getting off, and I know you are getting stressed out from this job." "Come smoke with us, you ain't got sh*t to do later." But there was no way I was getting caught up with that, seeing that I was only about making my money at the job and nothing else. When we were on some downtime one day, I decided to take a poll to see who was either sexually active or had smoked something occasionally. Almost everyone that had smoked weed had confessed to tossing some salad or getting theirs tossed as well.

Floating Angel: And Y'all wanted me to smoke with y'all? Ew, butt breath no thank you! I'll go find some people that aren't active like that, if I decided I wanted to smoke with somebody.

Once I did get comfortable in the workplace, I will admit I did get a little handsy with a couple females, trying to check them out and see who would feel me back. I got motorboated while I was trying to Facetime Jess in the crew room. I was just chilling and the girl caught me lacking, while I was waiting for Jessica to set her phone down in the classroom.

I also got twerked on and grabbed, but I didn't play about getting my butt grabbed. But this one girl was working on the prep table and she had the yams. She was a hoodrat but that butt was looking natural & ready for a thirst trap on her phone. So I waited until she walked back to the sink to clean some dishes and we got to talking and she said she had a boyfriend. I said to her, yeah that's cool and all, but I heard you said you do squats at home. "You said sixty squats right?" "Can I feel it?" She poked her butt in my direction and I felt my hand disintegrate from the softness of her right cheek.

*Floating Demon: Oooooweee. So this is what homegrown feels like? I'm trying to do something with this boy… Yes Sirrr. *hits the nae nae and the reverse.*

She gets off before I do around twelve, but when I clocked out and walked out to the lobby where she was still waiting in the chair (Red Flag #1). I keep talking to her while touching up on her thighs, and get her Facebook from her. She tells me to stop playing before her boyfriend comes and sees us.

Floating Demon: I told her I don't see this guy anywhere. But something in my head just then told me to chill out because we were out in the open, regardless of how empty it was looking.

Floating Angel: And who would've guessed that there would've been a 6 foot light skin, grown man standing outside the door staring right at her. He didn't even come inside to get her.

Floating Demon: Boyfriend?! That's gotta be her pimp, not her boyfriend… These girls getting pimped at Mickey D's like that?

And just like that, I haven't heard from her since then. Which was a shame because those yams were something else.

On October 31st, I decided that today was the day I would purchase my own Iphone from Tmobile. I saved enough money and finessed my clock out time to make sure my checks would be just enough. I took a Lyft from my house and put down at least 600 dollars on the Iphone 6 plus. It was the upgrade from the cracked Android that had been dropped by Mr. Rok's daughter while I held her on my shoulders in New York. I didn't even have to look down at the phone face down into the sidewalk; I could just tell that by the noise it made on impact that it was over with. But I wasn't mad because it wasn't entirely her fault and I could still use the Samsung anyway.

On the way home my Lyft driver was giving me the whole rundown of why getting into the stock exchange was a good investment for life, especially if you start at a young age. He even gave me a couple names to research, which went in one ear and out the other. Maybe it was the fact that I was too focused that I just spent this much money on an Iphone, being that it was my first one.

I opened it up as I immediately stepped into the frame of my doorway, quickly sifting through all the apps and changing the wallpaper and lockscreen to my liking. I recorded my unwrapping to my Snapchat story and who decides to reply with her usual sly and fresh remarks? Jessica, who decided to tell me that it was about damn time that I got an Iphone. She didn't even make an effort to call me on the regular; let alone Facetime me. Meanwhile outside, everyone was trick or treating all the houses while I was the lucky kid inside the house with a brand new Iphone to call his own. By Thanksgiving, I caught some type of cold in my immune system and anything like that keeps kicking me down never leaves my body until I'm in a better mental and physical state. I had to take that breather in the crew room because I felt like I was either going to throw up or die. My head was spinning and getting hotter while the noises of orders being placed and kitchen utensils being slammed on tables rang in my ears.

Someone told one of my guys to wake me up and I staggered towards the grill area, putting my hand against the wall as he rushed back to this position. I kept working through it and occasionally sanitized and cleaned myself off in order to keep my yucky germs off the food. Once my shift was over, I felt like a Walking Dead zombie shifting one foot at a time towards the lobby and slammed my head into my arms. I wouldn't wish to feel this sickness on my worst enemy, but it was times like this when you ask where is God going with this now? I took my ride home and collapsed in bed, with whatever I had on.

I didn't care that my family was heading out with their nice clothes or coming back only to get what they needed. As long as I healed up from this illness, I'll be good on the turkey and apple pie. I was woken in the middle of the night to a cold towel around my head and medicine on my window sill. Apparently, my dad and his girlfriend stopped by to make sure I was feeling better and that his eldest baby boy was doing okay. He saved me a tinfoil plate but I pushed it off and demanded to know what time it was. As I checked my phone, I cursed myself for forgetting I had a second job to go to. I forgot I had to go to Sketchers for my second shift, and now I was hours late behind schedule. I told my family thank you for checking up on me and called an Uber to head over to Tanger Outlets. Coincidentally, the lady that was driving me was one of my friends named Ty's mother. I told her that I worked with her son at McDonald's, but had no idea that she was the reason behind the birth of a "handle god".

Every pickup game at school, I played with two kids named Ty and Jalen once we had next on the court. It didn't matter what sh*tty players we had on our team or how many points we were down. Ty had Kyrie Irving handles and could score at the rim by adding some English on his finishes. Jalen was a 3 pointer shooter but had enough speed to drive in the paint, and I was there dishing out assists to anyone that was open or scored when I had the chance too. It was the three of us but we either would lose together as a team or won as a team. We all had AAU experience so it was nothing for us to compete against anyone that thought they could take us down. We didn't join the school basketball team but that gave us the edge over anyone that underestimated our chemistry on the court.

I thanked Ty's mother for the talk that we shared as I got out and hurried towards the back to find my manager, Justin. He told me that he was sorry but due to the fact I was very late, he would let me go and have to probably pass on my position to someone else. . I just thought that the more money at the time, the better my family would be happy to see that I was a hard working young man.If I could have foreseen the events in the next few months to come, I would have made sure to put my health in check first.

The month of December was something in itself, because I didn't get anything real special for Christmas. The Iphone I bought was enough for me but Aunt Evelyn surprised me with some socks and a sweater that I don't know where I stashed to this day. She had her beau at the time named Fisher come through to spend time with her and for the first time, I got to see a black miniature Santa Claus. It wasn't black Jesus, but it was something alright. Everything was chill and unbothered, and no one splurged on gifts because the money was tight but as long as I had my aunt in the house, rest assured that would be enough for me.

CHAPTER 21

A FAMILY TRAGEDY

"Death is not the greatest loss in life." "The greatest loss is what dies inside while still alive." "Never surrender." (Tupac shakur)

No one saw it coming. I don't think we didn't expect it to happen so soon, for us to grasp the reality of what was happening, how it could have happened & why, only God knows that answer. Anna and Gabriel had brought Aunt Evelyn to see her grandsons, Ari and Gabe Jr. and we had just gotten past New Years so no one had taken into full effect of what was going on. But I noticed the patterns, so I guess this sixth sense can also be a curse as well. The way my aunt had stayed in her room longer than usual, and only came out in her red robe to get something out of the fridge.

She didn't cough or say anything when I came from work or outside which was odd but Aunt Evelyn always kept how she was feeling inside. That Friday afternoon, Lauren texted me to wake up aunty up so she could have a ride from basketball practice. I thought nothing of it because Lauren had enough friends at Luella to take her home if she wanted and everyone in our family knows that Aunt Evelyn will cuss you out if you wake her out of her sleep. I stood at the door for what felt like with my curiosity telling me to open the door and see if she was alright, but the voice in the back of my head telling me that she just needed some rest and she'll be fine by tomorrow. So I went to bed and thought nothing of it.

On January 6th, Aunt Lynette called to let us know she would be over at the house by the morning to take us to church. Lauren and I brushed our teeth, and threw our shoes on and I waited in my room for the moment Aunt Lynette would tell us to go inside the car because I wasn't going to freeze my butt off outside.

She asked Lauren if we had checked on Aunt Evelyn and we both responded around the same time that she was asleep so we didn't want to bother her. She knocked on the door and opened it slowly only to soon let a bloodcurling, horrifying scream that could be heard around the whole house. "EVELYN!" I rushed through the living room only to be frozen with shock, not being able to process the scene unfolding before me. Aunt Lynnette was trying to revive my Aunt Evelyn's lifeless body, which had seemed to be getting colder and colder by each minute. She yelled at me to call 911 several times, but I started to shake and tremble as I reached for the phone in my pocket. I had to walk over to the dining room table and take a couple deep breaths to process what I had seen.

Black was banging around his cage and no one in the family had been made aware of the situation at hand. I don't remember who came first and who walked out last, with all the EMT's and the coroner walking in before my family even made it to the parking lot. When they all had arrived and did their silent moments of grieving and prayer, hoping that the coroner had made some mistakes, it was confirmed that she had passed away in her sleep. She had an enlarged heart, among other things which could have only meant that her stress, as well as her unhealthy lifestyle and other factors contributed to her passing. I think what scared me most wasn't seeing my aunt lifeless but how everyone reacted to the situation as if the death was so unreal at the moment.

Gabriel clutched his wife's hand and kept muttering to himself that he should've been a better son, yet little did he know that he would play a huge role in developing the young man I would become to this day. Ashley, Ryan, Lynell and Aunt Lynette had already lost a husband and a father a while back, so this one really hit home for them as well. Anna, Gabriel and Ebony would learn to set aside personal differences to unite as siblings for what was to come before and after the funeral.

And my dad, who had been fashionably late and had some business to attend to outside of the state, came to find that he lost his twin, and his sole flesh and blood. He punched the chair in my sisters room over and over again as everyone took their seats around the house, yelling and crying "Why wasn't it me, God?"

I didn't say anything to him because the only words that projected into my mind were of malicious and foul intent.

Floating Demon: She'd probably still be alive if you didn't curse her out all the times when she was just trying to help you raise the kids right.

Floating Angel: To be honest, It was really no one's fault. We all had no idea that we would lose someone close to our hearts that day. What we can do now is figure out how we can come together and turn things around for the better.

I didn't say anything and still couldn't find anything to say as the days went on, but tried to hug everyone that was crying or that needed so comfort because my family deserves some reassurance and comfort. I kept the guilt and pain inside my own soul as I struggled to find answers to questions that were too far out of my reach to answer.

Why God?! Why now?! I asked her to stop smoking those Newports and she promised she would. But I could always see through the screen door, the trail of nicotine and gray smoke clouding up from the patio as she would ash her cigarette into her tray. I cried in my room, as soon as I was aware that everyone was sleeping inside and or had left to be elsewhere. Was it my fault that I didn't wake her up to get my sister from basketball practice? Maybe if I poured out all the Cokes she stocked up in the refrigerator down the drain, or helped her out more in her Special Ed classes that she was taking, she would still be here with me.

She wanted to help out the less fortunate, the kids with disabilities like her alcoholic father who had a stroke and she had to take care of for a long period of time. She was sooo f*cking close, and didn't pass her test. I told her every time that she would be closer to her goal even after we all chipped in and helped her with any spelling error, margin misplacement... because it was the least we could do at the time.

She taught me so much in the past year and seven months that I lived with her. She would wake me up in the morning for school and kiss me on my cheek, telling me she knew I was tired but wanted to make sure I had a good day at school. Then she would wake me up around 2-3 AM, with just her robe on, yelling about the dishes that were piled up in the sink, as if she couldn't have taken that same energy to my sister. And then she dragged me out and made sure I was in the kitchen before she slammed the door back to her room.

I remember when you brought me out to the kitchen and told me that it was time for me to cook some food; that I couldn't feed a girl just cereal and ramen noodles all the time. I muttered under my breath, that whatever girl I was with was gonna humble herself if she had to eat ramen noodles and cereal with me. Otherwise she ain't the girl for me. We cleaned the chicken in the sink and you showed me which seasoning to use over it before you put it in the oven to be baked. We broke spaghetti noodles and sauteed the onions in the frying pan with vegetable oil. I remember when we were playing Heads Up on the tablet with Dad and Anna and then, when Anna asked you who Dora's cousin was, and what was your answer? You didn't hesitate to say Pablo because your competitive spirit to win forced you to get the wrong answer and make us all laugh. We knew it was Diego, but I wish you had gotten it right, because you always made everything feel right. You yelled at me to pay attention to the landmarks and get off my phone so I knew my way around back roads in Henry County and always got mad when I never finished my projects on time.

Remember when I had that skeleton project for Ms. Williams? You still cursed under your breath and made sure we got the glue and pins to put him all together on the carpet of my bed, along with Lauren's help. Remember when we drove in the car and I asked you why you saved up money for Ari and Gabriel's insurance and you told me that in the case that you were not here, that they will be able to have a good future and be the successful grandbabies you know they were capable of becoming.

I called someone to vent too while I was down in my loneliness, and I even tried to play some J Cole but even the song was breaking my heart into pieces. It was "Intro" from his 2014 Forest Hills Project. "Do you wanna be... "Do you want to be happy?" "Do you wanna..." "Do you wanna be free?" "Free from pain, free from scars, free to sing, free from bars…" "It clears your mind, learn to fly, then reach the stars…" "You take your time to look behind and say, "look where I came." I couldn't even finish singing the song because I felt like I failed you in a sense, Aunty by not being there all the way for you.

I was so selfish about my reasons to not move to Georgia, that I didn't even come in the bed to watch movies with you because my sister would be resting her head right on your shoulders. The same person I pushed all my anger on once I left. You invited me all those times with an open door and I turned to my room with only my music and writing to calm me down. I called Jasmine to tell her about it all, and I don't know if it was the fact that I was an butthole that only spoke acrimoniously towards other people that bothered her. I don't even remember if we spoke after that call or I got blocked for just being the stupid insecure jerk I was to her or anyone else at the time. But Jaz cared about me enough to tell me it was going to be okay and that I was going to get past that storm that I had over my head pretty soon.

Fast Forward to the funeral, where my aunt's lovely church members opened up their doors to our family. I sat in the back of the family members and looked for someone to walk in with and to someone's hand to hold. Luckily as we all filed two by two like Noah's ark, I had a lucky lady that called me her handsome cousin as we ushered ourselves to the pews in front of us.

Thanks @ChampagneMommii, because if you are reading, I need that reassurance from you cuzzo. I kept telling myself in my head that I would be fine and won't let my nerves get the best of me until the damn PowerPoint presentation came on. The stupid PowerPoint that got my heart pumping as if it was racing a 10k on its own. Everyone stood still and wiped their tears as the pictures flashed left, right up and bottom. My blood ran ice cold and my eyes stopped on the graduation picture of myself in the cap and gown with my aunt by my side. Everything hit me at once and I bawled into my knees, as someone rubbed my back telling me that it was alright baby and I could let all the tears out.

As the service ended, everyone had ushered back into their cars, and we piled into the black limousine ready to pull off. I wondered to myself if I would be able to keep myself together when the casket dropped in the grave and then woke up to the reality of Gabriel trying to bring important details about Uncle Gabe and Aunt Evelyn's past. He went on to tell us how the relationship fizzled out and they divorced after one had cheated on the other. I could tell by the energy in the car right then maybe that wasn't the right time to mention that your mom had done dirty back to your dad. It sounded like he was telling the truth but then again, that was the wrong time and the wrong place. Neither of us weren't physically present at every step of their lives to shed a true answer to that problem. Sometimes it's better to just move on from a situation like that, because life isn't always black or white where we can either deal with the problem or move on to find peace in something else.

My father decided to make plans of his own later that month to separate himself from the chaos but also take us kids along with him. "What the hell are you trying to say?" I'm saying that he discussed it with me while I was sketching a layout of my brand and that I needed to get out of the house by February and move in with my grandmother. I asked him why I needed to do that and he said to just do it because he told me so and there was no questioning behind that.

Floating Angel: "*He didn't know that I already planned to move in with Aunt Lynnette.*" "*Because we created a system of our own where as long as I paid the rent and stayed out of trouble, then I could do as I please.*"

Floating Demon: "*That's fair!*" "*So why does he have to control what I do because he's mad that he lost his sister?*" "*And how he's telling me never to reach out to my aunt ever again?*" "*He does know that's gonna strain our relationship right?*"

Floating Angel: "*He's always been about self man. I try to explain it literally every time and he tries to hide it with his ego. It's so damn annoying, especially when everyone in the family but my mom is in denial about it.*"

I moved out to my grandmother's house around February in Mcdonough because I clearly didn't don't have a say-so anymore on the situation. I would end up staying there for at least another year before I decided to move out again.

CHAPTER 22

GRANDMA'S HOUSE

I packed all my bags upstairs and moved everything around in the attic to my liking. My cousin Ebony had moved out because she couldn't deal with being in the house and already had plans of getting an apartment of her own. I tried to plan how I was going to get out of this jam of being with Grandma being very particular about her space, her glasses, and her things being touched a certain way. Her OCD was driving me up the wall and I knew it was going to be a matter of time before I left. The way I didn't wash dishes all the way through so she called me back and said I needed to wash them again. The way she said I left crumbs on the floor because I left them behind and being careless.

My grandmother had cancer, back pain from the stab wounds she had received from an attempted murder on her life, and a broken arm from different accidents in her early days of college. Whoever decided along with my father for me to stay with my grandmother didn't make the best judgement call because to put a kid that hasn't gotten over his aunt's death with another person of the family was not a good move at all.

I was still at Mickey D's, before I decided to put my two week notice in and ended up having this conversation with Marcus about how all the general managers could just come in and tell me what to do and run things like I was a slave there. Unbeknownst to me, "Lessy", the new GM managed to eavesdrop, as all women do, on my conversation with Marcus.

Floating Demon : Well let's be fair. You weren't whispering when you were talking to him. She wasn't even ten feet from you in her office.

Floating Angel: Yeah bro, you can't just say f*ck everybody because they didn't help you with your work problems yet. You gotta be patient.

I heard a lot about Lessy before she came back to Mickey D's… Some comments were rude remarks and others were compliments, but once you got to know Lessy, she was a very sweet person. She had the best interests of other people at heart and never said anything slick *unless* you did her dirty at the job or said something rude. Then she would turn on you. So I tried to stay on her good side and she stayed on mine & we got along just fine. The first thing she said to me when I decided to leave was to make sure I found a better job if I was going to be sure I wanted to leave and wished me my farewell. It hit me because I didn't think she would genuinely hope for me to find something better at that point in time, but it felt great that she said it on good terms.

Back at the house, my grandmother was interested in me getting my license in Georgia and all I had for a form of ID was my permit. The driver classes cost too much and I was already applying for other jobs on my phone and weighing my options to see what would help me save more for my drivers ed course. Fortunately, all the courses I could have signed up for were booked for August, as it seemed as the state of Georgia was only letting certain people that were registered for school to drive these courses. I just wanted my license so I could get a car to go to and from where I needed to be. Simple as that.

My grandmother decided to call up her next door neighbor Ms. Katrina to give me some driving lessons in her Chevy Cobalt. Ms. Katrina was skeptical at first because of how inexperienced I was, so she would take me to a parking lot in Stockbridge after my work hours at Luxxotopica. She would have me either come to her door or call me, depending on what kind of day it was (she was never consistent) and I would come inside the passenger ready to head off to her physical therapy classes.

She damaged her finger at her workplace, but didn't trust me enough yet to drive so she drove the whole way there & smoked those nasty cigarettes in the car. When we reached the parking lot that I would practice in, I would start off light with orange traffic cones, and the garbage cans circling over and over. Then she would rush back to get on the highway so I could make it on time to work whether she dropped me off or I walked from my grandmother's house.

CHAPTER 23

JOB NUMERO 2

I started working on March 1st, 2018 for Luxxotopica under a contracting temp agency. On my first day there, I said hey to the cute looking security guard who was tatted up from shoulder down, but she had a natural softness to her face and looked like she stayed in shape as well. The warehouse was huge and had boxes for name brand sunglasses stacked high and low. I had to make sure as I walked to my orientation that I didn't get hit by oncoming traffic or anyone in a moving forklift.

I kept my questions simple and answers sharp as I was introduced to my reporting supervisors, the break room and the locker room. I was placed to work on the first floor in retail but the issue was having someone to train over me and teach how to scan codes, and look through aisles. So they found an older white woman named "Susan" to train me until around 10-11 because she was a senior citizen who could work a flexible shift to her liking.

Susan was polite and helpful, but was an Energizer bunny when it came to work. I swear it seemed like no one would see me speeding past the boxes of Raybans or Gucci's trying to ask why I needed to punch in three buttons to continue and only two to make sure the product was scanned. She walked and talked fast so the only time anything made sense to me was when she slowed down for break and explained the rules of the breakroom to a science. Susan pointed out where to put your food in the fridge because people will (and they did but not mine) steal your food, how long breaks are allotted for and what supervisors to watch for if you come in on break late or stay later than usual.

After that, I needed another senior person to watch over and it was this guy named Mike, who was very laid back and chill but kept chewing gum on him, as if it made the halitosis go away. He whispered to me, "I saw you running trying to keep up with her and I felt bad, so I'm going to show you how to keep up at your own pace." He slowed down everything for me so I would get it the first day with him and by the third and fourth, I liked learning from him so much I forgot all about the bad breath.

The checks were looking so good at Luxxotopica that I was soon making around 500 dollars a week, even as a temp because my hours were from 3PM to 1:30AM. I decided that if I kept this up, I could get hired permanently no time. However there were strict rules in place of working at Luxxtopica. They demanded no talking between or in aisles, no food or chewing of any sort, and definitely no personal music playing in the warehouse. I broke just about all three of these in the short period of time I was there being the rebel I was.

I did have friends within the warehouse that also were in my group for attendance. There was Pigg, Darius, Franco, and Vernon as far as the guys were concerned. Pigg was into muscle cars like I was, Darius was into investing into his money and saving up into property. Franco was the relaxed out of them all because he came from a different agency than I had, and didn't talk much but he stood out because he had tattoos that were pretty decent quality (not like mine though), and always came to work with the freshest pair of shoes on. Where he had the money to pull out shoes like he had all the VC in NBA2K, I don't know and it wasn't my business to ask. What I do find interesting was the inside conversations that we had before work and during our breaks. We talked about the girls that he used to smash in college, his tattoos and the meanings behind them if he had any, sports teams but one day he said something to me that really caught my attention. He said "Bro I don't know if you noticed at this job but everybody is working like they are sheep waiting to get a dollar because all their minds are fed by a paycheck and nothing else." Vernon was all about being a friendly, but flirtatious hood dude, in the sense that he could be a player, compliment any female he approached but only treat them as friends because it was work and he had a girlfriend that he was loyal to at the time being.

Deep down, I knew he was a good kid and had a very generous heart but he smoked a lot, which made him lazy and didn't come to work on time. Also his transportation wasn't reliable at all even though he stayed in Griffin.

Now Vernon tried to put me on to a lot of females at Luxxotopica, however I wasn't trying to approach them in the same fashion he was because they were either girls from 1st or 3rd shift which meant they wouldn't give you a chance unless you worked with them. It got to a point where he would corner me on the aisles if he saw a girl that he had spoken to, give me the details like he had a Dragon Ball Z scouter then "pushed" me towards the girl by making a scene behind me.

And the girl would already be walking in my direction so it was as if he had forced them to grab their attention.I got at least six girls numbers and out of five, none would respond or leave me on delivered. Three out of the six girls had told me, "uhhh you not on my shift so I don't know how this going back and forth is gonna work." Vernon told me to never cry over it, which I didn't because I felt like an idiot wasting my time at the job. He said it was only practice for my confidence, so that I could get girls outside of my job like at the movies or something. I swear if he actually was smart enough to get out the hood, he could have written a book on how to get girls for dummies, the way he carried so much pride about himself. He had conversations about bulking up and gaining muscle because I told him in the near future I'd focus on getting stronger. Sometimes we would do push up contests to see who could beat who, but would get caught because just like school, there was no horseplay in the warehouse.

Floating Angel: I'd ask him all the time, where he got all this knowledge about eating with good nutrition and the diet that you would incorporate if you wanted to be in good shape.

Floating Demon: Then Vernon finally spills the beans… his dad was Vernon Forrest aka The Viper, who held world championships in two weight classes until he was gunned down in 2009. Now that I googled it, he has his dad's face and everything.

I showed Vernon some texts between Jasmine and I. Her number had changed and she sent me some photos she had taken at this photoshoot for feedback. I don't know what it was about this girl wearing an all black dress, but I know she looked really good with it on. She told me later on, she had even got some looks from these guys that were looking her up and down from the side.

Vernon: Damn n*gga! She is fine as hell and she looks pretty thick too. I know you are hitting that because I would hit that if I were you…

Floating Demon: Ohhh no! Don't you start with that blushing and getting shy sh*t now. You better say she's just a friend, playboy.

Me: Naw bro! We are just friends and she is staying in Florida anyway so there would be no chance.

Meanwhile, There was this one girl that I did have my eyes on that I'll call K.P. but I ended up getting shut down quickly too. Vernon once again tried to put me on but all I needed was the introduction and we made some light conversation. I mean she had brown skin, long braids and she had the yams poking too? No questions needed.

I tried to get her number at one point while I was moving around handling orders, but she kept putting me off while we were in the aisles. So I kept handing my phone off until she told me that she had a boyfriend in jail and also a child of her own; so trying to kick it with her wasn't going to be an option.

Floating Demon: And that's great that you have a child and all, but I was asking for that number. I didn't ask for the whole backstory, beloved.

So we kept it strictly platonic at work, despite all the guys that would whisper in my ear telling me to get her number for them or the "Okay I see you nephew" from the older guys. Ugh. Soon I found out K.P. had an art major she was pursuing and even worked in her family restaurant business, but the warehouse money was just a cushion for her child, now that she was being more independent. Every opportunity we got to converse, K.P. would tell me how she had some artwork that she was putting up for clients around the way so I told her I had some ideas for my brand that I wanted her to illustrate for me. Sad to say she never reached back, but hey I tried and was willing to pay her to work on it too.

Around this same time, some dude approached me around the corner and told me that I needed to mope over K.P. because I wasn't getting any action from her as a king and I needed to keep my head up. Now the man that approached me was Thomas Gillie Jr., although I didn't really give him the respect that he was showing me based on how he was dressed. But sometimes God can send you an angel in disguise and you'll never know it. He approached me one time and had me come meet him in the locker room.

Anyone at that job can vouch for me... that was my personal hideout to go take a nap when I got caught up on any cart orders in Luxxotopica but today I was going to get schooled on some motivational stuff. He started his story off about how he went from being homeless through apartments and the hood in the south trying to make ends meet and come up on the next meal. Then he went on to tell me about how he had fallen in love with a girl who he thought in turn liked him for his character and would be willing to support his pro football dreams.

Around this point of his storytelling, I asked him if I could record him on my cell phone, just in case I got too comfortable in my chair and dozed off lol. He continued stating that when he makes it into the NFL, "his ex's mouth is going to drop, because she will remember that guy tried to marry her and now he's making millions of dollars, all because she didn't believe in him when he told her too."

"And she's going to understand bro why I'm so blessed to have all the money and fame because I was the same man that was trying to lead you to God. "I was that same man praying for you and... it changed me, because I don't have any hate for her but I had to keep searching and doing me." I wish I had recorded more of him talking to this day because by the energy in his voice, you could tell he was all about pursuing his dreams and having some commitment in whatever he was doing. He told me that I had enough time to figure out what I wanted to do, because I was 20 and he was 27. I believe if he has the talent, and hard work he can accomplish that NFL dream if he gets around the right football people.

CHAPTER 24

MY BOY IS GETTING TATTED UP...

It was time for me to ink another tattoo on my body. The little leg tattoo of Aunt Lois's name that I had wasn't enough to rival anyone's huge sleeves or back pieces. Everyone had most of their ink done in a cheap shop or in someone's house, but I wanted the tattoos I got to have some meaning and be worth having on my body for the rest of my life . I didn't want anything to just be inked onto my body. I wanted it to be something with a nice aesthetic and some memory behind it. "It looks great and I wish I could go to your artist when I got the money" is what I wanted people to say when they would see any of my tattoos.

But where would I go in Atlanta, and how far would it be and how much would I have to save? Fortunately, these guys I bumped into put me onto this guy named Slim in the Downtown Area. They showed me his Instagram and his work so I gave him a follow and DM'd him for more info. I don't know what I thought I was doing trying to go back and forth on the tattoo I was planning to get.I figured he'd been doing this for a while so I could improvise once I saw him in person. I called up Carter after I set up the appointment and left my grandmother's house to meet up with him in his car.

The whole car ride consisted of Carter talking about his personal tribulations with women not giving him the time of day like he wanted them too and trying to live beyond the means of what his daily life was like.I listened to him as he shifted his emotions from working back in Mickey D's to a new car detailing shop he was working for. I didn't know if I should've drowned in with his pity or try to give some motivation to take off with.

All I do know is that you can't let a bad job or life change the outcome of how you want to live your life. But I do know that I was going to get some food to eat before we got there so I could tolerate this tattoo session. I went ahead and got a burger with fries to-go and we kept heading down the interstate until we got to our exit. We took some backroads leading us to this huge warehouse. I waited outside in the parking lot until a really tall black dude with a relaxed, distressed outfit that was slim fitted from head to toe came out to dap me up. It's like his whole character really defined his name which is really dope and to see him be happy that I showed up eased up about 95% of the tension I had for my tattoo.

We follow Slim up to this apartment, which from the inside looked like a traphouse for an artist that had been locked in against his own will. The upstairs portion was his tattoo area, where he had paintings galore as well as the unfinished ones, graffiti art on the walls and tattoo equipment lying on the table. Carter and I took our seat on the couch and Slim got his laptop with his drawing tablet at the ready. As I snarfed down my burger and sifted through my fries, he started going through the images of African queens on Pinterest and asked me his opinion on each of them. I wanted that tattoo in order to represent that having a black woman to me, as a partner for life meant that I could look at her, pleased she would be trying to seek out self improvement for herself everyday. She wouldn't be perfect or stagnant but rather see some kind of harmony within everything that she does for herself and others.

Floating Demon: You want to get some queen from Africa and get it tattooed on you, huh?

Floating Angel: No, man. It's about expressing how I feel about black women in society. I've had strong independent women such as my mother, aunts, cousins and they are strong, fearless, loving, compassionate, nurturing...all the things that you can ask from any other woman in any other race as well. Shout out to all the true queens out there.

As Slim laid the outline of the now finished design on my upper arm, I was still a little antsy from what I had learned about in Anatomy on tattoos. The dangerous chemicals that are in the tattoo ink, and the risk of skin infections from unclean needles.

I expressed this out loud and Slim personally unwrapped each new needle in my face for a swap out as if to let me know that he was serious about his craft and he wouldn't intentionally give me skin cancer or some disease. I looked over to Carter who was fast asleep with his right hand in his pants and sighed out loud. "Damn bro this ain't your house, you can't just be doing that anywhere." Slim laughed it off and I wondered how it seemed like nothing bothered him at all while he worked, like he was so unfazed about what was happening in his comfort zone.

We talked about how we both lived different lives, but both shared that phase of being the same quiet black kid that just watched how life was going by and trying to take advantage of the good things life offered us. I told him that his paintings of all the black women, literal black art was what attracted me to even coming to his shop in the first place. It was something about his handmade style, the way that all his old artwork compared and contrasted to his work now that set him apart from all the other artists I had on a recommended list in my Iphone. He told me about getting girls was a strenuous task for him in school as well, until he had a mentor to teach him the game, on how to be sociable with women because you can *either befriend them or get to know them intimately but it's all about how you do it* for yourself because what works for him might be way different from the cheat code I have in mind.

A mentor… Someone to teach you the ropes of how to pull women for yourself. I've had guys that have told me that I had to Jedi mind trick women in order for them to f*ck with me or groups of guys that told me to stop trying to respect women out in public, because "you'll never get any play trying to be the nice guy all the time." I just wanted to learn how to be in control of myself while also getting some girls here and there at the same time. And not being in places where I could attempt that left me depressed until I started talking to my guy, CJ on Snapchat. I watched him post the no face no cases on his story and always having a good time whether it was walking out on the strip with his friends or going out on a date with his girlfriend.

So I asked him what his secret was and it was simply making people like him for who he was and going with the flow. You have to ask yourself, who are you really, before the lights turn off and you look into the mirror? Are you trying to be a follower or do you want to stand out and set trends for other people? We both liked shoes and clothes and materialistic items more than socializing with people, because people always tend to show me their true colors in person or I'd have them figured out by then. I was never given the spotlight of attention so I hid from it and made my own rules as I went along.

I would post pictures of Instagram models, and half naked pictures of girls at that, because I wanted that but didn't know what it took to be that guy. CJ would reply to my photos, that one day I would be getting those same girls if I got out of my comfort zone and believed in myself because they'll dig the confidence first. I said I don't know bro, so CJ said don't stress over girls, because it may not happen now, but it will when you are older. I had literally made up the name @theladies_man on snapchat because "I want women to cry and pour their heart out for me and tell me how much they hate it when they are apart from me." (Drake-Dreams Money Can Buy). Because to live that fantasy as well would be more fulfilling than an average kid would settle for. CJ and I would joke around over the whole Orlando Brown situation on DJ Vlad video and posted videos from each other's Snapchat story if we found the same TMZ videos each week.

I also remember mentioning to him that if Orlando Brown can get a girl pregnant, then that was a sign that I could get some play from a girl too… but I'd also make sure I wasn't a mental train wreck either. I had aspirations to become a real father and husband one day, not someone's baby daddy, so I'll wait until I put myself in a financial position to raise my children with a mother that would genuinely love them with all her heart and soul. After I kept giving him the whole "woe is me " talk back and forth, CJ let me in on some details about his past, that he had been in a couple home invasions, while going to school because the struggle of maintaining income from a 9-5 was tough enough. I didn't believe it until he had sent me pictures and screenshots, that this double life was really his day to day thing.

But in his spare time, he also worked hard on his paintings, making music and being a content creator. I posted his work on my Snapchat and tagged his snapchat name, begging people to f*ck with my mans work because his raw talent and how he managed to come up with a new canvas every other week was incredible. He thanked me for the shout outs every time but I told him that I looked up to him a lot because he was like a big brother to me, the one that I wish I had in my life.

He taught me to never be envious of another man's come-up because every man will find happiness in their own way. Then he had vanished from snapchat before I could make a new one, and I searched his accounts, but all I had was his inactive Twitter account. This was before I made a new Snapchat, but when I saw my dawg had gotten a patent for his brand from Twitter, I shed a tear because if he maximized his talents to his fullest potential then he could make a name in this world and never have to look to the streets for a hustle again.

Hey CJ, I made it bro. Remember when you told me, "if writing is your niche, then you should take all the stories you talk about seriously and make it a real name for yourself?" Hit me up if you ain't dead or in jail because I miss you, big bro. Thanks for believing in me when I didn't know how to believe in myself or if I could for that matter.

Back at the shop, the tattoo took about 10 hours but between all the talking and vibin we did to the music, the pain really felt like nothing. My dad once told me that when I was eleven years old, I was standing on the balcony walkway and when my mom began to yell at me for cleaning my room I started to claw at my neck because I wanted the anger in my mother's voice to go away. I kept scratching my neck until the crimson blood began to drip in between my fingernails and my father yelled for her to stop before I ripped my vocal cords out and stopped me.

So I guess compared to my nails, tattoo needles weren't all that painful. I think that it just was therapeutic to see the work being done in progress and it also put me in my happiest place in mind, whether it was looking over a huge ocean or riding into the sunset with some chick in the passenger seat. There was this one song by Playboi Carti called Love Hurts that Slim was playing, that I had listened and added to my playlist. I'm not a huge fan of Carti but the song was dope and listening to it helped ease the pain. I paid my finished tattoo via Zelle and he dapped me up along with Carter, who had woken up with his hands finally out of his pants (Thank the Lord).

He said "damn bro the hoes gonna be all over you with this one." I said thanks to Slim, but as I headed out the door, I knew that all of my tattoos would leave a lasting impression for myself, but if the girls ended up liking them, then good for them. Carter dropped me off early that morning after we drove through the dark and I made sure that he had got his gas money before I walked into my grandmother's house.

Unfortunately, my grandmother had to find out about my tattoo in the worst way possible though because I couldn't hide it forever. I wish I could make this story up because I felt so ashamed at the moment but it is what it is. I walked in from work with the wrap still around my arm peeling off and I tried to bypass my cousin Shon who happened to be sweeping in the front porch. I didn't even know he was dropping by but that's how everyone was at my grandmother's house, trying to check in and help where they could.

He said what was up, which I said nothing very quickly and started in the direction of the stairs. My grandmother had stopped me and asked about the wrap,which I quickly said on the fly, that it was an accident at work that I got involved in and my arm got caught in. There was an awkward silence as Shon came downstairs and his footsteps creeped towards the living room. I didn't see them talking but I already could tell what was coming next…

"Tell the truth about where you really got that wrap from." Dang Shon… "Whyyyyy". I dragged my feet from the steps towards my grandmother, where she examined the tattoo and then dragged me with some unnatural strength, that I didn't even know she possessed towards the front door. She almost dislocated my shoulder, trying to look at it in the sunlight.

Floating Demon: Hey, hey Mary Jane… The tattoo's still fresh, and I can't have it in the sun right now. Take it easy, please grandma.

Floating Angel: Grandma is only disappointed because she did all that lecturing and reading scripture, only for you to go out and do that. Before you say anything though, slow down and convey your emotions with words, slowly. We talk about this all the time bro.

Floating Demon: I didn't do it to go behind her back or because my family members have them. I did it to make me happy but I'll take being misunderstood over being miserable any day.

CHAPTER 25

YEAH AIIGHT, IMMA HEAD OUT!

"So do not be afraid of them, for there is nothing concealed that will not be disclosed, or hidden that will not be made known." -Matthew 10:26

Fast forward to the end of May, where people are getting cut left and right from working because of their temp agency calling them to a new location or because they weren't the right fit. Guys getting fired for a simple whisper, or having their back turned to talk to someone only to get walked out by the Italians or warehouse supervisor. They don't play no games, it's either you working and you talk on break and hopefully find a new job. People were getting tense, senior employees discussing stories with me about how they worked on holidays and never got their bonus check added after the holiday passed.

I'd ask, "why did you never leave" and they said, one check wasn't going to stop them from making more money though. I shook my head as I realized the reality of the warehouse situation I was in: that the older people were working traditionally for paycheck to paycheck, while the younger kids could easily find a new job on their phone and make their money elsewhere if they were unsatisfied.

I had to leave soon if they didn't make me permanent and with the July V.T.O, my plan of action had to be sooner rather than later. Back at my grandmother's, I didn't know how I was barely getting any rest or shuteye. I would be tired from playing video games at 2-3AM after I came in from creating a social cocoon from giving Ms. Katrina money for her utilities and making money at the job. It was always money that she was begging for rent or helping her cut the grass...

I couldn't live like this with waking up early just to make sure she had the means to get by. And she never put any of her disability check money back into my pocket, but I always caught her getting a new hairdo or having a friend come over for the day. So if I'm giving you money, and helped you buy a phone plus another one from Wal-Mart, then how come you could return the favor back? Then I had to help her when online hackers posing as a virus protection company hacked her bank account! When I decided I was reaching my breaking point, I reached out to a couple people at Luxxotopica for some feedback to make sure I wasn't tripping about the whole situation.

Floating Demon: You could make her your sugar mama!

Floating Angel: If I'm the one giving her money then why would I have to be her sugar- Ew, no! I don't even like old people in that way.

Floating Demon: You could take some of her money and blackmail her.

Floating Angel: That would be a lovely idea, EXCEPT SHE'S RIGHT NEXT TO MY GRANDMA! I'm not setting myself up to get backfired.

I had fun buying shoes, talking to friends and spending money on pizza and takeout. But it's time to get serious. I came to work and get a car so I can go find my own place to be. I even video called Shaniqua for some advice on my work issue, but this chick was in the shower butt naked. I had to throw my phone in my pocket because I was just in the middle of the warehouse where everyone was too busy cleaning and I put my headphones in my ears as I walked towards the exit. I signed out and we had a normal conversation like this girl wasn't scrubbing away. I could barely hear her talking over all that shower water, so I told her that I'd talk to her later and we ended up going our separate ways after that, because she got in a relationship.

Floating Angel: I don't even know why you bother wasting that time on that girl. Grow some balls and figure out what girl you are going to spend some time on.

Floating Demon: I think he's trying to make up for the absence of cheeks he's not clapping yet. He's too chicken of a guy to shoot his shot elsewhere, but hey live your life bro.

On June 1st, on that very afternoon, I had completed a huge order when I noticed myself getting drowsier than usual. I don't know if it was the lack of sleep or my feet hurting on the hard floor but I had to rest my eyes before I passed out in one of these aisles.

Floating Angel: Oooh ooh. Let's ask Darius up ahead, he might know something. I know I have too much pride to be going to sleep on some toilet seat in the bathroom.

Floating Demon: If they hadn't been catching people in the locker room, I would doze my eyes off. Too bad getting caught sleeping means instant termination; especially during this seasonal peak.

Darius had the same idea in mind but I figured that I would improvise with the boxes in the area. I told him to keep watch over me as I walked to the farthest end towards the entrance because the corner I was trying to occupy would block off the view of anyone coming straight ahead of me.

Floating Angel: Now if I could adjust this box to the left and hope they don't see my legs poking out while I sit up on this floor.

Floating Demon: What are you doing trying to sleep on the floor man? I know it's a quick shut eye but they're gonna catch us forreal. They ain't got time to play any Games with you!

But it was too late it seemed because as soon as I fell asleep, I woke up to feel someone tapping my chest and opened my eyes to see all the supervisors around my body, which was now stretched on the floor. Apparently someone snitched and had all the supervisors headed in my direction. Darius,(being the awful watchman he was), was on the other side of the warehouse and couldn't make it to my spot in time as the managers all alerted each other on their walkies. I wasn't mad because it wasn't his fault. You just hate to see it happen though.I had someone walk me over to the door and give me the whole should've- known-done- better bro speech. What they didn't know was that since they were having a potluck that following afternoon, somebody was going to sneak back in as a worker since he got to keep his badge.

Floating Demon: You can take the job from the kid but I'mma take the food from y'all like I'm Robin Hood and eat good tomorrow.

I walked in that day with my chest out high and sneaked through the long way and via the middle of the warehouse like the true ninja warrior I was.

Only problem was that one of my old supervisors had recognized me as I made brief eye contact with her. Dammit, I should've kept my head down. As I peeked past the tinfoil, a stern female voice called me by my full name and asked me to follow her to the exit.

Floating Demon: I say we grab the food, then juke her because she can't catch us if we run out of here quick enough.

Floating Angel:I don't know about that one dude. I already got caught sleeping, so the last thing I want them to know is that I tried to run out playing Hot Potato with collard greens, turkey, rice or whatever is in these pans.

I followed the guard and gave her my badge in her outstretched hand. It seemed only fair that I had tried to get some food, working most of that shift off last night. I walked with my head low back to my grandmother's house and avoided any direct questions about why my job was seriously letting me go.

It was just a minor setback because I would find another one pretty soon. In the meantime, I decided to go to Anna's house on a regular basis, to avoid any of Ms. Katrina's sass and to get some actual driving done for my license. Anna let me practice on her Hyundai and I was a nervous wreck because I had gone from someone instructing me outside to actually being in the car, speaking calmly.

I learned quicker from Anna after going out and driving her around places with Ari. It was just something about making sure they were safe in the car that made me want to drive better everyday. By July, I was ready to get that license. And I already got another session with Slim booked again. It was just something thrilling about getting those tattoos, man. I planned to finish my whole arm and Anna had promised to drop me off before she made it to the wedding she planned on attending.

She wanted to meet Slim in person before she left, just to be sure that I was going to be in good hands. This should have been a clue to me that she would trip over me later but I thought nothing of it. I walked up with him to the room and he had a friend of his finishing up his client on the left side of the room. I sent him the photos of all the black people I wanted on my forearm, down to my wrist.

There was Jackie Robinson on the inside of my arm to represent fearlessness in the face of the oppressors because Jackie Robinson still played and did his thing regardless of how his white teammates and the fans treated him. Angela Davis on the other side because her history on activism speaks for itself. MLK Jr. because he spoke about unity for all races and he still got assassinated. And Malcolm X, because that was Aunt Evelyn's favorite movie.

As we got started on my arm, we got started on my armpit area because "we gotta get the hard sh*t out the way first, even if it was the painful part." I cursed under my breath and bit my tongue but I kept telling myself that it was only temporary over and over and that the finished product was going to make all the pain worth it. We stopped on Angela Davis because of the shading and Anna being worried about me being out all night. She just kept calling over and over in the middle of the session like I couldn't have taken an Uber back.

So I talked it over with Slim that we could get this done later that week. The next time I came back, the session was just as long as the other due to the shading for the tattoo (I think it was 10 hours for both sessions and that's including the breaks I took as well). I cursed, and writhing my neck around a bit, but I wasn't going to tap out like a sissy.

Towards the very end, I had been holding back to use the bathroom and I almost fought Slim that day. I really did consider that he was still taking pictures to send to me and for his Instagram to brand himself, but I was very close.

*Floating Demon: *pinches fingers really close together like the emoji. You see my fingers bro? Them b*tches is close! It was either pee in the seat or take this n*gga out while he took the pictures because I'm dying over here lmao.*

Anna had pulled up once again outside with Ari in the car seat, with short shorts and a regular top, like my guy you just woke up lol? She gave me a hug in the car because she had gone into mommy mode to come get me. We drove back safely and in one piece. The next day, I went to take my drivers test, and my emotions were on another different type of high as the instructor took her seat next to me. I literally finished a tattoo sleeve the night before and now I'm up taking this drivers test, looking for Anna to send a prayer up that I would pass. I scored a 77 on the test and decided to go for a redo because the instructor said I could've done better with my parallel parking and speed changes. But my man behind the counter told me to just take whatever I got on my test and just practice behind the wheel for yourself. Great, now all I needed was the car and I would be straight.

CHAPTER 26

BACK TO SCHOOL VIBES (2018)

It was out of my hands, but I was going back to school. My aunt Lynnette and Aunt Denair had put in the work to go back and forth to college for my sister and I. The school transcripts, the calls back and forth to make sure the paperwork had gone in fully. Reaching back to my cousin Lynnell who had pulled some strings on her own time by making sure I spoke to my academic advisor and would get put into the right classes.

The only issue I had… the problem was that the Financial Aid superintendent was giving us a hard time on granting us Financial Aid because of the circumstances that my parents hadn't put their signature on any of my work. I sighed as my family had gone too far just to quit on my education now, and I knew they would keep pushing. I had a father who did his work under the books, but didn't sign off on anything and a mother who made too much for me to get approved for Financial Aid. The day we handed over Aunt Evelyn's death certificate and reference letters to the school is when I knew I wouldn't be staying too long to graduate. But first, I would do things my way and learned as much as I could, before I bounced.

I had three courses to take a Public Speaking class, an in lab science class and something about biology related online. I take them slow and all my own pace while working back at Mickey D's. I had just come from working at some shady warehouse where someone almost got shot up over some money and it wasn't even worth the paycheck they were offering anyway.

Floating Angel: You must be talking about when a random guy strolled into the warehouse, because there was no security in that unsanitized place. He started throwing punches on this helpless guy and it took way too long for supervisors to grab him off and escort him out of the building.

Floating Demon: It's like if he had pulled his gun out from his hip right then, nobody would have stopped him because they were all watching from the tables. All too scared to jump in and help buddy out while he cried for help, saying you got the wrong guy!

I would run into some trouble myself outside of work back at school, seeing as though old people run into your life from time to time like that. There was this girl from Luxxotopica that I bumped into and she would be going in for nursing classes or so she said… I told her that she could drive me back to my crib while she was heading out to go back to Griffin. All the while, this girl does not have any concern for either of us in the car as she's trying to pose for Snapchat filters on her phone while she's driving.

"Like can you pull over and let me out now if you're gonna try to kill us both?" We got to her crib first and I waited as she talked to her mother first outside and I watched through the windshield as she got inside and her mother pulled from the curb out of the neighborhood. I wait at least ten minutes to go by because I'm not burning up in the car but I need to think about what I'm going to really do before she comes back in.

Floating Angel: So I call up Gabe and ask him for some advice on the whole situation. And he pauses on the phone like I should know the answer already and says..

Floating Demon: "I think you should try to smash." Like I wasn't thinking about that but….

Floating Angel: Ain't this the same chick that got passed around by 5 guys, and then had a cold sore in the warehouse? Only to say it was just a cold sore and blew up my phone AT 2 AM AFTER WORK, telling me that I shouldn't be spreading rumors about her.

Floating Demon: I don't even feel sorry for her but if she got something fishy going on or she acts up, I ain't going for it.

I let myself in as she goes up the stairs to her room and grabs the pants that she needed for her job out of the dryer and closes the bathroom door behind her. I think to myself that this was my chance. I stood at the door but before my gut told me that this was not the girl I wanted to go for. So I sat on the edge of the bed with some lotion in my hand just putting some lotion on my legs when I could have been lotioning something else. I walked to the car when she was ready to go and we walked into Buffalo Grill to get some wings. She let me drive her car back and all I heard was how I could be driving faster from the same person who could have slowed the hell down while she had her phone in her hand.

It was around October when I left Mickey D's again, for the simple fact of someone's little brother telling me "Come help dump these nuggets in, boy!"

I was so glad it was a Sunday I quit because I swear all the guardian angels that day were keeping me from making the afternoon news after I heard that. I thanked Lessy for all the love and support she was showing me but I really didn't want the Fox News to have my nappy headed face on the screen over some little white kid calling me out like that. I went out with that little Griffin chick on two other occasions to see how she would move because, apparently if she's not going to give it up then what's the point of me hanging out because I'm not attracted to her past anything else besides her body. She had let some "upcoming rapper" bone her down so I figured if he can take advantage of her by seeing she was a pass around, then post him on her story as some guy she was so in love with, what was she going to do with me?

Would she let me smash or would she take advantage of the fact that I had a job with money and make me the food n*gga? We went to a nearby restaurant and she was convinced, by how relaxed and poised I was, that I didn't know what I wanted from her and started talking in circles about her so-called boyfriend and getting out of town for nursing. I assured her that if she wanted to find out, we could leave and go to a hotel or something instead of dropping me right off back to my house. Of course she wasn't falling for it. She recorded the food that I posted on my story and I knew right then that it was time for me to go back home. The third and last time we would go out was to the Griffin Fair.

My aunt had told me to play it cool, buy her food to make her comfortable but I had my guard up the entire time. If you're gonna try to pimp me, you got to do better than that. We did a lot of walking around and didn't make any meaningful conversation other than "let's go to this line because this line is full or get some food real quick." We didn't hold hands until we got on one ride and I didn't understand why she wasn't trying to hurry up and leave until we sat at the table and she had to take her brother up and go home.

Floating Angel: Boyyyyy, she used your money to her advantage. I bet she knew her brother was at that fair the whole entire time hahaha. You should've listened to the other guys when they said don't mess around with that girl.

Floating Demon: I ended up getting the last laugh because I ended up blocking her after she started judging me about how I moved differently and how I was a fake christian, blah blah blah.... I didn't have time for no hoes. I've been a loner my whole life so I don't really need these girls anyway if they don't care about my well-being.

This brings me back to the conversations where Mr. Howard, a kind man in the neighborhood, would drive me to college for my classes and we talked about society and the people that got used by the government and the system and the people that took advantage of the system for their own purpose.

It's okay for black people to use credit cards like Jay Z said and pay money back on things, it's okay for black people to go to school and stay in college. But what do we do to the people that want the fast and easy way? We either got caught up with jail or become intellectual bums, as Mr. Howard called it where we loaf on other people because they got money or stay at other people's houses, because "they" can afford a house and we can't. So that being said, do we help those people get on track and steer them so they don't make the same errors over and over? Or do we leave them to make their own mistakes and figure it out themself?

That's the biggest question that I had because I knew what was going on in the world but what could I do to help the black community? How do I help the ones that want to grow that want to live to see another day outside of the jail cells or be out of handcuffs? These burning questions imprinted a mark on my brain, because I didn't know whether to talk to my family and they tell me I need more Jesus in my life or do I go help the kids out around me that are obviously in need of guidance and need someone like them who's willing to overcome great odds and create some vision of a better future.

CHAPTER 27

NOVEMBER 2018

I ended up landing a job at D.H.H.L. in McDonough. It was another one of those jobs that I would walk across in the morning to go to work my shift and then clock out after I could go home. It was Nothing too hard, because a check is a check at the end of the day, it's what you do with that check that makes the difference. I had my bright orange Prologistix badge and got to wear any kind of outfit I wanted underneath it; as long as I didn't keep a hoodie over my head inside the building.

The only downside of working at D.H.H.L is that there had to be 60 or so people willing to work those lines, so if you didn't make the cut to work that day then your ass was grass. Sometimes I took that literally to heart, as I walked back home in the grass to my grandmother's house in the morning. I knew I was more fortunate to walk home than the few that had to drive hours to get here but I wanted something stable, somewhere people could treat me right.

If my grandmother wasn't poking fun at my deposition by saying I had another free vacation from work, as if it was my fault I was getting sent back home, then it was the question of did I like my job, besides the fact that people get cut from working there in the morning? I said yes I do, because there's black people, hispanic people, white people... all different ethnicities that I can have smart and rationalized conversations about the world around us.

There was Ogechi who was my chubby smart homegirl, "Trey" who was a hustler and jack of all trades, Abdul who was a friend of my sisters and later one of my closest, and last but certainly not least the older guys that we worked with, Bruce and David.

Now how did I meet all these people and get them to get along with one another as mutual and respectable coworkers? Well it took a lot of time and moving through different lines because as I said before, there wasn't any consistency of keeping the same group of people working together.

So I just want to thank my work mom at the time, Sam. If it wasn't for her pairing us with each other knowing that we could talk and work as a group of minorities who all wanted the same things, which was work so we could go home and talk so we could forget about how boring the work was.

We didn't care about who the fastest line was sometimes or who was trying to outwork us. We individually wanted to be the best that we could at the job. Bruce and David were the older black men that brought a lot of wisdom from the outside world while making the world load much easier for the rest of us.

Floating Demon: We never b**ched about the small stuff at work that could easily get fixed. Bruce told me about the benefits of the army and how you could make an easy hustle as a civilian after you get out of the army.

David told me about how he ran a small business for himself and was able to take care of his son, and his girlfriends at the time by working odd jobs. He worked as a bodyguard for Offset, Og KK, Scrappy all while he was in Memphis. He also was a bodyguard for drug dealers and congressmen too and made what he could so he could stay out of illegal activities.

Floating Angel: Abdul was young but he wanted to go into the Marines so Bruce gave him a lot of advice on how to be consciously aware of what to look out for and what to stay away from. David was just an old ass n*gga that made jokes and they picked on me all the time because I had no comebacks. I didn't want to go to the army but I didn't want to go to school either. It wasn't until they told me that they were joking around and made me feel included over time that I learned they weren't bad people to hang around.

Floating Angel: I made my jokes and comebacks soon as I learned where I fit in with the group. I was the little brother that the older guys could talk too but also listen and take advice from if I knew something more than they did.

Trey taught me how stocks worked in the stock market and how to move my profits up or down, what the red and green lines meant. I could've googled it or went on Youtube, but it felt better that someone who was a little older than me could break it down in terms that I could understand. He had a little over 10k in stocks and I wanted to get way more than that.

I downloaded my own apps from the App store, but didn't put any real money in until later; just small amounts from my checks until I found a job where I could add more money to the stocks. We would hang out every now and then to smoke or talk about life in the system of the world and how we as black people had to move to survive or walk around, looking for a handout. And the real hustlers never asked for a handout. Cute girls came around with the same old gossip and cries of "man these n*ggas ain't sh*t and they all want the same thing." That's only because you are looking for the same dude at every single workplace. You are not going to find the next Drake or Future at some regular warehouse job. You have to get in where you fit in or go find that love somewhere else another job.

Fast forward to Thanksgiving at Shon's loft. I was walking alongside my dad and his girlfriend Lori, if they were still dating at the time. We were packed in and the food was out but we still had some people that hadn't stayed too long. The Garcias needed to grieve and get over their own personal loss of their mom but it was no hard feelings to the rest of the family. I just felt weird eating and talking about my aunt without having her there. It felt weird praying around in a circle and taking pictures without her there. I wasn't sad but part of my soul had died in that house and I couldn't find what I needed if I didn't even figure out what my purpose was in life.

I barely touched dessert because I didn't need cake or ice cream to fill the void that my heart was missing from my aunt being gone. I needed some guidance from someone in my next course of action, because my stomach may have been physically full, but my mind was lacking the nourishment or gas to keep my mind from being sad and depressed all the time. I knew I wanted to be somebody, but what would I be?

CHAPTER 28

DECEMBER 2018

It was approaching the holidays but I needed that job to keep my mind off from that loss of my aunt that would still linger in my mind. Yes I'm aware that I am using the memory of her being with me as fuel to be successful but I can't let it define me because that would only hurt me in the process. I needed to be around my friends at work so find some motivation, to get some help and figure this purpose of what my life on earth is about. That day would come in the form of getting sent home with three other people in my work shift. It was the four of us- Ogechi, Monica, Tay and myself.

We went out to Waffle House and I got kidnapped in Tay's truck to go on the way there, when I specifically said, "Bro take me back to my house." "I don't have money like that to be hanging out with y'all." But Tay loves an adventure like the n*gga is Diego the Explorer or something, so Waffle House we went. I'm a very picky person so while the girls dined in with waffles and eggs, I got plain cheese and grits after I saw that Tay ordered it too. We all stood outside in the parking lot afterwards and Tay had plans to at least get one of the girls before he went back home. He told the girls to meet up at the Wal-Mart down the road, and we let the girls drive off while he went to go get some Black N' Milds from the gas station.

I told him that I don't smoke blacks, but let him do what he wanted because I was getting kidnapped. As we headed across the intersections, he asked me if he could give me some suggestions on his idea of creating a music label with his brother. I told him after listening to him pitch his ideas, that he should get this many people and focus on this type of music. He thanked me and asked if I could be the manager for their label, but I politely declined his offer. I gotta figure out what my dreams are first before I figured out how to help anybody else reach theirs. And I definitely don't want to be a record label manager either, but good luck trying to find one. It was still early in the morning when we got into the Wal-Mart so we decided to just explore and look for what we needed if we were going to buy anything. Ogechi wanted to walk with Monica and Tay to grab the electric shopping carts.

We followed the girls through the hardware, gift cards and electronic department only to find that we were driving around in circles. I posted some videos on Snapchat to pass the time and then turned around back to the hardware department. Tay ended up making a hard left to play catchup with the girls and I turned a hard left too but a little too late as the cart snagged one of the shelves and everything came crashing down.

Floating Demon: You know how black people get when they hear something they didn't break! We either look one way or run the other way. They didn't stop to help me or nothing. They took off running, some friends that I had brought with me….

Floating Angel: I helped the assistant pick up all the nutcrackers and Christmas ornaments off the floor and promised I would be more careful. But I felt like everyone's eyes were on me as soon as I peeled out of there, and eventually I had a guy come tell me that he needed that electric shopping cart for a gentleman outside.

Floating Demon: Of course I followed him from a distance to see where he would go with the cart and I didn't see anyone come to get the cart, so who the hell was the cart going too? Was it just a distraction to keep me away from my friends? Luckily, Tay stood back and waited with me so I could keep walking on foot throughout the store.

Floating Angel: We walked to the checkout and when we got to the parking lot, Monica realized that she lost her car keys.

We didn't know what we were going to do. Should we wait out and call triple AAA? Would one of us stay until Monica got the replacement key? We all decided to just dip and come right back to the parking lot as fast as possible. We hopped in Ogechi's car and as soon as she took off on that interstate, she started to *zoom through the cars like this was GTA V and not real life.* If I could put on a second seatbelt, I would have over the first one because we were all bunched up in the car as is. She played some rap music that only Monica and her would know all the words too of course and we made it there in a good amount of time. We didn't get pulled over by any cops and made it back to the parking lot in a good spare amount of time.

While we sat in the parking lot, we decided to tell some stories to pass the time. Monica talked about her experiences in relationships and how she felt like she had carried every single guy in the relationship. Why depend on her all the time for emotional support and comfort? She wanted a guy who was going to man up,while she got to go to work or take care of other responsibilities. Most guys she associated herself with, ended up thinking she was cheating or out being a hoe, simply because she didn't answer her phone. She had friends that she loved to hang out with,but hated being with insecure guys that couldn't accept the fact that she wanted her own space and her own friends outside of a personal relationship.

When she started telling the story about how her boyfriend was in the drive thru and put his head into the window because he didn't know what he wanted to eat, I busted out laughing. She was such a good story teller, when it came to being funny. I don't know why she didn't try becoming a standup comedian because I'd pay to see her shows.Ogechi was having her own man issues and couldn't get over her boyfriend that was clingy but she was clingy too as well. I ignored it because all that back and forth of "I love you but I don't know if he loves me back forreal forreal" was making my balls itch. She did share a personal story about her school teacher who ended up motivating her to become an engineer. It was an interesting turn of events because when she said that her future career was to become an engineer in class, her teacher stopped her and told her "no you're too ditzy to be an engineer." And that she'll be off choosing something else.

It made me say, "Damn bro, you still want to be one?" She said "hell yeah, I ain't letting no teacher tell me what I can or can not be in life." That's when she and I instantly shared a mutual bond and decided to become close friends shortly after. I love hearing or seeing people motivate themselves to be what they want to be, despite what anyone says about them. Tay, however, was still unsure about what he wanted to do because he didn't know what he wanted to be. He loved nature, plants and animals but didn't know what his true calling was to be in life.

He had a couple run ins with the law, and even tried to run off once on a raid where he got caught up and then arrested.In addition to his legal issues, he had a baby mother and child so he was trying to his best now to keep out of trouble, but his baby mother was also giving him a hard time about everything. For him it was "do I keep on hustling for her or do I leave and do me so I can finally be happy in what I wanted to do ?" I thought to myself as he grappled with his own thoughts, that if I ever had to question my happiness with someone in life then I shouldn't even be with them if they weren't trying to make me a better happier person.

Tay was still steadfast on his plan for us to go to Noah's Ark, because Diego The Explorer had to have something ready for us to do and I swear if he was given the chance, he could have planned the whole day out. Some people, like the two girls with us, would have wanted to go home and sleep but I, on the other hand, lowkey wanted to see where the rest of the day was going to take us as well. Tay was practically begging for us to go on this Noah's ark trip every 10 minutes. So after about 20 more minutes of talking, we decided it was time to head out. Tay and I left first, and Monica pulled off with her face saying otherwise in the opposite direction with Ogechi.

Tay stopped at a liquor store on the way and asked if I wanted something, I simply said no because I don't drink. He still grabbed some shots for the road anyway because he said he wasn't a lightweight. I told him if he started driving crazy or veering off the road, I was going to hop the f*ck out because I wasn't getting arrested or die over his reckless driving.

Floating Demon: He said nahhh, bruh chill out I told you I have been handling this sh*t. So I unbuckled my seatbelt and waited until he got to a rolling stop at the light to crack my door open slightly.

His eyes got a little wider as he realized that this big head kid wasn't playing, he'd really jump out if he started to drive crazy.

Floating Angel: I looked at the road and how far we were from the grass and estimated that the moment I would start falling is when I would hit the tuck and roll position to brace the impact. I didn't know where my glasses would go because I'm blind without them but I knew that I could see just enough to look for them if I hit the grass.

Floating Demon: Fortunately for us, we got to Noah's Ark safe and in one piece. We took all the backroads to get there so it's safe to say that he has done this before.

Floating Angel: We didn't stay too long at Noah's Ark because the animals looked just as tired and depressed as we were but caged up. It was so sad to see some deformed animals the way that they moved sluggishly in circles with nothing to do, like they weren't really happy or sad.

Floating Demon: Tay took me back home and asked me if I enjoyed the ride getting there and the whole adventure we took. I said yeah, except for the fact that you took some shots on the way but I had fun. Coincidentally enough traffic was backed up on 155 South so the cars were moving slower as the minutes went by faster and faster with time. There were some cops directing traffic and they were in the middle of the entrance that we had to turn to get into my grandmother's neighborhood.

Floating Angel: All I could tell myself is Jesus Take the Wheel. Take it from his hands because if he gets too close to them "accidentally", I don't know what I'm going to do.

We got to my grandmother's crib and I dapped him up for the ride back. He suggested while I walked up the driveway, that maybe in the future we could do road trips or the movies when we all had free schedules. I agreed and he then took off to handle the rest of his business at his house. My grandma asked me if I had a good day today, and I told her it was pretty interesting but I'm home now and that is all that matters.

Christmas was an entirely different situation at Grandma's house. My dad was itching to use the television and his laptop to stream and watch all the sports games that came on. He tried to give me a present in the form of a teddy bear that morning, but I told him that I was good and didn't want it. I just felt down because I was thinking about the black Santa Claus in my Aunt Evelyn's house and the spirit of fellowship and love in the house that past Christmas. He tried to force it again and again, but I still turned it down because I figured that he was doing the most at this point. I just didn't want to be bothered with presents or look at any at that exact moment in time. Ephesians 6:4 says "Fathers, don't provoke your children with wrath; but bring them up in the discipline and instruction of the Lord." He ended up telling me that I was ungrateful for not being a part of the Christmas spirit and ended up taking out the stuffing that was in the bear to reveal dollar bills inside and handing it over to my sister. But I didn't care because I felt the money couldn't quench those feelings I had about my aunt being gone. I went downstairs because I wasn't letting someone in grandma's house stress me out that day and set up my PlayStation 4 so I could play some NBA2K19.

I ended up changing the channels for him because Grandma wished that everyone would just get along, as if it wasn't like this every other day.

CHAPTER 29

A HOPEFUL START TO ANOTHER YEAR...

"Do not be deceived; God is not mocked for whatever one sows, that he will also reap." "For the one who sows to his own flesh will from the flesh reap corruption, but the one who sows to the Spirit will from the Spirit reap eternal life." Galatians 6:7-8

I couldn't complain about life so far. I made it through another year and even though I expected as always, for the same negative things to come back into this year, I also hope that the positives of life would balance it all out. I was still working at D.H.H.L while my grandmother and family members were alive and breathing, and all my friends were doing good for the most part.

I talked to Jasmine off and on as the days would progress. She was staying with her family and living her best life and made me happy by knowing that she cared about my well being as well. She was moving away from her past feelings that she had with her ex girlfriend and looking for bigger and better things in life to look forward to. It wasn't until February that I knew that the lines in D.H.H.L were getting slower and slower as time progressed. People began to leave and come only when they got the text to come into work.

I began to seek comfort more in my bed than what anything the outside world had to offer for me. I was caring less about how much money I made because some days it went up in my bank account and other days it did not. I remember when I went to go take a withdrawal out of my account, only to find that the banks at Well Fargo were shut down due to some company error.

So I just went back to the house and chilled because I couldn't control what happened over there so it was only right for me to wait until they cleared up that issue to get my money.

Floating Angel : "Man when your money gets to acting up, you just gotta walk up to Wells Fargo and tell them like Sam Washington over at North Carolina said to the Aggies..." "Tell 'em to bring me my money!"

As for the benefits of D.H.H.L, I sucked in a lot of advice like a sponge desperate for water as the clock counted down in my head for me to leave that place.

Bruce had told me to A) take pride in anything I work at because minimum work will give you minimum results. And then B) "Respect black women and support them because if we as black men don't do it, then why should we expect anyone to respect her or yourself?"

Floating Demon: Um, excuse me Bruce. But I already knew that about black women, that's why I got my tattoo.

Floating Angel: Shhhh. Didn't they tell you to respect your elders while they're teaching you something? Watch and then speak young grasshopper.

Abdul pulled me to the side one day that he didn't understand why I was so stressed about pulling females because I already had the right attitude and confidence in me. I don't know why but I had squinted at him like why is it always the lightskins saying stuff to me like that? I felt like because I was dark skinned, I already had to put in twice as much as everyone.It was as if everyone had the juice and I ended up being the last sip of Minute Maid that someone just threw back in the fridge.By March, everything started hitting me that I needed to leave and find somewhere else to be. I told myself that it was probably for the better that half of the warehouse had cleared out and barely two lines could run for the entire week. I went up to my agency recruiter and let her know about my situation and then went ahead and put some applications.

Ogechi was going to leave too and I thought it was best that we both left around the same time. My last day was March 23rd, but I made sure I didn't come to work on my birthday because hey it was my birthday. I stayed home and woke up to my grandmother wishing me a Happy Birthday To Me, and I decided that I was going to get an ice cream cake.I called Ogechi when I got to Publix and even though she said that getting a small cake would be ideal; I thought, what the hell. I am not getting any younger and I get my sweet tooth from my dad anyway. I came home ready to slice up the cake and eat a slice and Grandma even had some of her own portion of her cake that she made as well. I know my mom says sugar isn't good for you and nutrition blah blah…. I was going to eat good, because it was a blessing for me to even reach another year in life.

Two days later, Mr. Promise (as Dave Chapelle would say) came to the house bearing open arms. I didn't get a card, or a present for my 20th birthday, but because he left me at my grandma's and came back happy, I'm supposed to forget all that and be happy too? Hell No! I told him whatever and he shook his head in dismay, believing he too had failed himself as a father.

I got a card from Pepa and thanked him and Aunt Lois for the money. I was grateful for the money but to see the joy on his face as I embraced him would mean the whole world. That man cooked, cleaned, and worked hard for his family. The least he could know that even miles away was that his oldest grandson loved him very much, even if I couldn't physically show it.

I didn't have the car that I desired for a very long time and I had been responding to ads for days. Searching OfferUp only to see that I didn't have enough money to put down. It seemed as if I didn't get the response I needed, I just left it alone. They'll text me if they want me to buy the car and if I had the right amount of money, then it is a deal. I believe that if I tried a little harder that God would come through for me, but in the meantime, focus on the end goal.

March was the last month that I ever spoke to Jasmine… at least for a while. I was very petty and insecure about the feelings I felt towards her and I didn't know how to pinpoint what I was feeling over the phone. I knew it would be best if I saw her in person because she knew what was best for me and she always made sure I was good. Flashback to my birthday when I facetimed her and she was coming out to the house to go to some dinner, I believe. I looked at her while she was walking out and said, "Damn gorgeous where are you going?" And you gave me that stank face of yours like you weren't all dolled up ready to be out somewhere. "So you are not going to talk to me and just walk up in the car?" "Wow, that's crazy!" Once again, silence. She waits until her mother calls from the front of the car, "Why are you not talking to that boy?" She then looks at me and says "Because he knows what he did last night."

Floating Demon: Why did she have to go and say that? Why can't they answer the question without another vague statement? I did a lot of stuff last night besides being on the phone with you. I was in the bed, I ate food and I was playing 2k.

Floating Angel: Anyway… I told her I didn't remember the terrible deed I had committed while all of the 100 Spongebobs ran through the file cabinets of my brain, not being able to figure out what it really was that I had done to her.

Apparently, she let me know that I had said something about her figure that made her feel very insecure, something about her not having the perfect figure I liked before I decided to fall asleep while she was talking.

Floating Angel: Oh no. no don't block him, don't block him. Aww she blocked you, it's a wrap my guy.

Floating Demon: Wowww, you were this close to being on good terms. And you still managed to screw it all up, just because you said some stuff going into sleep mode? Bravo, King… Bravo.

I wondered if this is what married people go on a day to day basis- having to fight the urge of arguing and letting it go because it's easier to love someone when you have nothing to be mad or petty about. And give me a break feminists, I was tired and I always say things I don't remember or don't mean when I'm sleepy. By April I was once again truly at a double path in my life. I was coupled with the fact that I didn't want to go to school anymore and although I told my family that I was sick of the college thing…. My dad's side of the family is very emotionally knitted together, so of course I could feel the disappointment in the room when Aunt Lynette, Shon and Aunt Denair all wanted to know why I lied about continuing to go to college and keep my academics up when I knew that I dropped out in January.

The truth was that as soon as I signed up again, the second time around and opened up that psychology course online, it was over with. I loved psychology and I loved using it on people and myself but to actually study it for a degree…Nah I'd rather read a book on it or something. I just decided that I'll finish school when I can control the time and effort I want to put into getting it done better because when they wanted me to do it… wasn't going to be a chance in the world that I'd do it just because they had done all the heavy lifting for me. It had to be for me and me alone.

CHAPTER 30

#DEWAFELS AND #FRENCHTOASTCRUNCH

I was working at this place, Dewafels, which was another warehouse that was further down the road and the job itself lasted for at least two weeks. It was a cold facility where you had to wear a smock, over your whole attire and you had to make sure you had warm enough hands before you went into the cooling area because there was a guarantee that you were going to shiver and freeze up within seconds. I signed up for the french toast line like a couple of my other colleagues did which then again, came with the drama and gossip of working in a warehouse as it did with other things. I met a guy I'll call Ronny who turned out to be an army vet and between shifts, he told me his story of coming up and living with his parents, getting in trouble with the law when he started hustling marijuana which led to him facing a certain amount of time in jail.

He got out and started changing his life for the better for his family and his children. He had multiple cars, learned how to finesse the buy here/pay here car system, but maintained a good reputation by helping his pops out with getting a job and feeding his family with side hustles that came and went. He was at the point where he was secure in his life and just needed a job to keep from being lazy and coupled up. I asked him since he was so good with cars, if he could help me when I ever needed a flat tire changed or fluid looked at. He said he didn't mind as long as he made time in his schedule. We exchanged numbers and were cool ever since.

Another brother was out in his early 30s and he was a cool cat don't get me wrong. But he had a thing for being sneaky and talking to other women outside of his marriage that he was in. I couldn't help but judge how conniving he was to the commitment he made to his wife. He showed us all the receipts, all the numbers he had pulled and in exchange he had made a ploy to leave his wife out of it.

He even had sex with someone else's wife that he claimed was his best friend, but in reality, that was a guy that he just used to get to his wife. And you would think that his wife wouldn't be aware of the situation but he told me how he had a fake name and would turn to lying if the girl confronted him outside of work.

Floating Angel: We all confronted him on what he was going to do about changing himself and he said he would be in due time. But your actions can be like a fuse. You can create a trail of angry babymommas, jealous brothers and sisters, kids with broken hearts all because you decided to cheat and keep cheating when you knew you were wrong.

One day I even walked in the breakroom to see if someone was going to spare any of the good stuff in the vending machine. I sat down once I put my bag in my locker and realized that there was a noise from the other end of the locker room. I told myself that it wasn't a coincidence that *Musiq Soulchild- So Beautiful* was playing as the phone's ringtone, but I wasn't going to think about aunt Evelyn and start crying. I came to make my money and that's all I was going to do. So I put my bag up and walked out of the room and kept it moving. I did fall asleep on my line a few times to the point where I thought quitting was a better option instead of letting people go on break before me. I was literally letting people walk all over me and no one had a chance to help me out; all they did was give me a warning.

I remember that there was this one man I met, that speaking to him would change my whole perspective of how I was trying to control my life; as being a millionaire in my 20s and retiring when I'm in my 40's etc... His name was "Lou" and he told me his background story on how he was born in D.C. and grew up in the hood and getting caught up in the wrong crowd.

Fast forward to now, he has about six kids but he finally settled down with the right woman and helped her get through college because she was in the IT department. He told me that it wasn't too late for me; that I don't have to repeat the past mistakes of what 30 year olds and the 20-30 year olds before me already did. I could live my life the right way or the wrong way, but I could make my own mistakes and not let affect my future I wanted to see come into fruition.

I showed him the brand I was working on that I called Nice Guys Finish Last. I told him the concept behind it and how I was tweaking bits and pieces of it last year. Lou was ecstatic about the idea of a clothing brand and told me if I ever came up with some jewelry for the brand that he would rock the chains everywhere about and put the whole hood on to my brand.

This all sounded nice but turned to be bittersweet news because my stint at Dewafels wouldn't last long. My last day working was my saddest. I had a 6pm to 7am shift which meant it would last all the way to *Saturday morning.* Grandma was going to have a fit once she found out I was trying to go to sleep on the Sabbath, and not to church. *Oh no, whatever will I do?* I was going to milk my hours and then dip at 6:30 AM because I needed the extra time so I could slip inside the house before Grandma would notice a thing. So I tried to work my way through telling people when I was leaving, but they told me that I needed to stay all the way until 7AM. *Last I checked, I'm nobody's slave* and I have to make it back home, whether I have to walk back or take a ride back to the crib. Luckily I found this guy working on sanitation called "Ghost" who promised me that he would take me back to the house in due time. All we needed to do was leave by 6:30 AM. So around 6:25

AM, I started talking to people and asking around if they could let someone know I was leaving early but I guess everyone was too focused on their work to hear me.

I ended up dipping with Ghost and after we got some gas in his car, he started to tell me about his other activities besides working in the warehouse. He helped people get cars for the low in downtown Atlanta and he did some flipping, packing and selling packs when he was on the move on the road. He wanted to know if I wanted in and I said nah. I already promised my grandma that I was going to become famous and rich and I already made a promise to myself that I was going to outhustle all the drug dealers, pimps, and those whores the legal way, whether it took me a year or two years.

Ghost did give me some great advice on my clothing line though. He told me to only make it exclusive at least one time of the month and upsell everything then take it down and put the regular stuff back when it's back in season. For a street hustler, that wasn't such a bad idea coming from him. Then Ghost tensed up while Ms. Katrina pulled out of her driveway and stopped in the road, trying to peek in and see who I was with. I told him to ease up because it was just my grandmother's neighbor being nosey.

I was notified that Sunday afternoon while I was preparing my lunch and happy that Jessica **finally** *decided to answer my Facetime call… I sat on the porch as I looked through that missed call log and reached back to the temp agency that sent me out to Dewafelbakkers.*

Floating Demon: Yes Edward Felder, we are letting go due to insubordination and hope you have a wonderful rest of your day.

Floating Angel: Insubordination? Me? I told those jokers I was leaving a long time ago on Saturday morning. That's not fair.

CHAPTER 31

FINALLY GOT THE WHIP!

So there I was, without a job again without an all black Mustang to show for it. No job, and the check that came back was $896 which was a spit to my face for me. The only thing that I did learn from that job though was how to finesse the system and make it work for me. But as the devil takes away blessings, God always gives you a blessing right back in return. Shon came in the nick of time to save me out of my jam and he decided to call up as many places we could because we had two options on getting a car that would be paid in cash, of course. We checked out the first car with my dad and they were all cool about it and the car drove but something wasn't all that about the car for me.

Maybe because it wasn't how I pictured my first car to be so I did my homework on the next car after Shon gave me pictures to look at. It was a 1999 Lexus Es 300. It had an all white exterior with the brown leather seats, and it had cupholders to go with the luxury of it all. We went ahead and checked the car out and the funniest thing of it all is when I started up the radio in the car, City Girls Act Up started playing in the car.

Floating Angel: Alright slow down Cowboy before you go out into the Wild West and try to get your boots wet... Let's see if you got the money to pay for the car and cover your insurance from StateFarm.

I put down the money and signed off the paperwork, then put the StateFarm agent on the phone while also trying to decide if I was going to swap out the temporary plates now or later. I decided later because it all seemed too good to be true the way everything was happening so fast. If I could just control one decision, then I could really step back and see the whole big picture. Shon and I prayed over the car and left everything else to God. Once everything was settled and we were ready to go, I said thanks to Roy once again for helping me lock in on getting the car. The first place we decided to go to Emmett, Shon's go-to mechanic in Georgia. I was so excited to have the car, that I didn't even move it in without thinking I would damage it. I pulled into the shop so he could hoist the car up and automatically troubleshoot the problems I needed to watch for the car.

There was no air filter, and the timing belt would need to be changed pretty soon since its last checkup was in '06. I also would need hood shocks for the car but I would forget about it long after, since I did basic checkups on the car anyway. He told me his package deal was $560 for the timing belt, water pump and the seals on the car.

I liked him already, because if Shon could trust him that much then I could trust him too and I promised I'd be back to pay that package deal for what was under the car hood. After we headed out and I prayed for safe traveling mercies, Shon decided to speed past everyone including me as if I wasn't the one trying to keep up and get to the house too. Yes he was one of those drivers, just going through traffic and expecting me to not die like he wasn't the one playing Fast N Furious in his Audi.

Grandma was glad I got back in one piece, and loved how the car looked inside and out. I was glad that I could keep up with Shon in the dark for my first drive in my new car and loved that my bed was calling my name for my head to be on that pillow. My dad checked out the next morning, admiring my brand new car and how the seats looked. He promised we would stop by and pick up some tools for the car although it sounded like he just needed a ride around a couple places. We got all the small essentials like black tape, flashlight and a funnel from Dollar Tree and then went ahead and thrifted for items I guess he thought would add personal value. I didn't really care too much for those specifics because if the car ran good and had no problems when I turned it on, then I would be alright.

CHAPTER 32

GRADUATION TIME AGAIN… FOR MY SISTER

As the last few weeks of school had slowly crept up on my family trying to prepare for Lauren's graduation, I was trying to think of what type of life I was trying to live for myself, being that I was just getting dropped by job after job. It was around this time as well that I decided to write a book about my life. I told myself that I would be perfectly honed in on that craft by the time I turned thirty years old (it seemed like it was a refined art, like how golf can be for senior citizens).

I would have seen much of the world by then and had enough experience to write about topics that the world or myself would be interested in. The idea to write an autobiography made sense when I spied a box of my father's books on the couch and floor. I had seen this video where Gary Vee was talking about the way parents pull a facade in public, smiling for the camera in Disneyland but acting a certain way after the camera is put away and the family gets settled back down. After my dad tried to get me to start that Messy Eddy chronicles, which now that I think of it seemed like his own way of being satirical of how I left my room a mess all the time and would be another way to profit on this huge idea that he didn't even ask my opinion for. It was like he was trying to force me to believe in a dream that I didn't ask for or want to put any effort into making. Yet he still bashed me when a young woman ended up taking the idea off Godaddy.com and ran with it as her own.

The title of his book was "Give Us This Day, The Devotional For Entrepreneurs". I could tell by the font type that he had portrayed this idea of him being this changed devout man, but that wasn't the case in my eyes because I knew different. My father seemed to devote so much time to those books that it seemed like he didn't even care to hone in on what my interests were. If he was trying to handle a business meeting or phone call, it would be in the bathroom and he would hold it up as if people that lived in the house didn't need to use the bathroom after him. The way that he had taken up his time to forget about the needs and concerns of others emotional and well being.

I didn't write this book to place blame or negativity on my father's platform. He acted as though his whole life of mistakes and empty promises would be fixed with fame and fortune, in hopes of fixing everything with what? The promise of financial wealth and materials to give back to the family? Yes all hail Edward Eugene Felder Jr. with his MBA and banking credentials and classes of credit training all to help people kick-start their businesses into high gear.. You did it all at the cost of losing what sight really matters.. Family. I know this because every time I spoke up for myself, you became this volatile person when I didn't feed into your ego. I didn't see you as a rags to riches story you proclaimed online or in business events… every time behind closed doors you yelled and raged on about how it was the last time you would get any disrespect in Grandma's house.

I looked into your eyes and saw the same young man from college trying to logically justify why his father would tear his car down and return it without any rims, and the inside smelling of marijuana and other substances. I analyzed the guilt in your behavior as you struggled with the fact that you never personally spoke to your father on his deathbed. I remember watching as you stood on the other side of the wall in the retirement facility, not uttering a word or syllable that would possibly mend the relationship between a dying father and heartbroken son. Everything that is written in this book and written afterwards is why Aunt Evelyn begged for me to break the cycle of father projecting hostility towards his son. Thanks for creating this chip on my shoulder because it's made me the writer I am today.

I typed everything that I could down into my phone that I could possibly think of, memories of the past, memories now… anything that would guide the flow of my emotions through torment and pain of having an emotionally absent and physically distant father in my life. The research and work of contacting those who played the roles in a journey would prove to be tedious but I would manage my time around the house so I would be able to get it done. I reached out to my Aunt Denair who told me about her own story and how she kept all of her trauma and confessions written down but only would choose to bring that information into the light when she saw it was fitting. I, on the other hand, saw that I couldn't waste any time and would move strategically in order to convey the perfect story that would express raw emotion but humbled with the purpose that others may take this book and use it only for pure motivation in their times of need.

I waited until Lauren's senior citizen day for school to come out and show love to her participation, and it would also be a way for me to bounce feedback off Aunt Denair who would be giving the necessary writing advice I needed. My aunt told me as we sat down, waiting for people to grab their complimentary breakfast from Waffle House, that I needed to find a title for the book so my ideas would be concrete and not all over the place.

Floating Angel: What should I call it? The 20 Virgin Commandments? 20 Years Trying to get it together? Nah, these titles are looking pitiful by the minute.

Floating Demon: You need to make it sound reasonable and make it sound like there is some purpose behind this book. Like you've been running your whole life and you want to be able to see an opportunity and kick the f*cking door down.. *Think about what you want to expose in this book and what you want to keep a secret.*

Floating Angel: I want to expose the truth about what I've been taught and how I was raised in order to give people awareness of issues that are prevalent in and out the home. Generational curses, bad habits… stuff like that.

Floating Demon: So like you're hiding from what the truth really is ? Okay cool.. Cool. We can work something out with that.

I began jotting notes in my phone down only to get an uncomfortable feeling on how to function once my dad and Brian showed up to the function. It always feels weird when you sense that you can't trust your family or anyone around you. Aunt Denair had urged me to be on my best behavior, to not start any trouble but trouble always seems to follow me everywhere that I go anyway.

I finished what I had to eat, and then went ahead to greet some of my teachers around the school to thank them for believing in me when my academics didn't make up for it. I walked around the corner to the middle entrance only to bump into my old homeroom teacher, Mr. Hightower . "SIRRRRRR!" I loved when he did that to me, just hearing the enthusiasm in his voice of seeing one of his old students almost made my day all the way better.

It wasn't until he got to talking about how my father had spoken to him about my outside endeavors, about how I had just gotten a car and jumped from job to job looking for the best paying dollar and couldn't stick at one job to save up from the last one.

I didn't ball up my fists but there was clear tension and some sorrow that I could just feel in the air. I laughed it off in my head, because if my dad wants to throw salt on my name like that, then I'll just keep making fried crispy chicken with the BBQ and hot sauce. Because one thing about me is that I don't shrivel up like a slug around salt, I just use it to season whatever hatred or malice that's in my heart and turn my negatives into positives.

I looked back towards my family, now with a purpose to just leave everyone here but my sister because I couldn't believe my dad would just speak on my name like that and then have the audacity to eat at the same table like everythings all good. But he's been acting like a troublemaker behind closed doors his whole life so I'll be keeping my mouth shut on it and just let it get exposed in due time.

Floating Demon: Dad asked me to get him some eggs and biscuits from the line. I told him that a polite "Can you please get it yourself dad?" would be the only response he was getting out of me. I'm already pissed off and I wasn't trying to make a scene. He made a face and I knew he was about to beg for his younger sister or his mother next to him to get his pacifier for him because he was going to start crying again.

I didn't budge out of my seat because it was a test of faith and to see if I was going to go against what I believed in. My sister got up with the rest of the seniors and I would start to head out like the rest of the people, which was my cue to go. I called Aunt Lois outside, and kicked some dirt off my shoes as I told her I was writing a book and couldn't wait to add her stories and name in it.

She told me that she didn't mind me talking about her because she was going to die soon anyway of old age. I felt my heart cave in my chest as she said those words and I know she didn't hear my tears fall from my face and hit the soles of my Concord 11s, but she could tell by my silence that I was hurt by her words. The same woman that taught me how to read people and their behaviors from a distance… The same woman that told me at age 16, "I can tell you're drifting around in life trying to make sense of the world and its purpose but if you find happiness in doing that, it's okay too." I couldn't see her leave my side, at least not any time soon.

I dropped my sister and her friend that was willing to do her hair and then went back to grandma's house in the driveway. There was still much more work that would be needed to be done and I'd call up Aunt Lois more often to get the advice and help that I needed to stay focused because she always told me how to keep my mind intact like that.

Fast forward to the day of my sister's graduation. There were a lot of factors that I didn't plan for throughout the week and day of, but I knew how I had to handle them in order to keep my sanity and emotions at bay for the day. For example, I didn't know that I would be stuck like chuck when my grandmother told me that I had to move out by August because she couldn't handle the fighting or bickering. It broke my heart that she couldn't have this same conversation with my father. Could it be that the favoritism in my family be that real or was I overlooking the reality of the situation? My aunts tried speaking to me as they came through the door and immediately got upset when I didn't respond, like all women do when I don't speak back immediately.

I apologized because I was so lost in thought and tried to piece together the puzzle of why my grandmother would choose today, out of all days to ask me. I rushed down to go get my brother and pick him up from the hotel my mother stayed at, but first I had to tell her the good news about my book about how I figured out my purpose. That maybe the son could learn from the mistakes of his father and become a better man in the end. We talked shortly in the hotel and you asked me about what my purpose of the book was, what the end game was from all of this manifestation yet to come.

As I type these words, I could almost taste the success from my bedroom, but as I sat on those white hotel linen sheets, I couldn't give my mother a concrete answer. I could only tell her that I'm writing to inspire motivation in people to not give up on themselves, because I've befriended gang members, felons, kids that got kicked out & ended up sleeping in their cars. Some of those people might acknowledge me in the future and some may not. Understand that it's all love but God has us moving in different schedules and different time frames. I told mom I was going to expose some things about our family's past for the betterment of the world and if she was ready for that pressure.

She said with mild sarcasm, "I guess I'm going to be stressed for a year but if you want to, then go ahead." I love you mom and thanks for giving me the go ahead on writing.

I didn't know where to park when I arrived at the school and all the cars by the time I got there, were parked all the way into the grass. So I just picked my spot and made sure I didn't pull up any further to get stuck into the ditch that was already in front of me. As I began walking up on the sidewalk, I had seen the Poughs in their red van and I waved hi to them because we would all end up speaking to each other later on. Then I saw Shon pull up on his motorcycle and make his way around after he nodded his helmet at me to find a parking spot as well. I took my spot outside to the left where the walkway was and kept my distance from my dad and everyone else surrounding me.

I hugged Iliana and Brianna and Tati, Maygon and dapped up Mr. Rok, because they were family to me no matter what and not being blood related couldn't keep us from loving each other just as much as a real family full of brothers and sisters did. They called me their big brother and I loved them for it. As my sister came through the field with her diploma and cap in hand, I made sure after all her little friends got their hugs and pictures that I gave her all the brotherly love I had for you.

Don't let anyone or anything in this world make you think I don't love you sis. You're a charismatic young woman striving to do big and great things in this world. I can't believe you're growing up faster than I would. I remember when you had a little afro walking around with mom's styrofoam heads for her wigs in her bathroom and now you're on your way to be a phenomenal registered nurse. I know I act lame and I gush about you alot and do the most but I will always be your big brother.

As we headed out after taking all the pictures we could, I couldn't help but smile from a distance as Grandma and Aunt Lois bonded over church ideals and how she had to come see Grandma's little church for herself. My two favorite elderly women were getting along together like two peas in a pod. I had to scoop dad, Ethan, and grandma so we could all make it back home in one piece. That Sabbath, I made sure I was up and moving early to take my family where they needed to go. I had my brother and grandmother in the car moving down to find out where Aunt Lois and Pepa would be at. Grandma wanted to direct them to where her church was in Jackson and I had plans to go to church with my mother.

We said our goodbyes before I headed off and I went to meet up with my mother at the hotel. We had our breakfast together and it was a little cold, but I was hungry so I didn't complain after I graced over my food. We took the rental car that she had out in the front and I begged and pleaded to let me drive. Mom never let me drive her Kia for the Drivers Ed course I had to take but she insisted that I now had to be safe and drive very carefully, because the car we were currently in was a rental. She looked at me sternly, while I was backing out and narrowly missing a car coming past us as if to say, "Now give me one more reason why we shouldn't swap our seats and just let me drive." I said confidently that mom, I got this because as long as I had you and Ethan in the car, I knew I would make it to our destination in one piece.

We pulled off and got on 75 south to get to Stockbridge in order to make sure we secured the package, that package being my sister. We sat for at least over 20 minutes in the parking lot and my mom started to work on my cuticles and nails like she used to when I was younger. It was so relaxing and almost made me forget how behind schedule Lauren was getting us by getting your clothes together. We already told her to get ready and now we were still waiting on her.

She came out after some time and we headed off down the freeway, still with enough time to spare. About 25-30 minutes to our destination, I asked my mom about my chest and how one side seemed more enlarged than the other. Was it cancer or some abnormal issue I should be worried about? She felt me up and said that my breathing and all my vitals didn't seem to be affected or changed in any sort of way, so it was normal. The church service was alright and nothing crazy had taken place, but I knew that my mind was set on getting back to Shon's crib for Lauren's graduation dinner. I met up with Uncle Kevin and Aunt Kay for church and they decided to follow us on the way home. They're just the perfect couple together, intelligent with amazing careers and no children but living happily in one home together.

If you ask me, that's the kind of love that you can't find with no kind of price tag attached to it. I tried to make sure that I didn't drive too far ahead and maintain a safe speed so they could keep up. My mom let them know her plans of getting to the hotel to get my car on the way to Shon's house and didn't forget to add in how great of a chauffeur I was to her.

Floating Demon: Allllll those times you didn't let me drive? And now you got me thinking I'm gonna be your lifelong driver? You got me fooled for someone else because I don't play those games."

She laughed and smiled with such pearly white teeth that it made me feel good to see my mom was smiling better now. I prayed that I could see more days where she was like that. All three of us were able to go as I took the lead from the hotel in my own car and I knew that we were going to make it while I sped through 155, my mind trying to prepare myself for what was to come at that time.

We came into the house one and the same, greeting each other with fellowship and peace for all those who were coming and going as we took our shoes off and made our places in the house. My mom and dad were getting along, as in not showing any signs of disdain towards each other even as they were less than five feet apart so that was cool. It's good to see growth from people when they have to co-parent for the sake of their kids.

When the slide show for my sister's presentation had started, I knew it was going to be a problem once Grandma took her seat and noticed all the pictures of her "crowned jewels" being exposed in the prom pictures would be on display for the family to see. After we bid our goodbyes,

I told Alex, Tory, and Alex's boyfriend, Caleb that we would meet up later at the lake like Alex requested. When we had our chance to just get away from everything, we left and took what we needed with us into my car.

Of course, Tory was the first one to complain as she always is about something I'm doing, whether it be good or bad. But I shrugged it off because I had to focus on getting to the parking lot and hoping they left a space available. As we walked through the grass, the kids to the right of us were setting up hammocks and blankets on the trees above us. I didn't even know you could bring your own stuff to the lake like that but it's all cool and maybe I could do the same with my family next time as well. We sat on the benches and talked about life ahead of us and the present life with us now. I asked them about the type of girls I should surround myself with and how it was getting harder and harder to find the type of partner I wanted to be with in the world. I didn't know if I desired to be with a girl for the rest of my life and instead thought that I should just grow old and write books for kids and adults all my life.

I'd probably start charities and put houses up for the homeless to stay in and live comfortably as long as possible. Caleb told me I just need to find someone of God-like character, just shift through all these girls and I'll find the right one to be with eventually. Then there was the issue of my tattoos that almost *gasp everyone had something to say about. I knew there was talk around the family, some disappointed and others thinking it cool that I wanted to express how I felt about the world through any form of art I could interact with.

After we got settled, I dropped them back off at Aunt Lynnette's and told them in the car my plans for the book I was writing. The subjects I was touching on were personal to my life as there were also other things that I had to share about others. We all prayed before leaving and then I drove back to grandma's house, hoping that God would guide me through this journey from being ambiguous to a state of peace and clarity for myself and those that surrounded me.

CHAPTER 33

JUNE 2019

I wasn't ready for the stress of trying to write one book would cause me on a day to day basis. I would take breaks from writing, but when I tried to get back into the flow of things, my thoughts would float around and then escape me for whatever reason. How musicians, artists and other creatives managed to come up with ideas and put it all together for a project of their own was a mystery in itself. I reached out to Jessica for her own permission and she said she didn't mind that I mentioned her name or our relationship in the book. I questioned some of the actions that she had taken with me in the past and if she was really trying to change her life for the better.

As we took a trip down memory lane, I had to make it clear to her about one situation where I was fed up with the foolishness. Back when I was in highschool, Jess and I would switch accounts on Snapchat just out of pure boredom. I also wanted to see if she had been talking smack about me to one of her friends as well, so I guess you could say it was really an excuse to be nosey. I stumbled across a much older conversation that she had with some random guy who towards the end, had threatened to expose her pictures and account out of spite. Maybe she thought she knew him fairly well to be doing that but I remember turning my phone off that day and telling myself that this was exactly the sh*t I was trying to save you from getting caught up in. Fortunately, her information didn't get leaked and that guy was blocked but I always made a habit of dishing out advice that she could avoid people like that. But of course, she never listened and always had to be hard headed anyway lol.

After we had gotten done joking around, I questioned her about a moment we shared on the phone which had taken a sexual turn pretty quickly. Now she did have her old boyfriend in mind, which did count as cheating but she had been slowly losing interest upon the fact that he had been flirting with other girls behind her back.

Floating Angel: I was so sure that she had done that thing with her boyfriend in mind and not me... I wish I wasn't so toxic sometimes....

Floating Demon: And then she added in the part that she had climaxed five times… I'M THE GOAT! Yeah I'm the man, I'm the man!

Floating Angel: You see that ego of yours? You let that get to your head so you better calm yourself before you get an aneurysm or something. It was the past, it was cool but let it goooo.

Floating Demon: Okay, Okay I'll chill. But she still did it for me though. That's all that counts lol.

Before I ended our call, I had to ask Jess one more thing, just to make sure there wouldn't be any bad blood between the two of us. I asked her if she would leave her current boyfriend for me if she had the chance to and she said no, simply because she didn't want to hurt anybody's feelings and was looking forward to having something steady with this guy. Personally, I wasn't interested in a relationship with her but I had to see how honest she really would be in order to keep the past as the past so I could look back one day knowing I made amends on our friendship.

Jess was probably one of the only girls that I had no real issues with, mainly because we joked around about everything and at the end of the day, she was still my homie. She had a stash of off guard pictures with me looking dumbfounded in each one, knew just about all my personal secrets and could read me better than almost anyone in my social circle. But to see that she was finally being more responsible and mature about how she handled her business and setting boundaries for herself, I couldn't be prouder of my little loser growing up so fast on me.On June 17ᵗʰ, I had enough of the tomfoolery that was going on inside of my grandmother's house and saw no other solution but to take the high road and get my bags ready for packing. I was at another warehouse that my cousin Anna had recommended me to and was very grateful for the opportunity of working somewhere else again. But on this particular morning, before I took off to work, I was about to face a dilemma that would change the whole course of my day.

As I got into my car to head out, I noticed that my dashboard had flickered once I turned the key in the ignition. I figured the battery was already going dead, but it could hopefully wait until I got back to the house. Once I clocked out from my shift and started walking into the parking lot, my phone had fallen out of my pocket and cracked in all the places I wish it hadn't. But as long as I could make calls and text, I would be straight until I decided to get it fixed with a screen protector.

But when I got in, I had to come to terms with the car not being able to turn, so I knew for sure I had to pop those jumper cables out the trunk and wait for somebody to come help. And help did come in the form of this little man "Nico", that I particularly didn't like for how lazy he had been on the job, but help was help anyway. He told me I needed a new battery by the sound of the engine when I had turned it on so I followed him to the nearest AutoZone. I paid for the 1 year warranty because I didn't plan to keep the car for that long and went along with my business.

I came back home only to find out that my dad had been waiting on me to get back with the car and asked me once I got settled in the living room, if I could go out with him and take him out to let him go buy groceries for the house and Ethan. I said no without hesitating, because the fact of the matter is that I knew that he helped me over the phone with getting a new car battery but didn't put any money towards it. My phone was dying and yet now that everything looks charged up and ready to go, I have to drive him? No you aren't going to guilt trip me. I reached out to Gabriel that day to see if I was just an emotional wreck or was my act of selflessness was a reaction from everyone's selfish intentions? He said he was glad I was thinking on my own and becoming more independent and trying to think of ways to move around the problem at hand.

The only thing I could think about in that moment was that in the past anytime I wanted to go to Barnes Nobles to see the books that came out, all he did was make an excuse about the car being messed up and that he didn't get the oil change he needed yet while we were in Tampa. I hated it enough that we were tucked in that house in that gated community but the fact I couldn't go to the bookstore to read? I would end up playing video games (Lego Batman 2 on the Wii) to let the situation go and keep the peace between my father and I, because if the video games weren't there for me to ease that tension between us, then I would've let it all out on him. So if he didn't have an issue going anywhere when his car wasn't looking so hot, what was the rush on taking him anywhere if I just purchased a new car battery? I couldn't catch a break for anything.

Gabriel continued his conversation on the phone with me to tell me how I should probably reach back out to Shon and make that move over to Shon's house. Just agree to the contract and sign the paperwork, and everything would be all good. He made it seem that much easier, but I just wasn't sure if I could handle it all. The living costs, the bills, the fact that my money would be eaten up on groceries and necessities rather than the money that I could put into Jordans, jackets, or whatever people cared about more than trying to live to see the next day on this earth.

I reached back out to Shon and we handled the paperwork over in Grandma's house in an orderly fashion. For some odd reason, the way that he had all his legal documents in his folder clipped and organized was pretty impressive to me that I couldn't help but note how professional Shon was about handling his paperwork. He told me to keep a copy and he would hold on to the other agreement as well. As long as he could be available for any maintenance issues, then I knew that I would be okay with living at the house.

My father had chosen to stay with Ethan in the house and as a token of my appreciation for having my brother with me, I let him play my video games. I tried to show him how to play Batman Arkham City. I lecture him on how he was to watch for the incoming attacks and when the indicator above enemies head flashes, that's when you counter and take down all the enemies. I'd go through the utility belt and always see what gadgets I had at my disposal before I engaged my enemy. Was it six of them? Take three down and before the smoke from the pellet has cleared out, batarang the two thugs that have guns and leave one of personal choice for last. I always made sure that I strayed away from the bullets because Batman might have that armor, but because he was human, he could still die at the end of the day.

There was a lot I could appreciate about my brother Ethan because I also saw myself in him too. He was fearless, and always ready to try new things whether he ended up liking it or not because Ethan never was afraid of anything. I tried to get him to use lotion on his legs but the poor kid always wanted to do his own thing. I remembered the phrase my parents used to tell me, "you look like you had a fight with the lotion and lost" because my own legs would look like pure white snow. The kids at school would make fun of me because my lips were chapped and all messed up. Aunt Evelyn would badger me at home before we went to church that I had to put on lotion because I got all that ash from my dad. It was all a presentation for her, as long as you looked the part when you went out and acted like it then you would be okay.

I reached out to Aunt Lynnette after work a couple times in order to get some background knowledge prior to having the book in order. I would come over to the house and she would detail the things I needed to know in order to be discreet with the information I used about certain people in the book.

She had let it be known to me that she was the keep- it- real aunt in the family, because if she had something important to say, she would let it be known whether her opinion was favorable to everyone or not. I watched how she talked about those she loved and cared most for such as her children, the rest of my family and any past relationships she had grown from. If we were in the car, I would try to tell, based on how she talked on the phone, if she was interested in the guy or not, that he was trying to take her out on a date. If I learned anything though from my aunt, it was that family despite whatever our individual issues were, always came around full circle because it was just how life was meant to be. We would find a way to push past the differences.

CHAPTER 34

ADJUSTING TO CHANGES

But can we live without them? *Memories* are what our reason is based upon. "If we can't face them, we deny reason itself." (Joker, The Killing Joke)

On the day that I decided to move everything out of my grandmother's house, I was fed up with the shenanigans. It was pouring down from the outside and on the roof so I tried to maneuver around wherever my grandmother was in order to stay focused on getting my things in the car. She probably figured I was trying to detach myself due to the chores and things she had me doing around the house. And part of me didn't want to detach myself from the bond I had with my grandmother; but with the way my father was getting treated there, I knew it would be soon before I did something I would later regret. And if I remember correctly, such a thing almost occured when my father had arrived from one of his business trips where he had picked up some type of illness.

He hadn't dressed properly for the weather so he came in coughing, and his breathing pattern was erratic to the point where my grandmother would regularly come upstairs and nurse him. I watched as she fed him a teaspoon of sugar, some medicine, propped him up and even had me run up a glass of water for his majesty, being that was how my father was being treated. I wondered if he really became the center of her universe due to his being sick or that because I couldn't resolve any personal matters with him due to his only focus being writing and working on his entrepreneurship. Not like I didn't want him to get better but it did strike a nerve somewhere and I couldn't let it go.

So I'd say on his fourth day being back, my father asked for a glass of water and I went downstairs and proceeded to walk up the steps with the glass in hand. I pondered on whether I would wait to see if he was choking on his spit first and then give him his water, or not to give it to him at all. I reached the top step and turned to face him, as his body shuddered at the serene look on my face. "Hand me the glass… please son." as his voice sounded weaker with each breath that he was taking.

I'm not a medical expert by any means like my mother is but the looks of how things were turning out, it was safe to say that he had severe chest pain. I don't know if it was from the weather in the cities he visited or if he was getting lung cancer from second hand smoke he's been exposed to his whole life.

Floating Angel:This is only a theory but since he's from Bronx Ny, lived in the projects, his mother was smoking and his father was smoking and drinking but only Grandma was the only one that turned her life around, so that makes sense why my dad is relying so hard on my grandmother while his health is failing. All the medical bills I saw on the table from that chiropractor…

Floating Demon: I say we don't give him the water. He's the one that has been treating us terribly, in the sense that he doesn't care about the family. He complains about his back pain but walks up the steps just fine. Grandma defends him by saying that he's sleeping upstairs but everyone that comes in, can hear him writing on his laptop. He's a fraud, He's a deadbeat, let him suffer!

Floating Angel: No. He may be an man that disregarded my feelings and other family members and people that love him. He was only focusing on himself but in the process, managed to shut out people that cared about him. I understood the feeling because I tend to do the same. But I had to do the right thing because he was my father and deep down, I did love him; whether I wanted to admit it or not.

I hand him the glass in his shaking hand and walk away… contemplating if I really made the right choice for myself or because his chest pain was flaring up. I thought about ripping up his credit cards, taking his money and deleting some chapters out of his books… because now the attention had been placed on him, when I needed the help the most. But if I didn't force myself to do the right thing, I would have to face consequences that I would ultimately regret later on. I had to be positive in spite of the bad, so that I can be the change that I wanted to see in this world.

I just knew that I was getting physically and emotionally drained of finding out who I was to be in life without some sort of instruction manual from my parents. I liked that my dad got to travel and meet famous people but I never got to tag along. Then he had wanted me to create online products with his help. I could create my own brand and have people reach out to me so I can fly out to wherever I was needed. I could sit down at HBCUs, and work with kids like myself to figure out what their talents were and put them to use so they could rely on those same skills wherever they went in life.

My mom was very goal- oriented and professional, but behind closed doors it made her become very demanding, strict and questioning my decision making on trying to figure out what my journey was. Her future was to be a top medical doctor so she already found her way. So why was she stressing me with questions like, "Why don't you have a job right now?" "Why aren't you in school right now?" "Why aren't you paying those bills right now? If it wasn't something productive at the moment, then it was a waste of time. But sometimes I didn't have a plan to go from A to B, then hop right onto C. I was already struggling to move past plan A.My only hope was to become financially successful enough to one day answer all my parents' questions by doing everything they wanted me to do in my own way. Attending school on my terms, making connections with people that would last for a lifetime and planting seeds in the necessary places so I could make a path for others who wanted to be somewhat independent.

CHAPTER 35

AUGUST 2019

"There's nothing you can't do if you try." - Senku Ishigami, Dr. Stone

The day I moved into the house was the same day I had left my grandmothers house, in the cold thundering rain and as my boxes tossed and turned in the backseat, I could only imagine what issues would be waiting for me. The house was so clean to the point that I wondered if any previous residents really stayed there before I showed up.

The downside was the months of not having any functioning A.C. But my cousin Shon was working on getting it handled so I didn't stress it. I got a roommate named Jameel, during my stay at that house. He was a guy in his late 20's who was really chill about how he carried himself and had some of the same interests that I did. I don't know who in the family pulled strings to make sure he got to the house, but that was pretty genius on their behalf. We played Need For Speed Rivals, which is one of the oldest racing games I had with me for my PS4. I always let him play because he was more experienced than I was, seeing that he made more money and unlocked a lot more cars than I could have if I hadn't stopped playing.

Getting along with Jameel didn't turn out to be such a problem as I imagined it would be at first. He woke up before me & enjoyed his smoothies in the morning to get his day started. I, on the other hand, would gulp down a bowl of cold cereal along with three cups of water or some fruit, if I wasn't in a rush to be late or on time for work. Jameel shared with me his experiences with females in college and told me never to settle down, but enjoy mutual friendship and love as it would come to me organically. He wasn't the best at NBA2K as I was but I had to learn over time to get better as with anything in life. Still the satisfaction of spanking him or another friend of my cousin, Reemo by more than 20 points before the fourth quarter felt undeniably good.

In the meantime, I had two jobs and it felt good making the extra money on the side. I had to learn to balance gaining a bigger check at the warehouse down the road while working alongside the people at Mickey D's that I was personally happy to see, like my friends Jermaine, Marcus, Lessy and others that I had worked with as well. Marcus and I bonded well together and over time we developed a secret handshake, played GTA V online together, and even posted some collab videos on my Youtube gaming channel together. All the hard work I was putting in came at a cost though. I needed love for my personal life because I felt empty and I didn't know who to put the effort into or where to start if that. I also was slacking on doing my book and getting enough sleep because of the energy I was putting into helping other people in my spare time. Was I really living the life that I wanted too?

I would talk to D.W. off and on via Snapchat with her reaching out on Facetime, giving her opinions on the outfits she bought and getting my opinion on the makeup she tried. It was great helping her out with boy issues and such, but talking as best friends over the phone felt like middle school. It was just another phase so to speak, because hearing about all her relationships got draining after a while but I decided to put up with it for some time because I felt like that's what friends were for.

After a couple weeks, this one girl I'll call Stacy, decided to get attracted to me while I was working behind the grill area. I couldn't pick up that she was feeling me at first because I was caught up with work, but as you can tell from my past experiences, dealing with younger women never had a good impression on me and wasn't something I wanted to continue anyway.When the opportunity presented itself though, we agreed to make plans to go out to the movies although I tried to make it clear that it wasn't a date but more so a friendly outing. Stacy had her eyes set on watching some other movie that I wasn't interested over the phone while I told her that I planned to go out and watch Spider-Man: Far From Home.

I had already gotten my work check that week and the thought of anything happening during or after never occurred to me. I told myself that we could just watch the movie and I'd end up dropping her back home right afterwards. After meeting her mother, who was a very nice lady, I could almost tell that it wasn't going to be that simple of a task. Stacy ended up holding my hand in the theater and resting her head on my shoulder by the middle of the movie. It was kind of cute for the moment and I was cold, but on the way back, I had let her get carried away with touching my face and rubbing my neck. I did let her know towards the end of the trip though, how I really felt and if she had been of my age, that it would have been completely different. So when Stacy attempted to kiss me, I had to pretend like I didn't see her and kept my eyes on the main road towards her house so I could drop her off back home.

We both made it clear that we wouldn't speak to each other anymore so things wouldn't further complicate themselves at work. When we got to work, she did her thing and I did mine, by talking to my friends and acting like she was dead to me. It worked just fine and I hoped to not run into another female situation any time soon. Boy was I wrong about that one. One day towards the end of August, I spied my eyes on this girl at Mickey D's who was dropped dead gorgeous. She had nice curves, her skin was flawless, and those yams were looking crazy in her work pants.

I asked Jermaine what the situation was with this girl. He told me her name was Mariah, and she was a mean looking thang but was turning down *almost every guy* that would give in to her good looks. She had a son, but still seemed to be open for a relationship, if the opportunity came along. Jermaine went on to tell me that she even went on a date but turned the guy down afterwards, because he had sole intentions of smash and keep it moving I looked at Jermaine dead in his eyes and told him that I was on a solo mission and I was going to get at her, no matter what it took. Whether we dated or I got to smash would have to be on fate but hopefully it would play in my favor.

We exchanged small talk over the conversation just so I could get some type of vibe of the person she was, but she always found some way to throw subliminal shots at whatever order I was doing on the table. I'd rush myself cooking on the grill and working on the table, and suddenly she would come around demanding to know why the order that was up on the screen wasn't done yet. Like as if she had any patience at all. When I had approached her on some slick side to the corner, I told her I was really feeling her and wanted to see if we could talk more outside of work. She appreciated the compliment but told me she didn't know me well enough for her to go ahead like that.

Floating Demon : ummm… Excuse me. Where have I heard that tone before? She sounds just like those girls back at Luxxotopica. Back off man, Back off now. Beep Beep, Beep beep that sounds like trouble to me.

Floating Angel: I mean she is naturally pretty, and she's light skin, and smells good bro. It wouldn't hurt to at least try and see where this whole thing goes.

And soon I had gotten her contact info and just like that, she had gotten me with the hook line and sinker. I messaged her on Snapchat and had a little conversation going, hoping that one day I would manage to get on the rollercoaster ride of a relationship and let her know that I would really be down for her and not play any games. Because how could you not attempt to date someone that looked just as great as she did? You couldn't and I was going to try to make good on my bet with Jermaine one way or another.

CHAPTER 36

"I'M NOT THE TOXIC ONE! YOU ARE!"

"In this world, there are very few people who actually trust each other."- (Light Yagami, Death Note)

There were days when I came home from work and glossed over my options of the people I could use in my book, I realized there were but a handful of people that I could choose from; knowing their background and the impact they had on my life. What impact could they bring forth to my project and could they spark some potential in me to keep writing? Could I trust them wholeheartedly or would it just be a one-time thing?

The first person I decided to call and check up on was my old pal Jonathan. He had started becoming enlightened with the world and with the way the system that was working against the people and he wanted to take it up by storm. "We got to expose the elites in power over us and all the crazy stuff they are doing", he would tell me. I had to tell him to slow his roll on trying to take control back for the people, because for him to say all that on the phone could have us looking crazy or in some need of help later on. He was the first open-minded person to tell me that we really lived inside of the Matrix and our lives everyday were being dictated by the ways of our society and our government; nowadays we end up getting sucked into the electronic devices we carried on an everyday basis. The question was could we step out of that box and make it possible for other people or would it be a movement that only the two of us could move forward on?

I don't know if he had ever watched the film Superman/Batman:Public Enemies, but this whole "save the black community from government oppression" plan that he seemed to be concocting was going to be a lot harder on the two of us if we didn't reach out to all the "woke" kids that we met in middle school, high school & college that also wanted a better future for the generations after us. We had to be able to take care of our own business first, move forward with finding the right people who would have similar dreams of our own while keeping a positive mind-frame to be able to resonate with the goals we set out for ourselves.

So every other day that I got off work and he was available for a phone call, we reviewed everything that we had known in the past, from growing up in church as little kids to what led us to becoming consciously aware of the world around us rather than just living a regular life and trying to be like everyone else. He told me that he gained spiritual awareness from a retreat with his cousin where she gave him a lot of insight on what spiritual energy was and who Yahweh was and the meaning behind him. In relation to that, I went over anything that had to do with freemasonry, evil spirits, and who God is and who he isn't. I also added the fact that I had begun reading the Bible for myself and was trying to learn how to stay connected with the world by a thread in a sense. Because I personally don't think I knew everything there was to life, but I was always willing to find out more and how that knowledge applies to my life as well.

We started sending each other different information via Instagram posts so we had a visual of the direction we were going to be taking. I let Jonathan know that being in a short term relationship was fine, but if you ever came across a special woman in your life, then you make sure you plant those seeds so that only the two of you can water that spiritual garden. That way if anyone or anything tries to come between you two, those feelings and spiritual attachment will never be broken.

Jonathan would send me posts about Flat Earth, human trafficking, and how our school systems limit kids creativity based on what they can learn outside of the classroom. I sent him back posts such as Prince Donnell's Instagram videos where he spoke on how to keep a good marriage, and this Instagram TV video about this pastor who talked about Solomon and all the concubines he had slept with. The way I interpreted that video was that it was God's way of saying, be careful who you decided to pass your body fluids with during sex. Lastly, I put him on to this guy I followed on Instagram for a long time who went by his Instagram name, @cocaine_papii.

After following him for a couple months after seeing him on my explore page, I DM'd him in 2016 asking him how he got all the girls, models he ended up being posted with, because it seemed like the grass was much greener on his end. And he had replied back to me that he had made all his connections, naturally by being himself.

Floating Demon: You really thought this n*gga was gonna give you the cheat codes to getting girls and having the juice? I already told you it's different strokes for different folks. Get with the program.

For someone that wasn't an FBI agent, I was really tracking his movements down to a science to figure out how he really had the sauce because I knew that Shy, his real name, had a lot going for himself even when he tried to be lowkey with it. He did have face tattoos, and made his own trap music, but he managed to carry himself as a normal person who didn't have a problem with acknowledging his fans over the Internet or in person. He talked about faith in God, reposted Twitter threads on perfect hygiene for men, cleansing of the mind, and why he believed black on black crime was another concocted conspiracy... So I would send all these screenshots over to

Jonathan so he could have something he could digest before making the decision on his own to follow him. If you end up reading this Shy, I hope you are still looking forward to making a collab happen bro. Last thing I touched based on with Jonathan was this book I had titled "Y'all Not Ready For This Talk" and how with his knowledge and with others that I had selected for it, he could be a part of what the book was generally about; which he told me he had no issue with.

Floating Angel: That's fine by me. At least you know what you signed up for!

However it wouldn't be fair for me to keep going into this book, without introducing one of my closest friends, Juan who also put me on a path to elevate myself. He was around the same age that I was and didn't have any noticeable tattoos, but when he was at the warehouse I was at, he always managed to stay in his little shell of privacy. That's probably why I always told him when I had the chance, that he looked like Franklin the turtle lol. I asked him about where he was headed in life and how he was moving, hoping that he could give me more than just some general answers and he replied that he was simply trying to find his own journey of peace and happiness too.

He had lost his pops when he was younger, but we had similar music tastes like soul music and rap. We planned to do some dope music parodies together. You know like reenact some R-Kelly videos and do some voice-overs on Youtube. I think it would be worth it to see how that would turn out, probably shock the world in the process. He would have no problem telling me about his sexual experiences with the girls he met here and even made it known that he was trying to go crazy on 'em like he had this dance move where he would naturally get the "Ooooweee" in for his own entertainment. I knew I really could kick it with him when we were both sharing bars off Earl Sweatshirt's song Grief in sync with each other.

But the way he said Ooooweee…. It was the funniest sh*t I ever heard and how he rubbed his chest when he said it made me laugh even harder. I believe the weirdest story he told me was when he was trying to stroke a girl and her coochie felt like a jar of mayonnaise! I was like, "we talking Miracle Whip, booger sugar, all that white stuff?" He said "yeah man, I ain't like it, I ain't like it at all." Between the two of us, I was very upset once I found out that you left the job, Juan, because you gave me a lot to look forward to when I felt depressed working at the warehouse. In the end, I learned from you though that to really elevate in life, sometimes we can't solely depend on the people closest to us if we really want to be happy and chase our dreams. So with that being said, I'm proud of you bro and keep growing and learning and being yourself Juan.

As far as finding people to write about for my book, the most essential person that I decided to reach out too was none other than Jasmine. It hadn't occurred to me that I would really need any of her help, being that we hadn't spoken in a while, but the seed in question had been planted in the form of a reminder of her birthday. I remember scrolling through my phone to see the words, "my baby's birthday" with a few heart emojis next to it in the month of July and shaking my head like why would I try to set myself up like that? I then thought to myself that reaching out to her, even if it was just for me trying to write my book would only result in developing feelings for her in the end. And I couldn't deny that, being that I had a reminder set for her birthday in the first place. It took a couple months but by September, I had gotten a hold of her new number that she sent to me and made sure to Facetime her when she was available.

I asked her if I could use her permission to add her in this book and she said sure, why not? Just don't forget to mention that the relationship she had with Stephanie was just a fling, despite how emotional she had gotten for her. I had been so certain that they were a couple, but it seemed as though the poor girl had been getting used as sexual pleasure for Stephanie's liking. All the pictures that I had posted with her on my Snapchat when I had gotten into my feelings… it would seem as though word would run back to someone that wanted to break up whatever situation we had together. I asked Jasmine about how we distanced ourselves due to the issues we had in the past and if the split had been for better or for worse. She didn't give me a direct answer, but instead told me how betrayed she felt when her friend Lecia had shown her messages that confirmed she had been wanting a split from Stephanie as well. From Lecia's perspective, she believed that the relationship was overwhelming for Jas and that she would be a more peaceful person by letting it be.

Floating Demon: Damn bro, it could be your own friends that end up hurting you trying to help you out with relationship issues. I don't blame Lecia though, because to see her bestfriend be in that much distress from trying to love someone back, I would have done the same thing.

Floating Angel: I will admit that Lecia was a cool person and I appreciated her for stepping in and trying to get Jasmine and I to work out whatever petty differences we had at the time.

Some time later in that conversation, I asked Jaz if she could remember back in the past, when she was going on about wanting to get her pregnant. She had tried to hide her face out of embarrassment, but I swear in that moment if she had been Caucasian, her face would have been as red as a stop sign. So I waited for her to stop blushing and asked her to look me in the eyes because we were both grown and I didn't want her to have any reason to lie to me. She stated that although she did have baby fever, she also pictured a future with some kids and having me as the father because the love and loyalty I showed for her would be shown to our future children as well.

Floating Demon: Nah, nah she is bugging, bro. You know how many times a girl came up to us about losing her virginity or having sex with me, and it never happened? Now I know how much you like Jasmine and all but she was talking about a future with kids… Whether this was months ago or not, I don't know about that one bro.

Floating Angel: Nah, bro you are the one that is trippin'. She's never had a reason to lie to me about anything so that has got to be the right answer! I don't have to settle down now, but…

Floating Demon: Um, I don't mean to cut you off but you need to snap out of this delusion that you got going on. This whole reunion that you both are having is cute and all, but you may have to cut her off again.

Floating Angel: Wait what? But why?!

Floating Demon: Because if she gets caught up in a relationship, or if you do something stupid and get the wrong idea at anytime because you jump to conclusions alot… that could probably mess up the connection the two of you have together. If anything, you should work on finding your own happiness before you make any of it centered around her.

Floating Angel: But she is very special to me and my n*gga, even if she said that in the past, that is a lot for me to take in. I got questions on why she would decide to be so comfortable with my loser behind out of everyone else on this planet?

Floating Demon: Well, first slow your roll. If you even think that she could be the right girl for you, then we'll just have to figure that out by the end of this book.

Then for some strange reason, my mind spaced out while she was still talking and I had this vision of the two of us getting married and right before I said my vows, I felt the beam of a sniper being placed on my chest. Was this God telling me that she wasn't the right one or that I was only rushing myself to get killed to be with her? Or was this another delusion coming from the fear of losing this girl again? It looked like it was Stephanie in the dream, trying to get back with her, and take me out of the equation.

Maybe I was the toxic one trying to have Jaz all for myself and she was meant to be with someone else like Steph, even if she knew that wasn't a relationship she didn't want to be a part of anymore. But I don't know because I can't predict the future as hard as I try, even with this book, so I could only hope that everything worked out like God planned it to be. And if Jaz was meant to be, she would have to let me know on her own how she really felt, because it would only work if the relationship was mutual love on both ends.

September 2nd rolled around and I found myself at Mickey Deez just chilling on my break. I called up Jaz to see what she was up too, and to make sure everything was alright on her end. She was already aware of the fact that I was talking to Mariah because I told her but nothing was serious between us because Jasmine was seeing someone else in her life as well.

Floating Angel: I asked her over the phone if I could call her babygirl, honey all the little nicknames I had given her… and she said no because I would be setting myself up for trouble with Mariah and I should focus my attention solely on her…

Floating Demon: The second she said her name … speak of the devil. Yes sir, it was Mariah in the flesh. It felt like a setup from the moment I heard her come around the corner.

Floating Angel: Mariah asked who I was on the phone with and I said just a friend, as I muted the phone with Jasmine and slid my phone into my right pocket. Mariah started to move in and within seconds, had gotten way closer than I thought she would… her breasts were pressing up on my chest, her thighs aligned with mine and lips were barely touching. If there weren't any cameras back here in the crew room, boiiiiiii….

Floating Demon: Nah forget the cameras, because I tried to go in and she's gonna tell me that I was rushing it? If anything, she shouldn't have tried to tease me by getting that close in the first place. These females in Georgia were tripping on anything and everything else man, I swear.

After Mariah let me go from the little childish hug she gave me and walked back over to the drive-thru window she was covering, I took a moment to just take a breather from what had happened. I was so close to telling her, if you don't take that "hey cousin I'm here for the cookout" hug somewhere else… I reached back into my pocket and put my phone to my ear only to hear Jasmine giggling and telling me that I had sounded scared with Mariah the entire time.

Floating Demon: I could have sworn I had the phone muted. But I know she wasn't talking about being scared, because if it had been her instead of Mariah in front of me… let me stop because this is supposed to be an "inspirational" underdog type of story but all I was doing was taking L's after L's right now!

I let her kee-kee over the phone until I told her that I had to go, because my break was nearly over at this point. Then I took a minute to reflect over what I had just gone through and if I should have just waited until after work to make that call to Jaz. Not that it made a difference now that I couldn't seem to catch a break. It seemed whether I came off as a player or not, I was trying to take all these fadeaway shots and nothing was going into the net at the right time when I needed it too.

The next day, I was chilling over in my area in the kitchen and was trying to get this one girl's attention because I had given her some money to get something from Subway. She had been on Snapchat with one of her friends going out to eat so I figured since she wasn't as broke as she made herself seem, and maybe we could go out and I could get reimbursed for my money. Apparently, some girls overheard what was going on because they were grouped in the front counter, gossiping about who knows what. Next thing I know I'm getting called out for being a player, and how I can't handle my business at work. Now I know that Ogechi had told me before that I didn't need to really explain my business to anyone at the job because some things don't deserve an explanation and you just let it be. *But* I was the type of guy that wanted to clear the air on some things right away and let them know that it was nothing to take seriously because work was work and with that job being a female dominant environment, I couldn't let that be brought up again.

And just when I thought things couldn't get any worse, I had gotten into some hot water with Jasmine… You'd think that I wouldn't be catching any feelings despite the fact that we weren't in a relationship but I was wrong. She was planning to go out to dinner with a couple of friends and I had seemed to be undergoing a "physical reaction" while she was rushing to get ready and leave.

Floating Demon: Haha, that boy could not keep his wood in his pants, could you? You were over there sitting in your room, trying to take off like Buzz Lightyear, ain't it? Look at you being a horndog while she's only trying to get ready so she can leave with her mom. Get a hold of yourself man.

Floating Angel: But I couldn't help myself and didn't intend for it to happen, which was the weird part. The worst part was that I told her about my ongoing situation and she laughed it off nervously and told me to handle my business and this wasn't the time to be getting aroused around her. So being the loose cannon I was, I handled my business by flashing her, without any second thought of how my actions that day would affect the friendship or relationship I had with her. It was clear at that moment that I was the toxic person between the two of us.

Floating Angel: Now, was it called for? Absolutely not. I may have been joking around but I should've been mature enough to handle myself accordingly. Time to see how this would turn out.

My friend Tae decided to text me, trying to see if I could come over to Carter's crib on Sunday to play some video games and probably smoke something after work. With all the hours I was putting in, I figured that I might as well go over with them so I could relieve the stress I had weighing on my brain. Sunday came and I was leaving work, and I tried to reach out to Jasmine to see if she had let the whole situation dissipate or not.

Floating Demon: oooohhhhh you in trouble…. And I thought this girl was the one for you too man… She respects you like a king, gets attached to you with some feelings and you go ahead & treat her like she is whatever to you. Why do you just go and f*ck over good women like that bro, just use your brain.

When she texted me that morning after work that we'd be talking later that night and I saw that she didn't respond to my "talk about what" text within five minutes like she usually would have, I knew I was in big trouble. She had given me one task and I was in for a rude awakening for disturbing her peace. All I had to do that day was play it cool, and I'd probably would have been able to call her that evening. I guess I was just prone to catching L's straight out the air and letting them crash right down in front of me. I met up with Carter and Tae inside of my house so they could have an idea of if we would stay over at my place or go straight over to Carter's like we had originally planned.

We played two quick rounds of MW Remastered while we talked it over and Carter watched us go back and forth while eating boiled peanuts. They decided that it was best to go over to Carters because they had some sort of video game setup in place. As I escorted them out the door, I noticed as I grabbed my keys to head out that Carter had used my favorite blue cup for his boiled peanuts.

Out of all the cups that were in the house, he just had to grab my favorite one. But here I go overreacting, so I washed a couple of dishes and then decided to head out. I got inside and those boys were over there just already passing around a joint and drinking dark liquor on the side. I just sat back in my chair and watched on one side as Carter played Shadow Of War and Tae was playing Star Wars BattleFront II. Carter kept acting like I was tone deaf and the two of them had kept passing the blunt in between themselves like I wasn't in the house with them as well. So when I decided that I was tired of feeling like the third wheel, I got in between the two of them and made sure that I got a couple hits in.

Then seemingly out of nowhere, I began to pass out mid game while I was playing alongside

Tae. I managed to get back up, but ended up blacking out again on the chair. I woke up around the sixth time with Tae chuckling at me and then shortly after having a look of concern crossing over his face, asking if I needed to go home. I thought it was just the effect of THC passing through my body, but it seemed more so that my brain was still trying to weigh out the possibility that maybe Jasmine was overreacting that morning and she would probably pass off what I did as a careless mistake. I decided that her being on my mind heavy was my cue to go and told both of my guys that I would be headed out and I'd check in with them later.

As I got home and dragged myself towards my room, the texts from the morning were screaming headlines in my head, just rattling my brain back and forth. "I'M GONNA CALL TONIGHT!" "I'M GONNA CALL TONIGHT!" I slithered into my bed, trying to close my eyes and praying that the situation at hand would be something that I could laugh about later and leave behind in the past where it belonged. The next morning, I woke up to a jumble of text messages from Jasmine about how I was truly an inconsiderate and unthoughtful person who really had no regards for how other people were feeling but my own. She couldn't believe that I could be that disrespectful and made it clear before she blocked me that she didn't want to deal with my toxic behavior. I will admit that I was hurt, but I couldn't blame her because anytime I made some means to get comfortable around her, I always did something stupid off impulse and ended up regretting it later. Maybe the time away from her would help me push me to do right by myself later on.

D.W. ended up calling me later that day on Facetime to give me the rundown about how this relationship she was having had quickly turned sour. She had made it clear that she didn't want to have any type of relationship with this guy anymore, due to him blowing up her phone with calls and texts about her whereabouts. She declined all of his advances by trying to make him aware of her boundaries and soon this escalated to the point where she reached her house one afternoon, only for him to drive over and meet up with her there as well. He then proceeded to beg on her driveway for mercy and show in all the kinds of ways that he was so sorry for how he acted and that he wanted her to be back in his life by giving him one more chance.

She said after all the stress that her mother was putting her through school, and after putting up with this guy's foolery that she had even contemplated killing herself by using the gas from the car exhaust because her life didn't seem like it was worth living anymore. To her it seemed like she wasn't there enough for her friends and people that mattered in her life and it was hurting that she put such little effort into what really mattered. After the tears had stopped flowing down, I reassured her that life was going to get better and that she didn't have to commit suicide because she was a good person, deep down whether she wanted to believe it for herself or not. She couldn't let one toxic situation dictate how she wanted her future to play out. And she was studying her butt off to get into graduate school. As long as she stayed focused, she would cross that finish line soon.

CHAPTER 37

ARE YOU PLAYING CHESS OR WAITING FOR THE CHECKMATE?

"Come to me, all you who are weary and burdened, and I will give you rest." "Take my yoke upon you and learn from me, for I am gentle and humble in heart, and you will find rest for your souls." Matthew 11:28-29

Soon, I really started to question if the energy I was attracting to myself was leeching away at my soul and if trying to get by in life was worth it, because it seemed like I was sinking further into my depression more times than I tried to keep my head above water. Just thinking about that is funny because I've hated swimming since I was a jitt. Anyway I couldn't contemplate whether I would risk my friendships for a better peace of mind and solitude; but it seemed like that happiness was never present unless I found some value within another person that genuinely enjoyed my company.

"It was right then that I started thinking about Thomas Jefferson, The Declaration of Independence and the part about our right to life, liberty and the pursuit of happiness." "I remember thinking: How did he know to put the *pursuit part* in there? That maybe happiness is something that we can only pursue. And maybe we can actually never have it, no matter what." (Chris Gardener, Pursuit of Happyness)

I thought about my friend Dae Dae, back at the warehouse near my grandmother's house. He was the first person I met that made me aware that I was like a brother to him stating that, "if I had called you a friend then I don't trust you, but if I called you my brother, then I got you for life." He even reintroduced me to anime when I came over to his house for the first time and we shared interests in dark humor and video games as well. I would notice that although Dae Dae kept to himself a lot, he was very eager to lend a hand or look out for someone else to ensure the work would keep on flowing.

He was one of the few guys at work that I had given some insight on my relationship with

Jasmine, mainly because he had caught me slippin one day at work around September. He gave me his own take on the situation, telling me that you should only keep a couple of girls available but never try to get attached because at the end of the day, hoes were always gonna do what they wanted to do. I didn't see any flaws to his statement but I assured him that I didn't see Jaz as some hoe I was messing around with, but rather a young woman who had some class and morals. She wasn't perfect but we all weren't at the end of the day. I could only wish I had done better in my pursuit to be a better man instead of some clown who thought he had it all put together.

When I had time during work, I would go over what the bible meant to me with Dae Dae and after telling him that it was a book with scriptures and parables on becoming closer to Christ, he became interested to hear some of these stories. So I told him about the ones that I had from memory, which happened to be Job and Samson. Job had almost everything taken away when the devil had made a bet with God, but Job never doubted his faith in God, and in return was blessed with everything he had once lost. Samson was a man with incredible strength who ended up losing his hair by literally screwing around with the enemy, but regained it when he had gotten captured, by asking God for strength to take down his enemies again.

I do not have long hair with super strength, or and I can't walk on water, turn water to wine and back to water... I'm not a barber, firefighter, police officer, or Grammy nominated rap artist. But I do know that just like my father, I have the gift of creative writing. It didn't matter what others were thinking about the journey I was taking. Only a select few knew where I was headed and with God's help, I would get there eventually.

He stared in silence after I finished speaking and said, damn Ed, you should think about becoming a pastor. I looked at my tattoos and rubbed the naps in my hair and told him no because I didn't feel that becoming a preacher was my calling. God can be anywhere and be in anyone he chooses to put in your life, but it is up to you whether you want to find him or not. It's not hard to make the right choices in life, but we often stray from it so he'll put us through some tribulations only to direct us right back on that path. With that being said, I ultimately couldn't decide what people's choices were for them, but I do know that along with my writing and future endeavours, that they can hopefully learn from my past and teach others what the right choices are in life and how to help them find their way as they reached out to me from time to time.

That morning on October 3rd, I woke up in my bed with a pillow full of tears, probably from overthinking about the past and simping over relationships that I had messed up on. I should have been getting up so I could get a move on but here I was, slumped like a dead man.

Floating Demon: Now I know your grown ass ain't crying over... Come on man, get up and get up for this job man. You can worry about shorty later bro...

I decided to reach out to my friend at the time, Dommy who had just come to pick her dog from the house, due to the fact that I was dog sitting for a while while she got herself situated. After getting the vibe that something was troubling, I texted her about how I felt selfish about doing and saying whatever I came to mind with people only to feel sorry when the tables ended up turning on me. She texted back shortly after that "I probably wasn't in the wrong at all, maybe that Jasmine just took it the wrong way and expected more out of me... but everybody hurts whether they want to or not because that's life, love and it hurts in every shape and form." So I ask the readers this question- "Are we too busy looking for love and find it in the wrong people or are we trying to recreate love from the things in the past we miss out on?"

If I was truly honest with myself... I don't expect anything glamorous out of a "traditional" marriage. Being in love and having a partner is a great thing, don't get it confused but in my opinion I feel like it's just some written paper that could be changed and ruled out, once those two people that had that mutual bond forget the reason why they fell in love in the first place. So what is love when the trust is nowhere to be found? And why do we choose to hurt those same "loved ones" when we can easily forgive or respect them? I guess that's just one of those things that you have to just let play out because you'll never know until you get in that situation.

Regarding my personal life, what most people may not know when they see me play with any basketball team on NBA2K19 is that I used to watch a bunch of Kobe "Detail" and analysis videos on Youtube prior to even buying the game. Not once did I ever select the Black Mamba and his team from the menu setup, but I did pay close attention to his Youtube videos on how he knew where all the players were or would be during an offensive or defensive play. It was so intriguing to hear how Kobe dissected each play that I couldn't help but replay those same videos so I could try to *watch those films with the same eyes he had*. After some practice and getting dusted by family members or friends alike, I tried to apply that same mentality towards the game because when I was in a more focused state of mind, I could pick my shots easily and not be so rash to break my controller when the possession didn't turn out to be in my favor.

If at anypoint I had thought about giving up on my writing, I would try to think towards the memory of Kobe making that bold statement in the 2009 NBA Finals... "What's there to be happy about?" "Job's not Finished." You could always take a break from everyday struggles when needed, workout, talk with family because we need that break from reality, but were you willing to take the extra mile to make sure you were focused on your dream rather than your nightmare taking over your dream.

Yeah my laptop may have shut off on me, and Google may have had a couple errors so I had to rewrite a couple pages over again. But when I went back over to assess my work, I could feel a sense of pride while doing so because to try to pursue that dream without any fuel or passion would be like attempting to gasp for air when you're just floating around in space. When Young M.A. said in one of her songs that she was rapping into a microphone since birth, I could only think back to when my grandma told me stories about me being a toddler trying to read out novels to my family in her house. Some things you are destined to do or as fate would have it, born to do.

On October 4th, I made sure that I came prepared with what I needed for the day. I had a letter for Mariah ready to go and to give to her along with some flowers that Dommy was showing up with. She was a little late meeting up with me, but I knew she would show up because that was my homie, and I knew, if she could come through for me then I would be there when she needed it. She asked if I could hold the flowers, because she had felt like recording me like some parent at their kid's sports game and added in the fact that she was also a hot mess. I looked her up and down because she wasn't a bad looking person at all, although she did look a little rough running out of the house like that. Nonetheless, we walked in and I instinctively pulled back because of all the people that were in the restaurant just staring at me. I couldn't take all the looks from managers to the side, the crew members and nosey kids over the counter.

Floating Demon: yeaaaaa, GOT THAT ANXIETY ATTACK coming through, ain't it? You might as well turn around because she doesn't want you bro. She would have given you the chance already but you over here air balling. Face it, she's for the streets.

Floating Angel: If you feel like this is the right thing to do, then f*ck what anyone thinks, even your negative thoughts. If she doesn't reciprocate it, then yeah she for the streets bro and you would be dumb to keep chasing that.

I walked over and asked for one of the managers to get Mariah from the back because these were for her. I waited for some time until she pulled up from the back and saw me shaking with the flowers. The people behind us started recording and she got shocked saying that they lied, saying that her parents were up here and it's just me with flowers and a card. I smiled because of course they would lie to get her up there, can't knock those people from trying to help a brother out. We hugged and I passed over her the things that she wanted. I told Dommy to hush after she yelled out, "And you better take my boy out on a date." She always had that confidence to go ahead and say what she felt in the present moment and that was one thing that you could not take from her.

I walked back and she said that she was getting through an altercation that just occured before I came and that she was glad that she didn't get sent home for it and ended up getting surprised with flowers. I gave her a moment to look over everything in the back. I wish I could lie and tell you that I didn't want to keep checking to see she had read it, but I waited until some girl walked by me as I made my rounds and told me that she was looking through it.

I watched as she covered her mouth and then took her time to read through it some more but the funny thing to me was the process that I had to go through to write that letter. There were four crumpled paper balls by my door and 3 different draft pages laid out on the floor to revise the new sheet on top of the others. I had MoneyMan going on repeat so I could keep the emotions straightforward to match with the words that I needed to finish this one thing.

I thought about what my mom said about teamwork and partnerships and a lot of crap in my head that didn't have to do with just a little work crush. Then when I stopped the halfway mark and I literally thought what the hell else do I write, because I feel like I've said all I really could.

Floating Angel: Then I hear Jasmine's voice just say in my head that she's heartbroken and not healed entirely… and it came in calm and reassuring as the ocean is when the tides are low…

Floating Demon: Hey, Hey, hey cut it the daydreaming crap out. Jasmine ain't the focus of this letter, so get finished with this so we can hit the bed and take this good nap.

Back in the present, Mariah questioned a couple parts that I wrote and even asked about the 70-30%, and 80-20% statement which was talking about the energy that you put into someone you want to pursue… and I said "yeah, you got to reciprocate that same energy and love back that you want, otherwise that relationship or friendship isn't going to work out." It's that simple. She asked me while looking up at my face if I normally wrote like that, and I shrugged my shoulders with a cocky look on my face saying, "Sometimes, depends on how I'm feeling at the moment I guess."

Floating Demon: Alright, she liked the gifts. Now all you have to do is see how she's going to treat you before she ends up clocking out. Now if she gives you that little hug that she keeps doing, then it's over with. If she gives you anything else, then we are in there like swimwear my guy.

Safe to say that didn't happen for me but she did take her gifts home with her. The whole time I questioned if she really did keep that letter like she mentioned because, if that was the case then she would've trusted me enough to let me come through to the crib, right? Or maybe I'm just waiting for Mr. Krabs soft sweet violin music because I should have known better.

CHAPTER 38

TELL HER HOW YOU REALLY FEEL

On October 6th, I was playing Middle Earth: Shadow Of War and had just gotten back from Steak N Shake, ready to find a captain as part of the objective in the game and taking him out in the fortress I wanted to capture. I had just given D.W. my honest opinion over Facetime on how I felt about giving Jasmine some kids in the future, and there was an awkward silence; even if it was just for a few seconds. She looked up at my face through her camera and said "do you really want kids right now?"

I said "Ehhhh" and bit my lip nervously while I kept playing the game, as if I didn't hear her the first time. "Eddy..Edddieee I'm talking to you…" "Do you want kids right now, yes or no?", she said. "Yes and.. No." "Explain yourself, ." I sighed as I looked toward the memory of Jasmine blushing and repeating those lines over in my head again. I was in no rush for any kids, or marriage of any sort but when it came to Jaz, I felt some kind of conviction… like I didn't have to second guess myself for once in life about if it's right or not. She was the kind of person I could see myself holding hands at a kids sports game & making sure our kids were the ones kicking the other teams ass, or letting my daughter know that she better ask mommy how to do the doll's hair because I sure couldn't…

I told D.W. about how back when I had confronted Jas on the whole matter and seeing that Jasmine was so comfortable because having kids ain't nothing to play with.. "I could tell there weren't any flaws behind her statement and she meant what she said." "But she's gone now so it's whatever. I have to keep moving with my life."

On October 8th, I made a promise to myself that I was going to make out with Mariah and then try to move on from there; if she was trying to take that route outside of work that night. We were closing the lobby down and only running through the drive-thru until she wanted to move out the way and not be seen by the cars still trying to come through. I told her to bring her behind over back to the crew room, but she once again complained about the cameras. So I told myself, why is she really caring about them now if they are going to say something about you & me together, anyway?

I waited for her to finish messing around with our closing manager Brittany and clean whatever she was going to behind the counters, then headed over to the bathroom to change. No sooner than I had come out then I had realized that she was already back at it with the jokes again. Complaining about how dirty I was and just checking into regular clothes to be dirty all over again, when I should wait until I took a shower at home. I looked at her with disgust, but it took me only a couple seconds to really comprehend what she had said. She didn't even know about the Bath salts soap I used at the crib and now I regret that day where I cleaned up the whole house like she was going to do something over there. Jameel comes over to ask "You got somebody coming over because I see you got those candles." And I wish I did but now I was going to go blow them mf's out, because she thinks she can play with me? Play with my heart?!

Floating Demon: You know what, hahahaha…. I'm feeling very petty and evil today. I don't know why, must be the Georgia weather getting cold out here or something.

I waited until she got over to the table I was sitting with her legs to the opposite of the direction she was, and made it clear that she didn't want me touching her thighs either. Once she was done talking to Monte, the kid that was begging me to drop him home, she had turned and started on me, listing a bunch of questions like if I ever went to jail, ever gone to any clubs, if I ever drank alcohol all to which I gave simple no's or shrugged my shoulders. She started off on this rant that I don't do anything that's cool and I must be such a lame blah blah… Then I cut her off before I get up and walk to the door stating, "If that's the case, then why are you f*cking with me?" To which she got quiet too, because I guess she didn't expect me to answer back.

If you expected me to cry or beg for her to get the hell on with that, then you got the wrong guy. I don't play those games, and I'll be cool if she could just go ahead and just leave. But she followed me out the door, with Monte walking slowly in between us… like if you don't get the hell on messing up my flow, with all that slow walking you doing to my car. She cracks the door with her leg and then presses it against her shoulder and I turn back at her thinking, "Was I really about to go ahead and make a move on this girl?"

This girl wasn't even feeling up on me and here we are. I go in and hope her lips are relaxed enough to even kiss her. She stops after the third peck to only tell me that "you can't really even kiss forreal."

Floating Demon: Yeah that might be so, but you ain't pulling back either. So you better press back up on me and kiss me like you really want to, like you really mean it.

So at this point, I already had gotten enough from her soft lips and I moved towards her neck and started planting down on her neck where I moved slowly but passionately, to her collarbone where I had then suddenly stopped because of the reaction she was giving me. We both hear a slam and look back to see Brittany making this face of envy, and I laugh until Mariah turns back and looks at me saying, if I was going to try to record her and put it on Snapchat.

Floating Angel: This is my time with you, so why would I dare put it on Snapchat… unless my intentions were different than yours right now.

I say no very calmly and turn back as I see Monte in the car waiting for me to wrap it up and go. Damn, I completely forgot about this kid in the car. She asks what my plans were for tonight, and I look at her with wide eyes like, are you serious right now?

Floating Demon: I was about to follow you back to the crib and dig in them guts but hey it's really up to you. Sadly, I have this kid in my car that I have to take back home, so that'll have to wait until who knows.

I got in my car because it truthfully was going nowhere and I was going to have to just take it with my chin up and get straight home. I couldn't even laugh along with Monte because I felt like my pride had died somewhere inside of my heart man. This dude over here telling me that she probably got wet from all the kissing… "Yeah and I was going to get my feet wet too… in the shower because you were cock-blocking my moment right now." Oh well, at least I got my work hours and did what I said I was going to do.

On October 9th, I was on the phone with Ogechi while heading from work down to the nearest AutoZone because I was growing irritable from the noise that my steering wheel was making, while it was desperately crying out for a bottle of power steering fluid. She had come to the realization that being single was a blessing and after seeing the in's and outs of all her close friends' relationships, she wasn't worried about being alone by herself even if it was for a brief moment in time.

She continued to say that people are afraid of dying and being alone but will have to come to terms with the fact that the coffin being put in the ground isn't made for two people but only one. I placed the phone down on the console, shocked by the acknowledgment that my friend had come to on her own terms. She cut through the brief silence by letting me know that "I know you are getting close to becoming a dog." She was referring to the dream I told her about a couple days ago. In the dream I was a couple years older, better dressed and had a lot more tattoos than I previously did at the time.

I was skating around backwards at a local skating rink, which was weird because the way I had learned was almost the same way I had watched my dad skate all the times we had gone to the skating rink. Hell, the black skates I had on looked like ones I would go out and buy for myself. I saw a girl that I got attracted to almost instantly and waited a couple laps around to get her number so we could make a move out of there. She told me she was waiting for her boyfriend so I told her to text him that her best friend was going to come pick her up instead. He pulled up to the front of the curb and parked, looking for her like any good guy would have but she was already in my passenger seat having the time of her life.

As we pulled up to my driveway, I remembered thinking how cool she was for not recording me because she would have gotten dropped like a burning Hot Pocket. She only came over a few times out of the week but I ended up breaking it off with her when she started complaining about missing her boyfriend, to which I took one glance at the text on my phone, laughed and then went all the way back to my bed with the phone on the counter. I woke up from the dream thinking, damn is that who I really am? Even if it had been messed up on her behalf, it felt good just to go out and be a player though.

On October 12th, I felt like I finally had all the answers for the book or at least the ones I thought I would need to have a complete story. My mind reverted back to the time when I felt guilty about going through Jessica's Snapchat and seeing those pictures of herself because all the years we had known each other, so it had caught me off guard with how her body really looked. I pushed that thought off to the side because I was immature at the time, but now I think of it... "So this is why I had one of her exes trying to beef with me over Snapchat and try to find out where my location was in Georgia." " All because he was over there hating and needed to let that whatever they had go." I was glad for my own sake that she was just back to being the homie, because all the drama I was causing about worrying over her was unnecessary. She went on to tell me that all these toxic guys were hitting her up out of nowhere and trying to figure out where her address was, or even get another chance at kicking it with her. I shook my head, only hoping that she could have more self awareness being in a relationship so she didn't have to constantly fight what she did in the past over and over again.

I thought about Mariah and if I could get her off that diet of Mickey D's and drinking soda. It wasn't her fault being a single mother, but she was over there feeding her son that junk and he was gonna get used to the same thing every time he came to eat fast food. I used to tell Dommy, before I would drop her off, that Mariah could have gone to the gym, made more money and then decided, if being in a relationship was the right thing for the two of us. Because it was strictly just work between us. I did peep all the red flags that Mariah was giving me but I don't know if it was her looks or her demeanor that made me overlook them.

The sad thing was that the girls at the job would pull me to the side and tell me to keep my chin up because I was doing all the right things to get her, but if she didn't reciprocate the love back then, why should I waste time chasing her?

I literally drove to see her, sometimes only to find out that she pulled off before I could get to the restaurant. I was so ashamed that I was waiting for her and wasting gas money, when I could've stayed home and went to bed. I don't know man...

If it hadn't been for those conversations with Jasmine and realizing that she was still trying to handle the heartbreaks that she went through in the past by herself... I would've made her feel bad for all the guys that were trying to take her out while she played with my emotions. I truly felt like I was wearing a Pennywise suit around these "regular people" on an everyday basis, because certain things and people held me back from feeling more like my true self. Love and life in general was becoming a huge joke to me and nobody was convincing me otherwise.

CHAPTER 39

"IS THIS … THE END?"

"Everybody is a genius. But if you judge a fish by it's ability to climb a tree, it will believe its whole life that it is stupid."

On the evening of October 13th, I was talking on Facetime with D.W. keeping the conversation centered around the two of us to keep the thought of Jasmine pounding against my brain. I couldn't begin to explain in words why or how she was still on my mind. Maybe I was trying to right my wrongs like Bryson Tiller? The only logical thing to do was venting out my issues to someone who would listen because trying to play video games or listen to music wasn't proving to be much of a cathartic process after all.

D.W. -*"I didn't know you wanted to become Batman forreal…"*

Floating Angel: I did because it looked great in my head but sounded stupid to say out loud at the time. I used to watch those Dark Knight clips at home when I would come in from school… I'd soak in the various ways Ra's al Ghuul trained Bruce on how to be stealthy, being able to anticipate his enemy's movements at the same time because it looked so cool even if it was a movie. I used to skim over this book excerpt from how to become Batman, because I felt like if you had the money and the time, you could really become Batman with all the gadgets and sh*t too.

D.W. - *"But your parents aren't actually dead so you can't be Batman forreal."*

Floating Demon- She's hating, man. I could be anybody I wanna be if I wanted to put the hard work in man. I could dream up all the ideas I had in my childhood and make it come true if I really wanted to.And if I got bored of the idea, then I'm going to pass it off to someone else to give them some inspiration.

We ended up moving on from that conversation by listing two things that we hated and liked about each other. For starters, I didn't like how she constantly found a way to degrade herself and said she had a elderly looking body. I would gas her up from time to time, letting her know that her body was looking right, whether she did her workouts or not, but she didn't want to listen to me because she had a lot of self doubt in herself. Number 2, I was sorry, but wasn't sorry for the fact that I called her thot or hoe in the past.

I knew it had hurt her feelings in the past when I had used that word, being that she was a sensitive soul but I just couldn't get how she messed around with the different guys that she was with. I had told her multiple times what certain guys would be capable of (because I am a guy for one) and you still came back crying and complaining. You should've gone crying to the guy that broke your heart and told him that he didn't need your forgiveness, so you could easily move on just like that. I, on the other hand, don't accept that fake pity because I ain't no love doctor.

I didn't care that you were having sex, but don't be a dumbass and turn into a sex addict, because you can't handle your emotions and wind up in a hole of self pity and shame. I was your best friend, but you'd forget at times that I'm not your man and as a result, I wasn't going to sit and listen to all your problems; over here acting like I cared about Mr. shouldn't have broken my heart again.

Last but not least, I also didn't like that you didn't like me the first time we met in person at school. No offense but F*ck whoever you had a crush on at the time. Because nobody ain't got sh*t on this sexy chocolate young man. (Man you get on a whole different spectrum when that self love hits you at the right time, and you don't need some woman to be telling you that you look good.)

So it was D.W.'s turn and the first thing that she disliked was the fact that she felt bad for me chasing after Mariah because she said I was a very sweet guy getting my hopes up for nothing & the second being my own personal insecurities ... I was over here liking someone that was taking advantage of my emotions in every situation, but I didn't have the heart to do her in the same light. Maybe it was because we were at work and we got to keep it professional, but I tried my best to be nice and polite to her when I talked to her in the parking lot before she left to go home.

Floating Angel: You know what song goes well with this situation right now? "Billie Jean is not my lover..." "She's just a girl that claims that I am the one." "But the kid is not my son."

Floating Demon: I think you got to hit that high note a little higher, or try to get up another octave... try something.

Floating Angel: "Unless you're gonna sing along with me, then don't tell me what to do bro." "That's the world we live in where we always try to control other people's actions." "So I'll respect your Michael Jackson and you let me sing whatever I want on this side."

She did have a point about me hiding the insecurities that I had about myself, like the big forehead that I didn't ask God for and my hair not being able to grow as long as I wish it could. I would get joked on for how dark my skin complexion is, but in reality having black skin to me looked just as beautiful as that girl from Belly. D.W. then decides to bring up that she was considering seeing me for spring break, just for a while and probably get a tour of Georgia from yours truly.

Floating Angel: Ooooweee. People will be twenty minutes away and they can't come check up on the man, but D.W. trying to slide for spring break? Say less.

D.W.- *Calm down. I said I was considering it, but the plan was to drive up and to see you for a good minute, then go right back to Florida.*

So when she went ahead and asked for my address, I hesitated because all I could think to myself was, "Now you just over here making false promises." "Either you are going to come through or you are not." So I said out loud to myself, F*CK IT and shoot my text over to her and she says after reading "yeah, I'm gonna go ahead & send this to FBI."

Floating Demon: "Alright bro, you can get off my line if you're gonna play around like that because I really don't want you to come see me." "If you are going to play around with my address, then go ahead and end up getting blocked lol." I'm already paranoid about letting people know where I'm at as it is.

I asked her about what she would try to wear and she told me whatever she felt at the time. It could be some jeans or a nice looking dress to go out to eat somewhere. Whether she decided to arrive looking like a snack or a bum that came out to the house with slides to my crib, all that is gonna come off when she comes to the room lol, but when she's in public, she can wear what she wants too. It's her life and not my right to judge how she wants to live.

I asked her if we got to cuddling and she got to rubbing up on me because she got that natural round thing on her. I know she would be rolling her eyes at these words, but they know how I'm coming. They know I only like them natural black jawns. She told me she would end up making a move, if I ended up kissing her because by then, she wouldn't be able to control what would happen next. I thought that was a good idea and she didn't because she felt like she'd be setting herself up for failure.

Floating Angel: It's only gonna be bad if you want it and she doesn't." And my n*gga, you better not rush in that thing if she gives it up too. "Don't go in shooting it up like a swat raid if she puts it in." Take your time and enjoy it like you're putting a spoon of delicious ice cream in your mouth."

Floating demon: Well, whatever she wants to do with you is between you and her is between you and her, my g. Don't make it your business of posting her all over social media like she is a hoe because if she doesn't want to, then you have to respect that choice and let her do what she feels is best for her.

Still skeptical about the hypothetical situation at hand, D.W. started to make it clear that she wasn't going for any type of relationship at the moment. And she said to do anything sexual with me would be a bad judgement call on her behalf. I told her to chill out because I'm the king of bad decisions, so I'll let you know if it's a bad decision to make or not. But she was still second guessing herself.

Floating Demon: Yo, boss.

Me: Yeah, wassup.

Floating Angel: I'm thinking we should drop her for right now. She is too wishy washy for me, even if she is just your best friend. You know we like any woman we are with to know what they want from a respectable man at that exact moment in time. As a guy, I'm too focused on making sure myself is secure before I get into anything at all.

Floating demon: Soooo is we gonna hit or we gonna quit while we ahead, and block her right now? Because it sounds like a no, because knowing you… you have any intentions of being patient unless it's something special and personal to you.

Me: "I'm feeling like this block button is the best option bro." "Sometimes you just need to always know what you need to do at the right moment and in the right time of action."

Then we ended the call after we said our good nights to each other. I layed down and stared at the ceiling, thinking about all the points we had touched on. D.W. asked me earlier on why I had a thing for talking to broken women. My first reaction to such a general question was to laugh, because the year before, Jasmine had asked me nearly the same question. So I gave her my response which was, "Everyone is broken but some people are just better at healing their scars far better than others." I didn't think I'd have such a prophetic answer but it's true because no one is perfect. You just have to choose your people like you choose your battles...wisely.

She had clowned me for talking delicately about Jas when I was feeling overwhelmed and I didn't respect that. I know I had my personal issues with her and needed to vent with someone but if the roles had been reversed, she would have wanted me to hear her out instead. I guess I thought talking out my problems would in turn help me escape my unresolved issues, but it seemed to make them more alive and present when the favor wasn't received in the way I hoped. As you come across these final pages, you may be thinking to yourself- "Why did he write this book and put all his business out there?' "Doesn't he have any common sense?" I'm not saying I am perfect because I've spent my personal time getting caught up in the life of video games and not stopping until the main villain got what he had been coming for since he showed up from the beginning cutscene(like Splinter Cell-Blacklist). But sometimes we need to come out of our comfort zones and enjoy the little things in life around us; being more realistic with what things are rather than what we complicate them to be.

Take some time off social media, some time off those books, turn down the radios and focus on your families or taking your dog out of the cage every once in a while. Get out of the house and get some fresh air. We get caught up in this fake reality of living to fill in all the emotional voids that comes with the hardships of life. Don't look at this book as a model to follow though… You can choose for yourself what makes you happy and what doesn't. Nobody else but you can make those choices and feel those emotions. Yes, we all have bills, and deaths and no one is free from any of these bad things in the world. But we can agree that we all need peace and love as well. Try to not hold onto grudges and bad emotions. Find that self love and balance that keeps you together as a person, before you begin to seek that from other things and people. I wish peace and prosperity to all those who have read this book to its entirety and want to live their best life moving forward.

EPILOGUE

You asked me for my reassurance and I honestly couldn't reciprocate it when you asked it from me. I thought I was better off handling my own demons than accepting the fact that you were an angel, pushing away the pain that makes my heart cold on the inside. Those times that I cried on the phone with you wasn't because I was sad, but because I don't know how to handle such undeserving love, and kindness that you would offer to me from time to time. It felt so surreal and powerful to the point where I felt as though every time I tried to treat you with respect, the self-doubt of "damn you didn't do enough for her" kicks in and I ended up taking things out of proportion.

You told me you would support my dreams when I told you to leave me alone. You wanted to be Queen and Slim while I was turning into Dumb and Dumber. You were flying high like a butterfly and I was still in a cocoon mindstate, thinking for myself on how to break my own cycle and find my own way. I love when you got that sh*t in your nose & act all petty by telling me to entertain my hoes, so next time I'll unlock my phone and let you do all the entertaining.

I can't be forcing myself to rush and think "yes she's going to be my wife, she's going to give me kids and we'll be on top of the world"… That's how I saw my dad mess up before my own eyes and I don't want to become that father for my kids. I'm only twenty and still growing, so understand that I just want the best for you. Focus on college, loving your family, forgiving your friends, dating and loving more people. I'm not forcing a meet up with you anytime soon, because sometimes the best things in life are worth waiting for.

I knew I had to meet you in person because I had to make sure that I wasn't just feeling these butterflies in my stomach for no reason. From the moment your dad let you walk over to me into that parking lot and you had hugged me… we may have been outside but in my mind, I felt like you had just walked down the wedding aisle and ya boy was on cloud nine. Remember that Anita Baker song, Lately and how I told you it made me think about you… That was true in the past tense but I had to question myself after you were gone and ended up telling myself, if I had to go back in time and give you the song that I really wanted, it would have to be my favorite song "Marvin Gaye- I Want You."

One of these days, if you change your mind and figure out that I'm really not the toxic asshole I make myself out to be, give me the heads up so I can make sure you get this ring on your finger and the three kids that are going to come along with it, Shorty.

Printed in the United States
By Bookmasters